Helsinki

Cities of the Imagination

Cities of the Imagination

Helsinki

A cultural and literary history

Neil Kent

Interlink Books

An imprint of Interlink Publishing Group, Inc.
Northampton, Massachusetts

First published 2005 by
INTERLINK BOOKS
An imprint of Interlink Publishing Group, Inc.
46 Crosby Street, Northampton, Massachusetts 01060

Library of Congress Cataloging-in-Publication Data
Kent, Neil.
Helsinki : a cultural and literary history / by Neil Kent.—1st American ed.
p. cm.—(Cities of the imagination)
Includes index.
ISBN 1-56656-544-8 (pbk.)
1. Helsinki (Finland)—Description and travel. 2. Literary
landmarks—Finland—Helsinki. 3. Helsinki (Finland)—Intellectual life.
4. Helsinki (Finland)—Guidebooks. I. Title. II. Series.
DL1175.28.K46 2004
914.897'1—dc22
2004004615

Drawings by Maggie Claringbull
Cover Images: Helsinki City Tourist & Convention Bureau

Printed in Canada by Webcom

To request our complete 40-page full-color catalog, please call us toll free at **1-800-238-LINK,** visit our website at **www.interlinkbooks.com,** or write to
Interlink Publishing
46 Crosby Street, Northampton, MA 01060
e-mail: info@interlinkbooks.com

Contents

CHAPTER THREE
MILITARY HELSINKI:
WAR AND WARRIORS

CHAPTER FOUR
ETHNIC HELSINKI:
LANGUAGE, IDENTITY AND COMMUNITY

CHAPTER FIVE
GOD AND HELSINKI:
CHURCHES, FAITHS AND RELIGIOUS DIVERSITY

CHAPTER SIX
HELSINKI AND NATURE:
WEATHER, SPORTS AND PUBLIC HEALTH

CHAPTER SEVEN
HELSINKI AND ROMANTICISM:
MYTH, EPIC AND ARCHITECTURE

CHAPTER EIGHT
HELSINKI AND MODERNITY:
URBAN GROWTH, ARCHITECTURE AND DESIGN

CHAPTER NINE
Intellectual Helsinki:
Science and Learning

CHAPTER TEN
Helsinki and Hospitality:
Hotels, Drinking and Saunas

CHAPTER ELEVEN
Helsinki and the Visual Arts:
Museums, Galleries and Artists

CHAPTER TWELVE
HELSINKI AND THE PERFORMING ARTS:
MUSIC, OPERA AND BALLET

Foreword
Helsinki: the Blue-White Daughter of the Baltic Sea?

The growth and planning of Europe's national capitals are closely linked to political, social and economic forces. Local, national and international changes are clearly visible in the history of Helsinki. Urbanization came late to Finland's capital city. Throughout the past two centuries it has appeared to foreign eyes above all as a modern city, even if the central part of the townscape is full of architecture dating from the beginning of the nineteenth century. As a Nordic capital, Helsinki's spirit has been, and still is, informed by a constant drive towards cultural modernity. This includes an ability to quickly reinvent itself while maintaining its historical roots.

The term "social capital" is often used when discussing the spirit of Helsinki. It includes concrete infrastructural assets such as a creative environment, functional institutions, buildings and support services, as well as various kinds of "soft" infrastructure like social and cultural networks. In the case of Helsinki, it is important to show the sort of glue that holds the two types of infrastructure together. Neil Kent's book deals precisely with how different local cultural players have acted together to create and build a middle-size European national capital, Helsinki. It mixes general political, national and commercial as well as military history with an account of urban development. The result is a literary portrait of Helsinki as modern and modernistic cultural city, where guests will receive a great deal of hospitality.

Cultural innovation can be viewed as a result of the equal contribution of the sciences, culture, economy and governance in shaping urban affairs and the local identity of citizens. The state authorities, for their part, act as an overall umbrella. Their role historically has been to create infrastructure and educational facilities and to ensure ethnic equality and democracy for the whole society. The railway turned Helsinki at the end of nineteenth century into a major exporting port and a real capital connected to the entire country. Throughout this book the history of Helsinki emerges as a continuous success story of cultural and political initiatives. The capital, as the most important port and the main center of communication, is also the natural channel for the spread of innovations and for the wider modernization process in Finland. Today Helsinki is a global symbol for a successful knowledge-based economy and hi-tech development.

The key to success in urban history are cultural diversity and renewal, present at every stage of this book. It traces the impact of Swedish rule, the Russian period and the personal influence of the "Founding Fathers and Mother" of the city—King Gustavus I Vasa (1550) and Queen Christina (1640) of Sweden and Russian Emperor Alexander I (1812). It reveals, for instance, how the heart of city, Senate Square, was planned as a monument to and symbol of a centralizing and imperial power. In that sense, Helsinki's development before 1914 was similar to that of many other medium-size capitals in continental and northern Europe. At that time, it was a part of the Russian Empire and can be compared with many similar cities in the other European empires.

The First World War shattered the old world, destroyed cities, and gave birth to new national states. Helsinki remained the natural capital when Finland separated from Russia and became an independent republic in December 1917 under the shadow of world war and the Russian revolution. A particularly valuable part of the book is formed by the description of how different cultural institutions (church, university, intellectuals, different language groups etc.) have since then formed the central image of the city. Indeed, the most significant innovations in Helsinki during the past two hundred years have been the work of people who have met the challenge of foreign influences.

Many of Helsinki's strongest meanings are embodied by waterways. This capital city is shaped and defined by the Baltic Sea. The river, the ocean waterfront areas, the bays, shores and coastlines, as well as the isthmus site have, to varying degrees, figured prominently in the historical development of the city. The sea has played a role in building the city's economic and symbolic image, as well as its spiritual urban essence, its blue-whiteness. The historic center, located on the narrow peninsula, is linked to the sea in an exquisite fashion, and its neoclassical waterfront façade is the well-known emblem of the capital. Extensive harbor and industrial areas express the economic vitality of the city. With the rapid industrialization in the early twentieth century, land was reclaimed from the sea for harbors and dockyards. Suburban planning has also moved along the coastline.

Helsinki has a particularly rich shoreline and very different spaces linking the city and the water. The presence of nature plays a central role in the city's urban image. As the seat of government in Finland, Helsinki was mainly created in the nineteenth and twentieth centuries, which were "centuries of capitals". As a result, there is nothing medieval or feudal in Helsinki's atmosphere. The first phase of the planning took place under the special circumstances of Russian rule, yielding a city of order and dignity. Engel's city plan created the white architectural image of the neoclassical parts of central Helsinki. The central area of the city still retains rather low roof heights, and any vertical element is highly visible in the townscape. Even so, Helsinki today is no longer bound by this neoclassicist framework. During more than 150 years that have passed since Engel's blueprint, alternative urban and planning approaches have been explored and a unique capital city has been constructed. With the 1952 Summer Olympics Helsinki joined the exclusive club of Olympic cities.

Although Helsinki is definitely an artificial and planned city, this book is not primarily concerned with town planning or a history of architecture. Instead, Neil Kent describes the development of the city—its changing architecture, the development of its infrastructure, its cultural creativeness—through its wider and eventful history, a history of wars and crises, as well as relentless urban growth. Here, as the author points out, lies the whole heroic idea of Helsinki as a cultural city. The last chapters, covering design, music and the arts, offer invaluable guidance for readers who spend some time in Helsinki. As this book reveals, the city deserves its high ranking among European capitals as *a city of the imagination.*

Laura Kolbe
Helsinki

Acknowledgments

This literary and cultural guide is a highly personal book. It is written from the perspective of a visitor to Helsinki, not a long-term resident, and in many cases does not always respect the orthodoxies of received opinion. It must be so, as the author has not imbibed these opinions as a child and to a large degree expresses his own impressions of the Finnish capital rather than those of established authorities, however learned they might be.

That said, I have been dependent on a wide range of existing scholarly research and expertise on many subjects covered. The assistance of others who have read over the manuscript and provided insights has also been indispensable. In particular, I would like to thank John Screen for his help reading my manuscript. Additionally, I wish to thank Edward Clark of the Tallis Group for his helpful comments on music. I would also like to record my appreciation to Marianna Kajantie, Assistant Director of the City of Helsinki's Cultural Department, who enabled me to stay at the charming Artist's House at Eläintarhantie, especially atmospheric with next door a former nineteenth-century brothel, frequented by famous Finnish literary figures! Finally, I should like to express my thanks to the Finnish Ambassador to the United Kingdom, Pertti Salolainen, who has consistently provided much encouragement and support for this project.

Linguistic Note

Finnish or *Suomi*, as Finnish speakers call their language, is the native tongue of the overwhelming majority of the population of both Finland and Helsinki itself. One of the Finno-Ugric languages, within the larger Uralic linguistic family, it is, together with Lappish or *Saami* and Estonian, one of the most north-westerly of this group. For political and social reasons, it only became an official language in Finland in 1863, its status enhanced by the publication of the epic *Kalevala*, compiled and restructured from folk poetry by Elias Lönnrot earlier in the century. It is distinguished phonologically by its vowel harmonies and consonant gradation, the latter a Uralic feature, according to which consonant stops are substituted by voiced and fricative variants. For example, a "p" would become a "v", as a word becomes modified by agglutinative endings. This, too, is a fascinating characteristic of the language, for words in general add suffixes and modify their spelling according to their grammatical status. Unlike Indo-European languages, Finnish prepositions and possessive forms therefore become "built into" the root words themselves. This frequently means that Finnish words strike the foreigner as extraordinarily long. Yet the grammar is remarkably logical and, though visitors to Finland are almost invariably terrified by the strangeness of the language, those who take the trouble to learn it are richly rewarded by their efforts.

In any case, the presence of foreign loan words in Finnish is also an aid to the learner. Especially in matters relating to the Church and the sciences, Finnish contains many foreign borrowings, from German, Russian, English and Swedish. Swedish was, indeed, the only official language of Finland before 1863 and, as an Indo-European language closely related to English, by no means difficult to learn. A basic knowledge of it also provides a visitor to Finland, especially to Helsinki and other coastal areas where many native Swedish speakers live, with a relatively easy means of gaining access to a better comprehension of Finnish life and culture. For those interested in more profound insights into Helsinki and its residents, at least a superficial acquaintance with both languages is virtually indispensable.

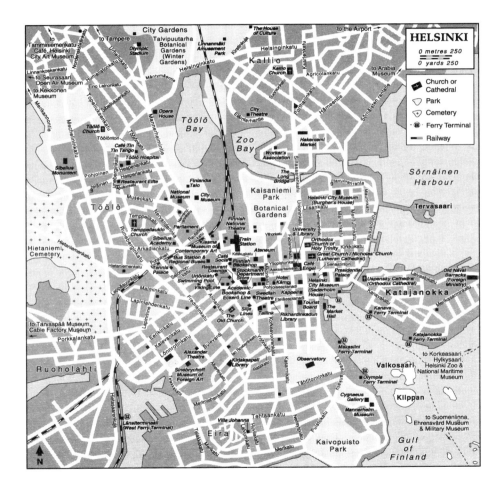

HELSINKI

0 metres 250
0 yards 250

- Church or Cathedral
- Park
- Cemetery
- Ferry Terminal
- Railway

City Gardens

The House of Culture

to the Airport

to Tamminiementie Café, Helsinki City Art Museum
to Tampere
Olympic Stadium
Talvipuutarha Botanical Gardens (Winter Gardens)
Linnanmäki Amusement Park
Helsinginkatu
Helsinginkatu

Kallio

to Arabia Museum

Linnankoskenkatu
to Seurasaari Open Air Museum
to Kekkonen Museum
Himalistonkatu
Mäntymäentie
Kallio Church
Agricolankatu

Eino Leinonkatu
Sibeliuksenkatu
Topeliuksenkatu

Opera House
City Theatre
Eläintarhantie

Mechelininkatu
Töölö Church
Töölöntori

Töölö Bay

Zoo Bay

Hakaniemi Market

Sörnäinen Harbour

Café Tin Tin Tango
Töölö Hospital
Pohjoinen
Hesperiankatu
Sibelius Monument
Restaurant Elite
Jeläinen
Museokatu

Worker's Association
The Long Bridge

Itävourenranta
Itävourenranta

Tervasaari

Töölö

Finlandia Talo
National Museum
City Museum

Kaisaniemi Park

Helsinki City Museum (Burgher's House)
Liisankatu

Temppelikatu
Temppeliaukio Church
Sibelius Academy
Arkadiankatu

Parliament
Finnish National Theatre

Botanical Gardens

University & Library
Orthodox Church of Holy Trinity
Kirkkokatu

Hietaniemi, Cemetery

Kiasma Museum of Contemporary Art
Bus Station & Regional Buses
Hietaniemenkatu
Tennis Palace
Urjönkatu Swimming Pool

Train Station
Ateneum

Yliopistonkatu
Great Church / Nicholas Church (Lutheran Cathedral)
Senaatintori

Malminkatu

Café Socis
Restaurant Cosmos
Stockmann Department Store
VikingLine
Academic Bookshop & Eckerö Line

Café Engel
Presidential Palace
The Ministry)

Hotel Kämp
Pohjoisesplanadi
Swedish Theatre
Etelässpanadi

Helsinki City Museum (Sederholm House)
Tourist Board

Uspensky Cathedral (Orthodox Cathedral)
Old Naval Barracks (Foreign Ministry)

Katajanokka

Lapinlahdenkatu

Silja Lines
Tallink
Richardinkadun Library
The Market Hall

Kanava Ferry Terminal
Katajanokka Ferry Terminal

to Tarvaspää Museum, Cable Factory Museum
Porkkalankatu

The Old Church

Fredrikinkatu
Eerikinkatu
Kalevankatu
Lönnrotinkatu
Alexander Theatre
Kirjakaspeli Library

Bulevardi

Makasiini Ferry Terminal

to Korkeasaari, Hylkysaari, Helsinki Zoo & National Maritime Museum

Ruoholahti

Sinebrychoff Museum of Foreign Art

Observatory
Tähtitorninkatu

Valkosaari

Olympia Ferry Terminal

Klippan

Cygnaeus Gallery
Mannerheim Museum

to Suomenlinna, Ehrensvärd Museum & Military Museum

Länsiterminaali (West Ferry Terminal)

Ville Johanna
Tehtaankatu

Eira

Merikatu

Kaivopuisto Park

Gulf of Finland

N

INTRODUCTION

Helsinki, or Helsingfors as it is known in Swedish, is not one of Europe's major capitals in terms of population or location. It has a population of only about half a million and stands in the northeastern corner of Europe, far away from the major continental crossroads. Stockholm and Copenhagen, sister Nordic capitals to the west, are twice its size and cover a greater area. Nonetheless, its stunning geographical position, extraordinary history and cultural *richesses* make it one of the world's most fascinating cities, situated in the innermost recesses of a wide archipelago, with seemingly endless islands, dotted by ancient and modern fortifications and the occasional summer cottage. And unlike most European capitals, it did not come into being or develop organically, in an accidental or haphazard way. On the contrary, it is an artificial city in its origins, like St. Petersburg, New Delhi or Brasilia, its creation motivated by the desires of its ruler.

It is also a city, rare enough today in our urbanized world, in which town and country enmesh in harmonious fashion. A busy urban thoroughfare can suddenly terminate in an unexpected wilderness of stark boulders and lofty pines, looming against a backdrop of blue sea and sky. As the French visitor and Fellow of the French Academy Xavier Marmier (1808-92) put it so bucolically after his visit in 1838:

> *This town stretches over a vast peninsula, dotted with rustic hills and cool vales; the sea surrounds it on all sides like a girdle of gold and silver, studded with woods and granite rocks. Here the sandy coast dips down level with the waves, which toss on it with a soft murmur their lace of foam, their fringes of mother-of-pearl and sky-blue. There the coast bristles with a rampart of massive rocks, topped further away by a pine forest. On the esplanade, on the quay, on the squares, there is activity, the continuous movement of people, horses, and, a few hundred yards away, there is wild solitude, the far horizon, and no other sound than the sighing of the waves or the moaning of the wind.*

Helsinki also lays claim to fame as one of the world's most northern capitals, situated on the sixtieth parallel, a little north, in fact, of Cape Farewell in southern Greenland. Yet it is a city in which the balmy warmth of a summer's day can be enjoyed along the banks of shallow ponds and lakes of almost spring-like warmth. Despite its cold winters, its environs have long sheltered human habitation. Indeed, its prehistoric settlement is far longer than its historical one.

Early History

The area around Helsinki had been colonized as far back as seven thousand years ago, at Kaarela, Pitäjänmäki, and Vantaa, though it was first during the early Iron Age that more permanent settlements were established. Yet an increasingly cold climate and the ravages of the Vikings and even of the Finns themselves, who sometimes pillaged the coast eastwards as far as Novgorod, curtailed the lives of these settlements as well as of their inhabitants. Yet as the centuries rolled by, the inroads of the Vikings were gradually substituted by the arrival of Christianized Swedish colonists, many from the coastal areas of Norrland and Hälsingland, but some even from the Swedish interior, especially in the years around 1100.

At first these immigrants settled the coastlands from the Gulf of Bothnia, in the west, to the site of Espoo, just to the west of present-day Helsinki. But, within a century they had moved further east, to colonize the coast of present-day Uusimaa, the province in which Helsinki is now situated. Only the outbreak of the Black Death in the late 1340s put a halt to this immigration, as the internal migrations of peasants, hunters and gatherers in Sweden itself reduced their need to seek work elsewhere. Still, numerous settlements on the south coast of Finland thrived despite visitations of the plague in the late 1340s. Koskela, a village near which Helsinki would later be founded, had already been long established by the time it first appears in historical chronicles from 1417, though virtually nothing remains to be seen from that period.

Swedish Rule

Although Finland, in political terms, had been integrated into the Swedish dominions as far back as the twelfth century, Helsinki itself only became a political entity during the reign of Gustaf Vasa (1496-1560), the first hereditary king of Sweden and the monarch who introduced the Reformation. It was during his reign that the first example of Finnish literature appeared in 1542: an *ABC*, under the auspices of Michael Agricola (c. 1510-57), Bishop of Turku and Finland's leading Protestant reformer.

After the foundation of Helsinki at the mouth of the Vantaa River by royal decree on June 12, 1550, numerous burghers from such Finnish towns as Tammisaari, Porvoo, Rauma, and Ulvila were obliged to move to the new settlement. The king's intention was to make his new "city" a mercantile rival to the Danish Hanseatic one of Tallinn (a name signifying Danish castle) on the southern shores of the Gulf of Finland, for it was hoped that it would derive its wealth from the prosperous Baltic and Russian trade. But fate was to dash his hopes since the shallowness of the bay and other factors frustrated his plan to create a good harbor, and within a few years the unhappy settlers, after ardent and piteous petitions, were finally permitted to return to their previous homes. Many did, but fortunately not all. It was their descendants, not great in number, to be sure, who in 1640 were relocated at Vironniemi in Finland, a name associated with Estonian traders and that part of Helsinki today known as Kruununhaka.

Yet the city's period of prosperity had still not arrived. In fact, in the late seventeenth century it suffered from a variety of disasters, not least fires, which ravaged the wooden town at regular intervals. As a result, Helsinki hardly grew in size and as the eighteenth century dawned, it had no more than 1,700 inhabitants.

When the Russian Czar Peter the Great (1672-1725) founded his new imperial capital St. Petersburg in 1703 on the southeastern shores of the Gulf of Finland, the portents for a new and even more ominous era seemed to have arrived, one with dire implications for Sweden-Finland. Already two years before, the Great Northern War had broken out between Sweden and Russia, a state of hostilities that continued until 1721. Despite the brilliant martial qualities of the Swedish King Karl XII, it became clear to the world that Sweden's brief position as a great power was at an end. After peace was made, the Russian border was radically readjusted to the detriment of Sweden-Finland, a situation that its rulers were powerless to change. Not only was the important province of Karelia, including the city of Viipuri (Vyborg, in Russian), lost to Russia, but Helsinki now found itself out on a limb, within a short journey from the new Russian frontier that was now literally on its maritime doorstep.

True, in the wake of the city's evacuation to avoid brutal treatment by the Russian forces, it was burnt to the ground by the departing Swedish administration itself, keen to insure that no practical use of the site could be made by the invaders. But with the subsequent return of Helsinki to Sweden, this was to prove the last catastrophe to afflict it on such a scale. Henceforth, Helsinki would accommodate its residents without a break and without the alien occupation of enemy troops. As a result of such continuity, a significant number of Helsinki families can even today trace their ancestry back to the sixteenth century. Later, the so-called War of the Hats broke out between Sweden-Finland and Russia and raged in the years 1741-3, taking its toll on the political and social fabric of the city, with a renewed occupation by Russian forces. But this proved a minor setback in the generally modest growth in prosperity that Helsinki enjoyed in the course of the eighteenth century. In fact, by 1800 Helsinki had grown into a rather large town, by Swedish standards, with around 3,000 inhabitants excluding an even greater number of military personnel and ancillary staff who resided on Viapori (now Suomenlinna in Finnish, Sveaborg, in Swedish) its recently built military fortress. As such, Helsinki had become Sweden's fourth largest town with a harbor, in terms of mercantile imports the third most important in the kingdom.

Imperial City

The upheavals of the Napoleonic period brought about many changes in the city, but by 1809, as the war between Sweden and Russia came to an end, a new era of economic prosperity and political importance dawned for Helsinki. With the Treaty of Hamina, Finland became an autonomous Grand Duchy under the Russian Czar, even if the administrative capital continued to be Turku. Yet the fire that in 1827 destroyed much of Finland's old capital—a city in any case tainted for the Czar by its close geographic, economic, social and cultural links to Sweden—made a major development of Helsinki, itself ravaged by fire in 1808, a necessity and so it came into consideration as the new capital. All the more so as it was much nearer to St. Petersburg, only 250 miles away, and thus more subject to Russian influence.

This provided the opportunity for the creation of what was really a totally new city, dependent upon the financial *largesse* of the Czar Alexander I (1777-1825) and conceived as a whole under the direction of the German architect Carl Ludvig Engel (1778-1840). The reconstruction included the building of both Lutheran and Orthodox churches, government buildings, and a new university. It was to take more than thirty years to accomplish, after the deaths of both the architect and his patron. Still, by the 1850s the grand designs of Engel had been completed and the city assumed a proud and elegant appearance, one of which its by now 16,000 inhabitants were rightfully proud. The outbreak in 1853 of the Crimean War, which was to last three years, had little lasting effect on Helsinki, despite the bombardment of Suomenlinna Fortress on islands at the entrance to the city's harbor.

The city's growth and development did not stop here. In 1880 some three-quarters of the city's architecture was still composed of one- and two-story wooden buildings, but this was soon to change dramatically. By 1900 Helsinki had grown into the Grand Duchy's most important industrial center and a city of 91,000 inhabitants. In the process, construction on a massive scale rapidly transformed the face of the city. In essence, this urban growth was a reflection of industrial development and change in the rest of Finland, leading to large-scale migration, not only from country to town, but abroad as well.

Other major changes were also underway. In 1906 Finnish women were granted the franchise, making Finland one of the first political entities to give women the vote, after New Zealand. This was a quite extraordinary feat, considering it was still a part of the Russian Empire, where such a political franchise was otherwise impossible. The city, meanwhile, continued to expand. By the advent of the First World War, Helsinki's population had grown to over 140,000. The First World War, independence in December 1917, and ensuing Civil War in the early months of 1918, created upheavals both social and political, but these were temporary and by 1920 the city had grown still further.

For many this was a time of great personal and social alienation. Such was the case with Ilmari Kianto (1874-1970), a novelist who had migrated to Helsinki from the province of Kajaani, in the far northeast. For him, during the second and third decades of the twentieth century Helsinki was "the world's most devilish creation", which sucked country dwellers into its perfidious abyss. L. Onerva, whose real name was Hilja Onerva Lehtinen (1882-1972), took a rather more ambivalent view. She saw Helsinki as a city of considerable charms and allurements, but one not without its dangers, moral and physical, as underscored in her 1911 collection of short stories *Nousukkaita* (The Parvenues). There, Helsinki's Siren-like nature was stressed, the city imagined as a vamp-like creature leading people willingly to their own destruction.

War and Peace

The city's greatest test was to come with the outbreak of the Second World War (there were actually three wars with respect to the region), when the Soviet Union attacked Finland. By the advent of the first, the Winter War of 1939-40, the population of Helsinki had burgeoned to 317,000 as large numbers of refugees from the east flooded into the capital. War against the Soviet Union broke out again in 1941, leading to Finnish recovery of the ceded territories and lasted until 1944 when the Finns were irreversibly forced out, resulting in the final resettlement of thousands of Karelians (from the former Finnish territory of West Karelia) throughout Finland, but especially in Helsinki. The lost territories were then ceded to Russia. Despite bombing, most of the city was left intact since relatively few bombs hit their targets and after an initial onslaught the Russians had other objectives to focus upon. One of the terms of peace between Finland and the Soviet Union was that the Finns turn on their erstwhile German co-belligerents, which they did, declaring war on and then driving out the Nazi forces stationed in the north of the country in the so-called Lapland War of 1944.

When this war ended with a return to normality in 1946, a large number of new independent communities sprang up around Helsinki and these, along with the older ones, were incorporated into the city. In contrast to the relatively expensive and more up-market accommodation of central Helsinki, the new suburbs were built as cheaply as possible, and with little attention paid to architectural details or the luxury of space; the desperate priority of housing large numbers of refugees quickly had made speed a necessity. Still, many incorporated a simplified modernist design and took advantage of the city's unspoiled surrounding countryside.

The 1950s was a period of redevelopment, but by the 1960s and 1970s the tide was turning and an increasing number of people returned to the inner city of Helsinki. There, during the 1980s and 1990s, old industrial areas, occasionally dotted with even older wooden houses, once again met residential needs as the industrial fabric was removed or redeveloped. To these must be also be added the fringe developments of Näckinpuisto, Ruoholahti, and Pikku Huopalahti, which served to link the older parts of the city with the parks situated on the inner periphery.

Despite such developments, the city's population increased to over 515,000 by 1995, of whom only 43.5 percent had been there for longer than one generation. As a result, Helsinki desperately required more housing. To fill this need other new suburbs came into being, such as Kontula, Myllypuro and Jakomäki, frequently less charming than those before and often comprising large and ugly cement blocks. Even so, the odd one such as Pihlajanmäki did receive some recognition for combining such largely unappealing elements as cement with a more successful urban plan and architectural design.

Helsinki remains a city with a sizable linguistic minority of long standing. Today, those who have Swedish as their first language make up some six percent of the capital's population, somewhat higher than the proportion in Finland altogether, albeit an ever-diminishing proportion of the population as a whole. Increasingly, during the last century, Finnish language literature has achieved a higher profile, so that writers, like Mika Waltari (1908-1979), have become famous throughout the world. His novel *The Egyptian* (1945), internationally renowned both as a book and as a film, also helped to give the literary scene in Finland an international profile.

With respect to the arts and most especially music, Finland long ago entered the international stage. The composer Jean Sibelius (1865-1957) has become a household name for music lovers throughout the world, and Aulis Sallinen (b.1935) may soon continue this tradition. The growth of the city and of its international profile are trends that will be explored in greater depth in the following chapters.

The Cityscape

Perhaps the best place to begin a tour of Helsinki is in the market place in front of the Swedish Embassy, not far from the South Harbour, near where the boats formerly arrived from Sweden, Estonia and elsewhere, carrying thousands of tourists every day to and from the capital. If one stands with one's back to the old Quarantine Basin, at the foot of the Esplanade, one can enjoy a panoramic view of the Finnish capital in all directions. To the west—in front—the visitor looks up the central promenade, extending through the leafy park, full of cafés, which makes up the Esplanade. This grand thoroughfare was laid down in the early nineteenth century, and the Swedish Theatre stands in the background, with the old red light district and working-class area of Iso Roobertinkatu beyond. To the left, southwards, towards the boat terminals, rises up the hill on which the Observatory is situated, at its foot the Kaivopuisto Gardens, where the famous Ullanlinna Spa was located, and some of the grandest of the old aristocratic residences.

To the right, northwards, however—and this is the most picturesque of the views—stands the true heart of Helsinki, Senate Square, the University, the old Senate House and rising above these neoclassical buildings like a crown, the Great Church of St. Nicholas. Beyond it, hidden from view across the Long Bridge, is the old industrial working-class district of the capital. And beyond this new suburbs extend, embedded among the granite boulders and gentle pine-covered hills, each representing a different generation of Helsinki residents. As the city has expanded to the north like a fan, it now covers quite a number of islands on either side of the peninsula on which old Helsinki is situated.

All this is, of course, set against the backdrop of the sea—the Gulf of Finland, with its countless islands of granite boulders, interspersed with the occasional pine. For centuries the sea has been the primary conduit of communication for Helsinki, for trade as well as for the less welcome arrival of foreign troops. More recently, it has also provided a splendid venue for tourists keen to experience some of Europe's most beautiful and pristine nature, where the colors blue and white dominate, the colors, fittingly, of the Finnish flag.

CHAPTER ONE

Commercial Helsinki: From Herrings to High-Tech

The name of Helsinki signifies that from its first founding its importance was as a commercial center, since the first half of the word denotes a mercantile base, and the latter the location of a stream or rapids. It was precisely to encourage such mercantile activity and to make Helsinki a rival to Reval (now Tallinn) that the Swedish king Gustaf Vasa obliged merchants from Turku, Ulvila, Pori, Rauma, Tammisaari and Porvoo to settle at the mouth of the Vantaa River. As a result, the parish of Helsinge, as it was then known, became the most affluent of the province of Uusimaa, with around 3,000 inhabitants in 1551.

Unfortunately, the king injured the goose that laid the golden egg, even if he did not quite kill it. After he visited the newly founded town in 1555 he permitted the merchants forcibly brought to Helsinki to return to their former homes if they so desired, which many did. The town's mercantile attractions were sharply diminished. Nonetheless, it still contained about 500 inhabitants in 1571, small for a continental European town, but still making it Finland's fifth largest urban settlement.

One of Helsinki's richest merchants and shipping magnates of the late sixteenth century was Hans van Sanden, a native of the Netherlands who died in the 1590s. His ships plied the seas from between Tallinn and Narva (in what is now Estonia) in the east, and to Gdansk, Lübeck and Amsterdam in the west. He married the daughter of a local family of German descent, Anna Jägerhorn, and began a dynasty of some importance. Today a black granite stone marks the site of his grave, adjacent to where the village's first church was built. (This site is not far from the Arabia Factory, where modernist Finnish tableware is produced.)

Early Days

Helsinki continued to grow during the early years of the seventeenth century, even if in economic terms it had failed to thrive as first expected. The Swedish government issued a decree on October 12, 1639, ordering the settlement to move further south to a coastal point near present-day Sörnäinen. The old settled area around the Old Town, Helsinge Rapids, was then abandoned. But not long after, Governor General Per Brahe chose Vironniemi by Kruununhaka as a location, a move further facilitated by the donation of land there by Sweden's Queen Christina in 1643.

Built on a grid-like layout, the town reflected the Baroque ideals of regularity so admired throughout Europe at this time. Twenty streets were focused round a central square and adjacent harbor, the whole of which was divided into four equal quarters. By 1670 a few streets adjacent to the churchyard were paved with stone, an indication of the wealth of some merchants who contributed to their construction and a rare luxury in Finnish towns at that time. Most were unpaved, as was usual throughout the Nordic and Russian world.

It was also around this time that the first private two-story residence was built on the corner of Senate Square, where Suurkatu meets Koulukatu and today the Council of State building stands. It was owned by the magistrate and ship owner Torsten Bergman (1661-1711), who had also served as a political representative in Stockholm in 1697. With chambers surmounted by vaulted ceilings, shop and kitchens, it was typical of large Baltic residences of the period. Unfortunately, it was destroyed during the Great Northern War in the early eighteenth century, with the other buildings, great and small, of the little town.

Baltic Port

Even if places like the ancient city of Hämeenlinna and its hinterland continued to prefer Turku in the west or Porvoo in the east as their partners, Helsinki finally, if slowly, began to establish its trading credentials. Today Helenankatu, Katariinankatu and Sofiankatu still form a central part of the heart of the city, just as they did when the rich merchants of the seventeenth century held political sway on the town council, even if the center of gravity of Helsinki has shifted to the southwest.

In those days wood was one of the most important commodities. The north of Germany was the main importer of Finnish wood, but Holland and England were also clients. These two seafaring nations were also keen to acquire tar, important for shipbuilding, stored on the island of Tervasaari. Tar soon became the city's most important export in the seventeenth century, though some iron and furs were also exported. Since Helsinki was a fishing port, albeit seasonal, the export of fish was also significant. Large quantities went to Stockholm, along with butter and other foodstuffs.

In return, a whole range of staples and luxury goods arrived. Salt was a necessity, essential for the preservation of food, while functional household items like nails, glass, crockery and cutlery were also needed. So, too, were fabrics and not least luxuries like wine, beer and the newly fashionable tobacco. Even hemp and jute, necessary for sails, were brought in small quantities by ship to Helsinki, the sails then shipped as far as the Mediterranean. Sometimes goods traveled even further afield. In 1789 the American brig *Bilbao* arrived in Helsinki and departed with a hull full of local products.

Wars may have devastated Helsinki during these times, but even during the periods of greatest disruption, as in the Great Northern War, trade continued. After the Russians succeeded in taking Helsinki, significant numbers of Russian merchants followed in the wake of Peter the Great's soldiers, carrying on a thriving trade. Then, as now, trade and money knew no political boundaries.

Shipping played a major role in the economic life of Helsinki, even before the city became Finland's capital. Then, as later, sea captains carried out a lively private trade, selling some of the goods they carried on their ships directly to the public at prices significantly lower than those in shops.

The merchant Johan Sederholm (1722-1805), active in political relations between Finland and Stockholm, amassed a considerable fortune in shipping, some of which he used to establish other enterprises, including a tile factory, at Herttoniemi and a glass works at Sipoo. A portion of his wealth went to construct his town mansion, the Sederholm House on Aleksanterinkatu 18, completed in 1757. It is the oldest stone house still in existence in the city and is open to the public as a museum, with exhibitions relating to life in the eighteenth and nineteenth centuries, having been acquired by the City of Helsinki in 1949. It was probably designed by Samuel Berner, otherwise famous for the old Ulrika Eleonora Church, named after the Swedish queen of the time. So rich did Sederholm become that he even became a moneylender to the French monarchy.

In the nineteenth century, shipping remained a major industry; over forty percent of the capital's merchants were involved in 1813, and because of this maritime focus Alexander I established a college of navigation. Families like the Sederholms and Heidenstrauchs remained active in shipping, and J. H. Heidenstrauch was so successful that he commissioned the building of a three-story residence, adorned by an Ionic colonnade based on that of a Parisian townhouse, which was completed in 1820. Unfortunately, if the Sederholms continued to flourish, the family fortune of the Heidenstrauchs collapsed, and their place was taken by others with greater business acumen. The mansion was duly sold to the government, to be renovated as an imperial palace in 1837. Six years later it was again renovated by Carl Alexander Engel, Carl Ludvig Engel's son, and is today the Presidential Palace.

The Hietalahti Shipyard produced its first ship in 1868, one of a series that seemed limitless in number. Then, in the 1880s, the Finnish Steam Ship Company initiated its lines, which by the advent of the First World War included 26 different destinations all over the world. In 1926 a regular shipping service from Helsinki to South America commenced, followed ten years later by one to North America. Not surprisingly, ancillary industries were also prominent. Already, in the late eighteenth century Helsinki could boast a sawmill, two shipyards and a sailcloth factory.

Trade and Industry

The backbone of Finnish industry was, of course, manual labor, but this was very poorly paid, especially after Finland was ceded to Russia. In 1819 a manual laborer could expect to earn less than one rouble per day. For entrepreneurs, on the other hand, there was much money to be made.

Feodor Kiseleff, the founder of a sugar dynasty, acquired his refinery in 1812 and made an immense success of the venture. Kiseleff House, completed in 1818 on a corner of Senate Square by Unioninkatu 27, had originally been built in 1772-8 as another residence for Johan Sederholm. The sugar baron had the three-storied edifice, crowned by a mansard roof, extensively remodeled by his relation, the architect Konstantin Kiseleff. The tarred boarding that had clad it was removed, while the windows were enlarged and those on the *piano nobile* adorned by wooden balustrades. The roof was reinforced with black sheet metal, and the façade painted yellow, in harmony with the other buildings abutting Senate Square.

The refinery moved from its site on Senate Square in 1823 to a new location by Töölö Bay. There Engel designed and built the factory that from 1837 to 1858 was the only sugar refinery in Finland. Kiseleff, a philanthropic figure typical of many entrepreneurs of this period, used some of the proceeds to establish a university grant-giving foundation, which still supports students to this day.

As for Kiseleff House, it was later acquired in 1879 by the great merchant Georg S. Stockmann (1825-1906), a native of Lübeck and founder of the eponymous department store. He had initially made a considerable profit by importing cotton to Helsinki directly from New Orleans while also supplying Christmas fare to British engineers setting up factories in Tampere. With a keen eye for the latest innovations, he also became an early stockist of the bicycle, which soon became one of the city's most important means of transport. Reflecting his mercantile spirit, a shopping mall was appended in 1911-12, under the architectural supervision of Lars Sonck, with an entrance on Sofiankatu covered over by large rectangular skylights. It was linked on this side to the department store itself, then situated near Helsinki University on the Senate Square. Today Sonck's building houses a branch of the City Museum, and adjacent is the so-called open-air street museum, literally a museum of Helsinki streets.

In 1930 Stockmann moved to its present site, opposite the Swedish Theatre, where a new German-inspired building, designed by Sigurd Frosterus, was constructed, a vast edifice of eight stories. Kiseleff House than became headquarters of the Police Department until in 1985 it once again was given over to commercial use as a department store. Stockmann's employee Julius Tallberg (1857-1921) also became a major figure in the business world of Helsinki. Awarded the title of commercial counselor, he established a building supplies company and filled in the area around Ruoholahti in 1889, among other developmental projects.

Stockmann was not, of course, the only department store to thrive in Helsinki. Sokos Department Store, designed by Erkki Huttunen, opened its doors in 1952. A five-story building at Mannerheimintie 9, it incorporates a hotel and two restaurants into its physical fabric of strong horizontal lines, the top three floors of receding in pyramid-like fashion to create an illusion of added height.

As the English mineralogist Edward Daniel Clarke, who visited Helsinki in 1799, wrote:

> *The foreign commerce, as well as that of the south of* Finland, *is, exclusively with* Spain, *to which country it conveys deal planks, and brings back salt; the return with this article being considered of great importance.* Helsingfors, *like* Åbo *and* Louisa *(Lovisa), is renowned for its deal planks; some of which we found to be twelve feet in length and two inches in thickness, perfectly fair, and very free from knots.*

The Esplanade, both North and South, was first planned as an elegant residential area for government officials and merchants, but by the second quarter of the nineteenth century the North Esplanade was a street of functional, hardly elegant, mercantile activity. There was an outdoor butcher opposite the corner of Mikonkatu and, in the vicinity, a tannery owned by a Mr. Kropp. Today the North Esplanade is Helsinki's most exclusive shopping street, and Mercury House stands on the spot of the long-disappeared butcher.

Even Suomenlinna, the fortress in the harbor of Helsinki, had its merchants, who included Russian traders, many of whom worked as victualers and shopkeepers. By 1820 about one-third of all merchants in the capital were Russian, but by the middle of the century this percentage had declined as Finns themselves became increasingly active in commerce. Even then, many Russians continued to be engaged in trading and industry on a more humble level. Most of the trade in glass on the streets of Helsinki at the turn of the twentieth century, for instance, was in Russian hands.

Trade was no means restricted only to the middle or lower classes. The Finnish nobility, for all its grand airs, was rarely averse to making a good deal. Some were quite willing even to offer up their private city residences if the price were right. Anders Ramsay's father, a leading member of the Senate, let his to the celebrated Admiral Lazarev, but came to regret it no less than many others in his position today do. As his son recounted: "upon our return in the autumn the place needed repairs that almost exceeded the cost of the rent. The parquet floors were torn by the young people's skating practice, the wallpaper was stained with oil where the icons of the saints had been, the furniture was badly damaged and the table linen had been used as dusters."

Markets

Despite the rise of industry and trade, traditional marketplaces remained important in Helsinki, which had long enjoyed a number of thriving markets. One, the Baltic herring market, had already been established as far back as 1743, and most continued well into the nineteenth and twentieth centuries.

By the end of the Napoleonic Wars the principal market for food was Senate Square, but in 1818 it moved to the aptly named Market Square or Kauppatori (Salutorget), adjacent to the Esplanade by the harbor. This location enjoyed the major advantage that it enabled fishermen to sell their produce directly from their vessels. Only in 1889 did the Food Market Hall or Kauppahalli, built by the noted architect Gustaf Nyström, provide an enclosed facility for Helsinki's shoppers. Situated at Eteläranta, its brick neo-Renaissance exterior clads a largely iron and steel structure, its central area flanked by two side wings.

Mrs. Ethel Tweedie, a British visitor, noted in the late 1890s:

> *The market is a feature in Finland, and in a measure takes the place of shops in other countries. For instance, wagons containing butcher's meat stand in rows, beside numerous carts full of fish, while fruit and flowers, cakes and bread-stuffs in trucks abound. Indeed, so fully are these markets supplied, it seems almost unnecessary to have any shops at all…*

It was to the peasant women who worked there that the principal charm of the market was to be traced. They were attired in pink cotton blouses, with brightly colored bodices, sitting beneath their "queer old cotton umbrellas, the most fashionable shade for which appears to be bright blue!"

Many of Helsinki's old markets like Narinkka, the precinct in which Russian and Jewish stalls were to be found until 1929, have now disappeared, but others such as Hietalahti continue to thrive, its frequent flea markets attracting visitors from Sweden, Russia and beyond.

Industrialization

Industrialization in Helsinki was a slow process, but by 1850 there were 27 factories, albeit traditional "craft" establishments where industrial technology had made few inroads. Henrik Borgström's tobacco factory, for one, had been established in 1834, initially employing over fifty people, a number which expanded rapidly in the following years. There were also five furniture factories, and four mirror manufacturers supplied the needs of Helsinki's growing middle classes. For them, no commodity was less important than the piano, provided after 1835 by Erik Granholm's factory. Between then and 1852 it produced over two hundred pianos of various sizes and types. There were also an almost countless number of tailoring establishments and even one manufacturer of scent. One factory produced playing cards, to the dissatisfaction of some more moralizing churchmen.

One significant boost to this rising industry was the abolition of the guild system in 1868. Then eleven years later total freedom of trade was permitted, further encouraging industrial growth. Even more significant, however, was the arrival of the railway. The first line opened on March 17, 1862, linking Helsinki to Hämeenlinna. Then, with far greater political, economic and social significance, a line opened, linking Helsinki, by way of Riihimäki, to St. Petersburg in 1870. Both passengers and goods could thus reach the Russian imperial capital in only a few hours.

The new railway station, which was built on piles on what had been swampy ground by Kluuvi, was a splendid affair, which even had its own imperial waiting room. It also faced a prominent new square, around which imposing edifices, both public and private, made their appearance as the century drew to its close.

Helsinki was now expanding well beyond its traditional borders, in part thanks to the railway along whose lines new urban developments sprang up like mushrooms. This was especially true after 1870 with respect to suburbs north of the Long Bridge, built in 1912. Sörnäinen developed in this fashion, with a linking road, formerly the East Chaussee (now Hämeentie) providing a principal artery for transport north and south.

By 1870 forty percent of the city's non-military population were active in industry, a state of affairs symbolized by the success of the great industrial exhibition held in the Kaivopuisto Gardens in 1876, when all manner of modern technology was displayed for a wider public. By the eve of the First World War at least sixty per cent of Helsinki residents were employed in industry in one capacity or another.

A significant proportion worked in the new food processing industries. Hartwall, for example, for decades producers of mineral water, began utilizing a steam engine in mechanized production in the 1870s. They were followed in 1894 by the chocolate and confectionery producer Fazer, who also adopted mechanized production as orders streamed in from Scandinavia, Russia and even Germany. Founded by a Swiss German journeyman tailor who had branched out into the trade of furrier, the chocolate dynasty was inherited by Karl Fazer, who in 1891 bought a site at Kluuvikatu 3, where, along with the production of chocolate and pastries, he published music. Having trained in catering in St. Petersburg, Berlin and Paris, he was in a position to make a success of the venture. And success it was, for even today that site remains a part of the Fazer chocolate empire, their historic café and restaurant. Another entrepreneur of German extraction was Eduard Paulig, like Stockmann a native of Lübeck, whose name became a byword for coffee.

Beer was also big business in the Finnish capital. Nikolai Sinebrychoff, originally from Russia, established one of the country's most important breweries in 1819 and was granted a monopoly on the brewing of beer in Helsinki by the city authorities—privileges which were later expanded to include the distilling of spirits. Others of Russian background like the Kiseleff family, whom we have already come across, took an important role not only as sugar producers but also as the founders of the city's gasworks.

Other enterprises produced metal, graphics and other food products. These tended to be based at Hietalahti, Hakaniemi and Sörnäinen, areas that acquired a large population of working people. The Swedish company Rörstrand was established there at Arabia in 1874, producing fine porcelain and ceramic ware. It was eventually bought by Finns in 1916 and despite changing hands on a number of occasions, still thrives today. A major engineering company, Kone, was founded in 1910 and became one of the leaders in the European market. It first manufactured electric lifts and joisting devices in 1918 and today supplies lifts and other engineering products worldwide.

Banking

The growth of banking was crucial to Helsinki's economy. As early as 1809 Finland had a central bank, its main purpose being to provide funds desperately needed for the running of aristocratic estates. In 1823 savings banks were founded for a much wider clientele. Whilst Turku, the former capital, was the first to have them, Helsinki followed suit three years later.

1862 was a red-letter day for banking, for it was then that the famous Union Bank of Finland was established, an institution that continued under that name until only a few years ago when it was absorbed in various mergers. It was the first modern joint-stock bank in the entire Russian Empire, and not surprisingly required a suitably imposing edifice to reflect the public image its shareholders wished to convey. This building, built in the neo-Renaissance style popular at the time throughout Europe, is situated at Aleksanterinkatu 36, where it still serves the banking industry, much as it did in the 1860s but with a much wider scope. Almost thirty years later, another important banking house was established for a mainly Finnish speaking clientele and with a Finnish speaking administration, when Kansallis-Osake-Pankki, founded in 1889-90, was situated within the hallowed walls of the Hotel Kämp, where it once again made its home after the Second World War.

Unfortunately, Helsinki high finance had its shadowy side as well, as Eino Leino's novel *The Bankers* (Pankkiherroja, 1914) indicates. Here, a rollercoaster ride alternates between prosperity and bankruptcy in a world of high risk. A more positive image is to be found at the Nordea Bankmuseum, located at Unioninkatu 32, where the appearance of a bank in the early years of the twentieth century by Gesellius-Lindgren-Saarinen has been recreated with National Romantic charm and elegance accompanied by historical explanations.

Workers' Metropolis

Helsinki was now a rapidly burgeoning city. With 32,000 residents in 1870, by 1900 its population was well over 90,000. This was only the start. By the beginning of the First World War, 250,000 people lived in Helsinki, and many of these were engaged in industry. Osberg & Bade opened an engineering workshop during the 1860s, while Tampella's dry dock in Hietalahti also took off.

At the same time, other grassroots organizations were developing. The cooperative movement was taking shape, larger and more effective than anywhere else in the Nordic world. A few years later in 1911 the Helsinki Stock Exchange was built at Fabianinkatu 14, to the designs of Lars Sonck. A symbol that the capital was taking its place on the world financial stage, its most striking feature is an interior courtyard overlooked by balconies, which seems to anticipate some of the modern shopping malls of today.

For the working man and woman, employment was arduous. In general, factory hands worked between eleven and fourteen hours a day, but in some enterprises like bakeries seventeen hours was not unusual, with working hours during the winter generally shorter than in the summer. It was typical at the turn of the century, for example, for a worker to do no more than seven hours in January but ten hours from May to October during that same year. Of these workers many were children, but in 1889 the Society for the Protection of Working People succeeded in lobbying for a new law prohibiting those under fifteen from working more than seven hours a day. By 1917 all factory work was restricted to an eight-hour day and that, in most cases, for five days a week at the maximum. A visit to the Worker Housing Museum at Kirstinkuja 4 provides an illustration of the domestic life of a factory worker during this period and into the post-war years.

Electrification and Electronics

The introduction of electricity to Helsinki during the 1880s, and its extension by a network funded by private companies, culminated in the establishment of the city administration's own electricity company in 1906. At first, electricity was limited largely to lighting, telephones and lifts, but by the early 1930s other household appliances were making their appearance in the more prosperous parts of the city. In 1932 the first electrical cooker was installed at Topeliuksenkatu 3.

Strömberg was a significant industrial actor, establishing itself near Sörnäinen after the company's original premises were burnt down. A vast concern, it generated not only electricity but was deeply involved in the whole field of electronics. Another company, Helvar, which produced some of Finland's first radios, settled in the vicinity at about the same time, to be joined by Slev, a manufacturer of cookers, in 1940.

The post-war years witnessed an extraordinary electronics boom in Helsinki and Finland as a whole. Recently, between 1990 and 1998, the sector's productivity quadrupled, exports now totaling 25 percent of the whole. That said, the benefits of these developments have accrued more to provincial industrial centers like Tampere and Oulu than to Helsinki itself, even if the capital still remains an important headquarters of high technology, with its multiplicity of research institutes.

Working-class Life

Nowhere in Helsinki epitomized better the life of the working man and his family in the early twentieth century than the old suburbs that lay to the north of the Long Bridge, such as Hakaniemi, with its famous market, and to the southeast. The working-class atmosphere of Punavuori is best evoked through the poetry of Arvo Turtiainen (1904-1989). Inspired by such American poets as Walt Whitman and Carl Sandberg, he grew up in the district and as a young man was a founding member of the society of writers known as the Wedge (*Kiila*), a haven for Communists and Socialists. Much of his writing utilizes local so-called *Stadi* or "city" slang. Sometimes there is modernity in his poetry as well as an unapologetic look at modern industry, as in "Goodbye to the Rööperi of My Childhood":

These streets, these houses, the sky above the roofs
these factory chimneys trailing their hair in the wind
these dinosaur-cranes in the harbor, these working dockyard voices,
the wild stammering of the riveting hammers
the sirening of these ships as they sail in
with flocks of seagulls from far seas
or sound their goodbyes to you
Punavuori Hill, old Rööperi, to you
Ever reflecting your face in the sea water
Ever and always making your face anew.

Yet in the very same poem, a different view of his neighborhood is presented, a nostalgic view in which modern industry hardly plays any role at all:

Where have the old wooden houses gone,
the lilac yards, the sailors with the Swedish twang,
the skippers' quarters and the fishermen's homes,
and where have the artisans, the horse-drivers gone,
leaving your streets and your lanes,
and where are the stables at the backs of yards,
the smell of the hay and the horses?
Where are sailboats in the harbor, the sand yawls, the ketches,
and the gallantest barque of all, the Tcherimay,
that many of your lads sailed off on to far seas and far lands
many not coming back?

Another poet, Viljo Kajava (1909-98), in his turn sang the praises of the working-class district of Vallila in the northern suburbs in his collection of poems, *Vallila Rhapsody* (Vallilan rapsodia). A native of industrial Tampere, a hotbed of socialism during the early twentieth century, he was another member of the Wedge group of poets. His works provide insights into the left-right divide of the 1920s and 1930s, important for understanding Finland's social development during this period.

The continuing growth of the shipping industry, exemplified by new harbor construction, along with that of other manufacturing meant that new housing was required for the workers. The 1920s and 1930s witnessed large-scale working-class developments such as that at Vallila. Among the most innovative, it was carried out to the designs of the architects Armas Lindgren and Bertel Liljeqvist, becoming a symbol of Finnish modernism.

The Depression
The outbreak of the Depression of 1929 had dire implications for Finland, much as it did for the rest of the western world. Even so, industrialization continued to grow by leaps and bounds in the 1920s and 1930s, even if companies like Arabia suffered a serious decline in orders during this period. This decline continued during 1931-5, though it was never as bad in Helsinki as it was in the smaller towns and rural areas of Finland.

For one thing, the city government was constantly at pains to stimulate the economy. With this in mind, it organized a British Week in the late summer of 1933, with no less personages than the Finnish president and the Prince of Wales acting as patrons. A variety of eminent figures arrived for the opening ceremony in front of the Great Church of St. Nicholas on Senate Square, including Lord Baden-Powell, the founder of the Boy Scout movement and then its Chief Scout. When the exhibition closed with a fireworks spectacular, 80,000 residents and visitors were present and the city enjoyed a modest boost.

Post-War Developments
In the aftermath of the Continuation War, Finland was obliged to make hefty war reparations to the USSR. Burdensome as these were,

they also had the effect of encouraging the modernization of many sections of Finnish industry. These benefits continued long after the reparations had been paid off, not least Finland's monopoly of supplying the USSR with icebreakers.

Another major development, in the immediate aftermath of the war was that large numbers of refugees from Finnish Karelia had to be resettled, many of whom had come to Helsinki. They required not only housing, but also work and not just any work. Those who were refugees from Viipuri, for example, and had worked on the trams were often similarly employed in Helsinki, an approach followed with other industrial and service workers. In many cases, this was no difficult task, since 171 of Viipuri's biggest companies had re-established themselves in Helsinki, the most noted being Hackman.

Within a few years, a rapidly growing workforce and a large number of refugees created a period of turmoil in Helsinki. Only in 1954 was the improvised accommodation established during the war—where people were housed in bunkers—finally phased out, as sufficient alternative housing was built and jobs had come to be provided. Even so, in 1956, the year of the Hungarian Uprising, the outbreak of a general strike seemed to herald further upheavals. But further disturbances did not occur and the city began to enjoy greater social and economic stability. The city authorities could now devote themselves to further considerations about how to improve the infrastructure of the city, especially in relation to transport. In 1959 a special committee was established to explore the possibility of building an underground railway system for Helsinki. Unfortunately, it would take over a generation for these ideas to be finally realized.

From the 1950s until the economic crisis of the 1970s, the composition of Helsinki changed radically as large numbers of people moved from the provinces into the capital. Many of these new internal migrants were entering the rapidly developing manufacturing and construction sectors. This movement required the development of new social and economic amenities.

During the 1980s new commercial areas grew up in and around Helsinki. One of the most important was Itäkeskus in a northeastern suburb. Forum, another shopping center at Mannerheimintie 20, was built in 1982-5, sprawling from Mannerheimintie on one side to

Yrjönkatu on the other, containing a vast array of shops, restaurants and cafés, the Amos Anderson Art Museum and the old interior of the Capitol Cinema of 1926. Gallery Kluuvi and a major annex to Stockmann's also followed in the city center, to be joined the following decade by Gallery Kämp, with its elegant shops, tucked away behind the recently resurrected hotel of the same name.

Soviet Collapse and New Beginnings

Trade with the Soviet Union had by now reached a high point. In 1989 alone 25 percent of exports from Finland went there, considerably more than to Sweden. In comparison, those to Britain were approximately 11.5 percent of the total.

With the collapse of the Soviet Union in the early 1990s and the loss of this important export market, an economic depression ensued, with a sharp fall in manufacturing jobs. Exports to Russia fell by two-thirds, creating a crisis that lasted until 1993, but one from which Finland achieved an amazing recovery, not least through the rise of its technology and communications industries.

Needless to say, in a country as wooded as Finland, the forestry industry has long been extremely important, providing exports worth some billion Euros annually. These activities are by definition largely based outside Helsinki, but the by-products of the industry are now used to generate energy, providing over ninety percent of the capital's heating. The technical innovations involved in these processes have been the lynch pins in the role of Finnish technology.

The shipping industry also continues to prosper. Shipbuilding is still important in places like the Kvaerner Masa-Yard, where eight major luxury liners, intended to cruise such regions as the Caribbean, began in 2001. Even more important is its contribution to Arctic shipping and the production of icebreakers, for Helsinki shipyards have contributed more than sixty percent of the world's icebreakers in recent years. A number of these can be seen during the summer months opposite the Ministry for Foreign Affairs at Meritullintori (Sjötullstorget). Much of the research behind this production has been carried out at Kvaerner Masa-Yard's Arctic Technology Center (MARC), the only private research center of its type in the world. A plethora of international companies, including Exxon, Shell and even

China's Bohai Oil, depend on the information gleaned there to facilitate maritime shipments of oil.

The importance of the medical industry in Helsinki should also be stressed. Finland had suffered severely in the twentieth century from such diseases as tuberculosis, generating the construction of sanatoria, of which Alvar Aalto's at Pemar is the most famous, as well as the development of new therapies. The unusual prevalence of certain types of incurable, malignant brain tumors (200 cases a year in Finland) has also encouraged the medical industry to concentrate on the exploration of new therapeutic techniques for combating this condition. This has resulted in the establishment of research programs in which the so-called boron neutron capture therapy has been developed under the leadership of the Helsinki University Central Hospital in conjunction with the Technical Research Center of Finland. As a result new hope has been kindled that the disease might one day be brought under control.

Ecological awareness pervades Finnish society and in the capital it has even reached the tourist industry where, for example, Scandic Hotels have built their new Scandic Hotel Simonkenttä in the city center with environmentally friendly innovations. A whole range of energy-saving technologies and appropriate construction materials has been employed, as directed by its ecologically conscious proprietor, Tapiola, and Skanska, the Nordic world's most famous construction company. Nor should the central role of the telecommunications industry in Helsinki in particular be forgotten. Finland was the first European country to introduce a digital mobile network and it is today a model for telecommunications worldwide.

Since 1998 most working people in Helsinki have been employed in the service industry. Commerce has entered areas formerly off-limits, as older, previously non-commercial bodies also began raising revenues. Manufacturing has still not recovered, nor has trade to the territories of the former Soviet Union blossomed anew. On the contrary, no more than four percent of Finnish exports made their way to Russia in 2000. In any case, the old industrial working class of the nineteenth and early twentieth centuries has long gone as Finland has moved from a resource-based to a knowledge-based economy. Perhaps the greatest symbol of this fact is that the Long Bridge, which formerly so sharply divided the traditionally working-class areas of the city from those of the middle classes, no longer does so. Now, instead, it is the gateway, through which contemporary yuppies enter their newly claimed residential territories to the north.

CHAPTER TWO

Imperial Helsinki
The Czar, the Architect and the New City

Today parts of Kruununhaka, situated between Senate House Square and Pohjoisranta, remain as the oldest area of Helsinki still in use as a residential area. An area of tall, eclectically inspired houses, its apartments tend to be large and comfortable. This district had been constructed long before the great re-development of the city under Czar Alexander I in the early nineteenth century. In those early days Finland was under the sovereignty of the kings of Sweden. Indeed, Finland had belonged to Sweden since the thirteenth century and would do so until the Napoleonic Wars effected its transfer to Russia.

During the seventeenth century the grandest residence, where the royal Swedish governor Count Per Brahe the Younger (1602-80) stayed on his rare visits to the province, was situated by the harbor. Two stories high, it encompassed a ballroom—an extraordinary luxury in Finland at that time—with a special suite reserved for Brahe, whose father, the elder Per Brahe, had been a courtier of King Gustaf Vasa. He it was who had made the younger Brahe a count and member of the council of regency as well as the governor of Finland during the years 1637-41 and again from 1648-54.

The Meilahti Estate
Other courtiers, government officials representing the Swedish Crown, and various dependents were also beginning to take up residency, at least occasionally, in Helsinki, even if Turku continued to be the capital throughout Swedish rule and well into the nineteenth century. Some of the estates they owned and occupied were situated in the countryside

outside Helsinki and were directly linked to royal *largesse*. Gustaf II Adolph (1594-1632), for example, had granted the demesnes of Meilahti, Munkkiniemi, Tali, Huopalahti, Latokartano and Lauttasaari to the riding master Gerdt Skytte, a devoted retainer of the king and an important courtier of his time.

Meilahti's history through the centuries is a mirror, in many ways, of that of the ruling circles of Helsinki itself. Thus, with political vagaries most of the lands connected to Meilahti had already been transferred to the ownership of the corporation of Helsinki in 1650, at which time they were used for both residential and grazing purposes. Then in 1682 the estate was again transferred, this time into the ownership of the war commissioner Johan Gripenberg. His proprietorship also proved brief, and by the eighteenth century the wealthy Dutch immigrant sea-faring Mattheizen family had acquired it. They embellished the Baroque country house erected there with the Chinese tapestries and other grand decorations still to be found on view.

After Finland was transferred to Russia as an independent Grand Duchy under the Czar, Meilahti once again acquired new owners. None other than the new governor general, Count Fabian Steinheil, purchased it during the 1820s together with the rest of Tamminiemi. His contribution was to add a small country residence in the empire style, a style much favored in the heady days of early imperial rule in Finland.

Under his daughter and her husband, Count Stewen-Steinheil, Meilahti enjoyed a period of splendor during the 1840s, never to be seen before or since. Among the guests who stayed there for lengthy periods while enjoying the seemingly endless festivities were the famous Count Vladimir Musin-Pushkin and his wife Emilie, as well as her sister, Aurora Karamzin, a famous beauty of the Russian Court who was also a lady-in-waiting to the Czarina Alexandra, consort of Nicholas I. The house and garden became the venue for a splendid cavalcade of aristocratic gatherings throughout the summer months. It was said that even the lawns were draped with fabrics so as to prevent the ladies from sullying the trains of their gowns.

Aurora Karamzin was also associated with another important country house of the nineteenth century, the Villa Hakasalmi

(Hagasund), today the City Museum at Töölönranta. Designed by Ernst Bernhard Lohrmann, the German who had succeeded Carl Ludwig Engel as the city's chief architect, and built in 1843-7, it was first the home of Carl Johan Wallen, an important administrator in the city's government and former governor of Viipuri in Karelia to the east. Situated just outside the city limits, it combined the amenities of both town and country. Of the two principal floors, the lower contained the kitchen, service rooms, and the rooms used every day by the family; on the floor above were the public rooms, used more rarely: two salons, the dining room and a guest room. Its stylistic appearance differed radically from that favored by Engel, eschewing strict classicism in favor of an Italianate villa arrangement and style. After the owner's death, Aurora, who was Wallen's stepdaughter, took over the villa. She continued to live there until her death in 1902. Strange to say, her descendant Catherine Oxenberg, the daughter of a Yugoslavian princess, became famous as the character Amanda in the famous American television serial *Dynasty*.

As for Meilahti, it was once again sold in 1847, this time to Count Alexander Kushelev-Bezborodko. He was the first of a number of proprietors who briefly lived there, including Captain Gustaf Jägerskiöld, until in the 1870s the city of Helsinki once again acquired it. Not only did the summerhouse enter Jägerskiöld's ownership, but the island of Seurasaari, too, on which the open-air historic village museum would later be created. Other principal parts of the property were then conceived as part of a new suburban villa zone, but since no one showed any interest in purchasing them, far from the city as they were, the area remained undeveloped for some years.

To the east, however, such plans for development proved more successful, and in 1873 the architect F. L. Calonius built the luxurious Villa Kesäranta, now used as the official residence of the prime minister. In today's context the most important building erected at Tamminiemi from imperial times was the Villa Tamminiemi (Ekkudden), designed by the architect Gustaf Nyström, later the residence between the 1940s and 1980s of successive presidents of Finland, most famously of President Urho Kekkonen.

The periphery of Helsinki still abounds with a number of other noteworthy manor houses from the Gustavian period. These include Tuomarinkylä Manor from 1790, situated at Kartanomuseontie. It had been commissioned by Johannes Weckström, an administrator of military finances, but changed owners several times until in 1917 the City of Helsinki acquired it. Restored in 1960 and more recently in 1986, it serves as a museum of country house life of the late eighteenth century. Also noteworthy is the late eighteenth-century Espoo Manor House to the west of Helsinki, which originally belonged to Governor Anders Henrik Ramsay, the scion of a Scottish family who had immigrated to Finland. It was considerably altered in 1914-15 by W. G. Palmqvist, who extended it and added a large colonnade that serves as a verandah. A bridge with stone vaulting, the oldest of its kind in Finland, is also to be found in its park, not far from Espoo Church, with origins in the late fifteenth century.

Fire and Rebirth

Like so many cities and towns in Finland at the beginning of the nineteenth century, Helsinki was a conglomeration of wooden houses and other buildings, prone to the ravages of fires. One of the last remaining examples of these wooden homes can be seen in Kruununhaka, where the Burgher's House, at Kristianinkatu 12, now a branch of the City Museum, is decorated, as it would have been in the 1860s. A relatively small house, its modest interior is furnished in the fashion of the times, including an interesting period kitchen. It remains unmistakably rustic in appearance, so unlike those built in other European cities during the mid-nineteenth century.

It was the very destructiveness of Helsinki's fires that also provided the opportunities for renewal, with wider streets, larger houses and more fashionable amenities than before. When in November 1808 a great fire ravaged the whole of the city, devastating the area between the two harbors to the north and the south, it presented a pretext for the rebuilding of this strategically important fishing port and garrison town. Originally, a military officer named Anders Kocke provided a plan for the reconstruction, based upon the earlier layout of the small town but with minor extensions along the "rational" rectilinear layouts prevalent in Europe and the United States at that time. But after Finland was transferred to Russian rule in 1809, many changes were in the offing. Helsinki was about to become the new and vibrant capital of the Russian Empire's latest territorial acquisition. This initiative was duly seized by the Russian Czar, who promulgated an imperial decree in 1812, according to which not only was the transfer of the governmental seat to Helsinki confirmed, but the creation of a new and imposing capital laid out. The plan was given its final form five years later in 1817 under the direction of Johan Albrecht Ehrenström. Ehrenström (1762-1847), an entrepreneurial figure, had lived a colorful life not without its up and downs. He had been put in the pillory in 1793 and was later imprisoned for treason, having had his death penalty commuted. Yet after 1811 his position in Finland seemed to change as he was rehabilitated and became actively involved in the redevelopment of the new Finnish capital.

It had obviously not been a very prepossessing place in these days, if the Pole Faddei Bulgarin, who had first visited the city in 1808-9 while a soldier in the Russian army, is to be believed. It was, he remarked, "one of the most insignificant and wretched little towns in Finland, a village, almost, a few streets of red wooden houses, built on rocks and impassable mud." Perhaps it is the old Burgher's House that provides the best illustration of this aspect of old Helsinki, though it is decorated in the style of the 1860s rather than of the time of its construction. Yet it was the end of a tradition, rather than the start of a new one.

Engel's Vision

Sensing the opportunity of turning this new rustic capital into a showcase city, Alexander I commissioned one of his favorite architects, Carl Ludvig Engel, to create a new and majestic city center for the Finnish capital. This was to be the beginning of the German architect's immensely significant relationship with Helsinki. He left his mark on the city as no other architect would do before or since, for he was to build thirty public buildings and to supervise the construction of more than six hundred others.

Engel had first come to Finland in 1814, when he carried out a design for a sugar refinery at Turku, and was shocked by the ruggedness of the terrain. As he wrote to his parents from Helsinki on May Day 1816, since:

all of Finland is nothing but a rocky cliff… boulders the size of build-ings must be blasted away where the new streets will be laid out. The crashing and banging of exploding stone is heard day in, day out, at all points where the new city is to be built.

By no means despairing, however, Engel saw this as a unique opportunity and eagerly took up the challenge.

Engel's first commission from the Czar was the restoration of the old Bock House, on the southeastern corner of Senate Square, at the corner of Aleksanterinkatu and Katariinankatu, carried out between 1816 and 1819. This structure had originally been built in 1763 for the merchant Gustaf Bock, but in 1801 had become the residence of an important city official. Under the Czar's scheme, it was to serve as the new residence of the governor general, the imperial representative appointed to live in the capital. To this end, it was enlarged in 1817 by the addition of an upper floor, in which a ballroom was placed and a balcony attached for public proclamations and such like. It was from here that Alexander I, on a rare visit to Helsinki, appeared before the crowds gathered outside on his name day, September 11, 1818. As he showed himself on the balcony, to great popular acclaim, the new façade provided a perfect backdrop, decorated as it was by a diminutive Ionic portico of four free-standing columns supporting a triangular pediment incorporated into the upper two floors. The renovated building also contained a large barrel-vaulted assembly room. Later, in 1837, it became Helsinki's City Hall. When that function was moved to the Society House, it was occupied by the Municipal Court, not far from where, on the south side of the square, the new Magistrate's Court was later built. As such, the Bock House was among the first of a number of important official edifices in the capital. During the late 1980s it underwent a major restoration, together with the Burtz and Hellenius Houses, and today also incorporates a new building in which the City Council Chambers are now located. Important receptions are now held by the City Council in Bock House.

Yet it was not so much the Senate Square but the Esplanade, that tree-lined avenue in the heart of Helsinki, that provided the central axis to join the new and the old districts of the city from east to west. Moreover, for all the modern building in stone, most of the houses continued to be of wood. Nor could the granite stone upon which the city was built always be relied upon to provide substantial foundations. On the contrary, some houses were also built not on rocks, but on sandy soil, where considerable preparations had to be carried out in order to make building at all possible. As Mrs. Tweedie, a lady who held strong views on a plethora of subjects, wrote in 1897:

The town stands either on massive glacial rocks, or, in other parts that have been reclaimed from the sea, on soft sand; in the latter case the erection has to be reared on piles. For the foundation of the house mentioned, long stakes, about 20 feet in length, were driven into the ground. Above this pile a sort of crane was erected, from which hung a large heavy stone caught by iron prongs. Some twenty men stood round the crane, and with one 'Heave oh!' pulled the stone up to the top, where, being let loose, it fell with a tremendous thud upon the head of the luckless pile, which was driven with every successive blow deeper into the earth. When all the piles were thus driven home, 4 or 5 feet apart, rough bits of rock or stone were fitted in between them, and the whole was boarded over with wood after the fashion of flooring, on top of which the house itself was built.

Unioninkatu, running north-south on the western flank of the Church of St. Nicholas, had now become the principal thoroughfare of Helsinki, like St. Petersburg's Nevsky Prospect or Berlin's Unter den Linden. Though it was diminutive in size by comparison to the former, it was taking shape as an elegant showpiece for its new imperial master's generosity.

Senate House

Senate House Square, newly created by Engel from what had formerly been a ramshackle area with small houses and a church, was the principal public space of the capital, a large area on which public demonstrations and festivities could be held. It was also the site of the Senate House, after which the square was named, a building upon whose construction little expense was spared, as the city's most prominent secular edifice. The Senate of Finland, as the Finnish government was called, had its seat here. Appropriately Engel chose for this, his first monumental building on the square, a Corinthian colonnade, the grandest of the classical orders, to adorn the exterior. An oval throne room, similarly decorated, overlooked Senate Square, with at either end a slightly projecting pavilion. The main block is rectangular in shape, while three wings to its rear, of lesser height, were decorated with ionic colonnades. The north wing was built by Lohrmann, in 1853, but later made way for another building, by C. R. Björnberg, in 1900.

The architectural inspiration for the Senate House derives from the Italian architect Carlo Rossi, whose works from the early nineteenth century include the Yelagin Palace and Alexandrinsky Theatre in St. Petersburg. Sources from ancient Greek or Roman architecture might also have played a role. In any case, a library had been included in the east wing, based on the Baths of Diocletian, but it has long since disappeared in the course of remodeling. In the 1980s the complex underwent a thorough restoration.

Costly Construction

Other building projects commissioned by Alexander I and carried out by Engel include (to name the most important) the university and its library, a military school for orphans, and a house of social assembly, all of which are discussed in other chapters. Together these formed a major undertaking, at great expense to the Czar. Yet even he did not possess unlimited money, and spending in Helsinki also had to be balanced against that in Russia proper, even if resources were largely raised in Finland itself. Still, all in all, by the time Engel's commissions were completed, a total of 4,229,743 roubles and 91 kopecks had been spent. This vast sum had been found not only from various local taxes, but also from an excise duty on salt as well as an export duty on tar, so sought after by foreign shipping. The State Loan Bank in St. Petersburg also assisted with substantial funds.

For those carrying out the work the rewards could be considerable. The building trade was very lucrative and some, like the Russian

Uschakoff family, made their fortune in manufacturing building materials. The villa at the North Esplanade, 19, now a city information bureau, would become a supreme example of Jugendstil in Finland, when Lars Sonck restored it in 1904. Others, like the Korastieffs, made theirs as building contractors. Still, it was clear to all that without the benevolence of the Czar, Helsinki would have remained a dusty village on some rocky crags. A suitable monument was duly commissioned to testify to the foresight and generosity of Helsinki's imperial patron. By the entrance to the harbor, against a backdrop of the Russian Orthodox Cathedral, the Empress' Stone was erected, a monument built to commemorate the visit of Czar Nicholas I and the Czarina Alexandra in 1833, when most of the rebuilding—though not the Great Church—was largely completed. It is still in Market Square today, despite the ebb and flow of political change, crowned by the Romanov two-headed eagle, symbol of the Russian Empire, and recently resurrected as the symbol of the Russian Federation.

Aristocratic Playground

Needless to say, when members of the imperial family went to Helsinki, their aristocratic courtiers were sure to follow and this they did in ever growing numbers, until the debacle of the Crimean War once again sidelined the Finnish capital socially. By then Helsinki had become totally altered from what it had been a few decades before. When the military officer Bulgarin returned in 1838 to the city of his youthful military days, it had changed beyond recognition: from a town of some 3,500 souls, it was now a city of 12,000.

It had also come to attract a large number of the Russian aristocracy under Czar Nicholas I, not so much for political reasons but as a summer resort. This was especially true during the 1830s, when by virtue of its proximity to St. Petersburg and the need to circumvent travel restrictions for those who wished to go abroad (introduced in reaction to the Decembrist uprising that had greeted the ascension of Nicholas I), many aristocratic Russians came to Helsinki.

Among the eminent, if sometimes extravagant, visitors who arrived at this time was the Princess Yusupov, notorious in the Russian capital for her Neronian feasts, during which the marble statues in her gardens were replaced by serfs in the appropriate poses, nude or not, as the fancy moved her. Her parties in Helsinki may have been more restrained, but her house at Kaivopuisto was built at great expense and with considerable elegance in the classically inspired style of the times. Legend has it that the proximity of her reputed lover, a certain Captain Isakov, imprisoned in the Suomenlinna fortress, was the true reason for her seasonal removal to Helsinki. It was believed that the site of her house had been chosen because of the proximity and ease it afforded her in surreptitious visits to and from her convict *amour*. History remains silent on the veracity of this hypothesis. In any case, the Princess Yusupov was not alone in her choice of Helsinki as a summer playground; the Princesses Gagarin, Trubetskoy, and Musin-Pushkin, also favored it, with retinues of paramours and personal retainers.

By 1850 Helsinki could boast a population of 17,000, not exactly a rival to Stockholm or St. Petersburg, but not insignificant by comparison to its size at the beginning of the century. Yet in the second half of the century, with the growth of the city westwards as well as into Kamppi and Kluuvi, the city burgeoned much further.

The upper echelons of Helsinki society now lived in Kruununhaka, especially in the vicinity of what is now Liisanpuistikko. But in many places vestiges of the city's older, more humble origins remained; many of the houses beyond Engel's monumental center were still comprised of one- or two-story wooden structures on plots separated by wooden fences. Houses of stone remained few and far between, even if the new construction of wooden houses was prohibited. In any case, the southern side of the Esplanade and the area around Kasarmitori still had quite a number of two-story wooden houses, so Helsinki's appearance, especially on its periphery, remained rather rustic and like that—except for Engel's city center —of Finnish provincial market towns in general.

Imperial Rule

One important aspect of the new imperial administration introduced into Helsinki after the Grand Duchy's incorporation into the Russian Empire was the official Russian nomenclatura of hierarchical ranks in 1826, which ordered both military and civil positions, superceding that of Sweden. According to this system long established in the Russian Empire, all official administrative positions corresponded to fourteen classes and covered 168 posts. Each entailed its own responsibilities and privileges and each had its corresponding uniform, edged in green, the color of Russian officialdom (this replaced the blue used on Swedish uniforms when Finland was part of the Swedish kingdom). Generally unpopular for its rigid regimentation, the nomenclatura, first established by Peter the Great in Russia in the 1720s, finally disappeared with the end of autarchy, only to be formally abolished in the early 1920s.

Yet some reform of Finnish political life was possible under Russian imperial rule and none was more important than the abolition of the estates and the introduction of the first Finnish parliament or Diet. This momentous event occurred in 1863 with its first convocation and was the first major political change since the cession of Finland to Russia. Within six years Czar Alexander II, a relative liberal, had ratified a new act, according to which a frequent and regular convening of the Diet was envisioned and greater liberties provided. Forever afterwards Finns would think of this Czar with great affection, the principal reason why even today his statue can be seen in the center of Senate House Square, the most important site for commemoration in Finland. It was created by the sculptor Walter Runeberg (1838-1920), a son of the poet Johan Ludvig Runeberg, and is flanked by other statues representing Law, Peace, Light and Labor.

Finns, of course, did not only look to St. Petersburg for political leadership. They also looked to what was then the Russian capital for work and career advancement. In fact, St. Petersburg was in many ways Finland's most important city throughout the nineteenth century. A large proportion of its population was from Finland and for much of the century St. Petersburg was home to more Finnish-speakers than Helsinki. Before the construction of the railways, transport by water to St. Petersburg from the central and eastern provinces of Finland was a relatively simple matter. Parts of Karelia, at Finland's southeastern corner, virtually abutted onto the suburbs of the northern Russian capital, while even Savo was easier to reach than Helsinki, connected as it was by a splendid series of lakes and canals. Moreover, many Finns worked seasonally on the railways, while in St. Petersburg Finns provided considerable seasonal labor in the building trade during the middle and later nineteenth century.

There were also several schools and churches in St. Petersburg in which Finnish was the main language, and many well-educated Finns made their way up the military and civil service ladders in the imperial capital. Indeed, they were an especially favored people there, with considerable freedom of movement in and out of Russia, not reciprocally granted to native Russians themselves with respect to Finland.

By 1840 at least 11,300 Finns, craftsmen, domestic servants and laborers, were at work in the Russian capital, making it by far the most populous Finnish-speaking city, after Helsinki (13,300) and Turku (13,200). By 1869 the number of Finns in St. Petersburg had risen to more than 16,000, making them the second largest ethnic minority there after Germans and a labor force definitely to be reckoned with. There were also many Ingrians who had settled in the Russian capital from the surrounding countryside, where they had resided for centuries before the foundation of the city and who spoke a language closely related to Finnish.

Unfortunately, the honeymoon of Finland with Russia, though long-lived, came to a sudden and unhappy end. The beloved and modernizing Czar Alexander II was assassinated in 1881 and his successors, Alexander III and Nicholas II attempted a more forced integration of Finland into Russia. This coercive approach was paradoxically part of reforms by Russian liberals to further modernize the government of the empire, to make it more rational and efficient and therefore better able to serve all its inhabitants more effectively. From 1889 onwards the growth of Pan-Slavism, with its emphasis upon a unified and unitary Russian state run from St. Petersburg, severely undermined the relatively harmonious relationship Finland had enjoyed under its various Russian grand dukes since its transfer from Sweden to Russia. In reaction, a new constitutional party was formed in Helsinki, bringing together both Swedish- and Finnish-speaking Finns of all persuasions. Focused initially upon a campaign of passive resistance to all attempts at Russification and infringement of Finnish political and cultural rights, its members in government office, often partisans of the Young Finns Movement, increasingly refused to implement the administrative measures that the imperial government demanded. This often led to sackings and the creation of a disgruntled segment of former administrators. As a result, it was the so-called Old Finns, "Uncle Toms" of accommodation as the Young Finns saw them, who came by default to fill their positions, taking the adage "bent, but not broken" to heart. It was perhaps just as well, for though on the surface more accommodating, their suppleness enabled them to endure the ever more vicious winds of change which blew westwards towards Helsinki from St. Petersburg.

Autonomy Under Threat

Russian imperialism in Finland, for all its negative reputation and frustrations, also encompassed many benefits, especially in the early days of Czarist rule. It offered a wholly new labor market to Finns, whatever their skills and abilities. Something of this phenomenon has already been mentioned above. Yet it is important to emphasize that these opportunities affected every level of society from the lowest to the highest. For by means of the fourteen ranks that formed the hierarchy of the Russian civil and military bureaucracy, a Finn, whatever his origins, if he possessed the requisite degree from the Swedish-speaking Åbo Academy in Turku, could in Russia enter the eighth rank, thereby gaining the status of nobility. Ironically, the structure of Russian society was such that these opportunities were very rare indeed for native Russians. Not surprisingly, then, the combination of career opportunities and status made Russia for many decades an attractive place for Finns to develop careers both in the army and navy and the civil service. Indeed, it was not until 1848, that the first Finnish flag— not the current one but the Grand Duchy's coat of arms against a white background—flew and the national anthem was sung for the first time in a public place, all under the placid eyes of the Russian authorities.

The more negative aspects of imperialism became apparent as the nineteenth century drew to a close, for it was during the period from 1890 to 1905 that the most concerted efforts at Russification were made. The Finnish currency was abolished and by virtue of the Post Manifesto of 1890 the Finnish postal system was integrated into that of the Russian Empire as a whole, losing all independence. The issuing of Finnish postal stamps was prohibited. At the same time, the use of Russian as the language of governmental administration and schooling was promoted.

With the promulgation of the February Manifesto in 1899, Finnish autonomy itself came under severe threat, as Russian intentions to remove power from the Grand Duchy's four-chamber assembly of estates became clear. Women dressed in black, and wreaths were laid at the foot of the statue of Czar Alexander II on Senate Square. The artist Eetu Isto produced in response his inflammatory allegorical painting, *Attack* (1899), in which his anthropomorphic embodiment of Finnish national identity, "The Maid of Finland", a beauteous maiden defending a vast tome of law against would-be attackers, acquired immense importance as a national symbol of Finland's vulnerability and defiance.

On March 13, 1899, a mass demonstration of discontent took place in Senate Square and a petition with more than 524,000 names was also submitted to the Imperial throne. As the Finnish author, Aino Kallas, wife of Estonia's first minister to the Court of St. James in the inter-war years, wrote at the time:

A telegram received by a certain Danish newspaper says that the Czar has not consented to receive our delegation, a group of 500 men. More dispiriting yet, it has been ordered to leave St Petersburg at once, otherwise it will be expelled!

It is not in vain, now, that Finns wear mourning dress, or place wreaths on the statue of the Law. It is as if a great funeral is being conducted there, the funeral of truth, justice, light and freedom. 'C'est fini!'

Extremism triumphed in 1904 when, with anti-Russian feeling reaching a crescendo, the Swedish-speaking Finn and son of a former senator, Eugene Schauman, took matters into his own hands and cold-bloodedly assassinated Governor General Nikolai Bobrikov before committing suicide soon afterwards. Another assassination of a Russian official occurred the following year, when Eliel Soisalon-Soinien, a government prosecutor, was murdered, but afterwards such events ceased.

The Russian authorities made no attempt to cease their policy of Russification, and as they persisted in the early years of the twentieth century so did the hostility of many Finns towards the centralizing tendency of the Russian government, especially among some Swedish-speaking segments of the population. Already, in 1903, some Swedish-speaking university figures had formed a conspiratorial society for the purpose of fomenting armed struggle against the Russian authorities. Yet a basic problem remained, for Finns as a whole were unable to come to an agreement on precisely how Russification should be resisted. As a result, great bitterness prevailed not only between Russians and Finns, but among the latter on whether a passive or active approach should be taken.

Revolutionary Stirrings

With the outbreak of revolution in St. Petersburg in 1905 and the General Strike in Helsinki that followed in its wake, conditions appeared for a while to improve. The student Hella Wuolijoki, later post-Second World War director of the Finnish Broadcasting Company, who hailed from the province of Estonia (until 1918 part of Russia), wrote many years later of her considerable relief at the time:

Finally, the news arrived that the emperor had signed a manifesto according to which legal conditions were restored to the country and an extraordinary meeting of the estates was called to deal with parliamentary reform and electoral legislation, with the aim of introducing universal and equal voting rights.

In any case, other political changes were also in the offing. In 1906 the Diet of Estates, only recently installed in 1891 was abolished by the Diet itself. In its stead a unicameral parliament was established. (Later, the Diet's premises at Snellmaninkatu 9, designed by Nyström and with a tympanum containing a relief by Emil Wickström depicting Czar Alexander I at the Porvoo Diet of 1809, was used by a variety of learned societies for meetings, although they too have now moved elsewhere.) The political atmosphere at the time must have been electric. This must also have been the case at the House of the Nobility, where representatives of the aristocracy had their seat, situated in Hallituskatu 2, with its pseudo-Gothic façade behind which a vast assembly room is located. (Like the nobility itself, it was less structurally sound than might have appeared from without, and steel reinforcements for the ceiling had to be added by Nyström as the Russian period drew to its close.) Still, the centralizing pressure from St. Petersburg to conform to Russification continued in the following years, only really to find itself aborted as a result of the First World War.

The outbreak of this war provided yet another push towards the approaching rupture of Finnish-Russian political unity. Instead of large numbers of Finns rushing to the aid of the Czar and so-called sister nations of the Russian Empire (some, it must be said, did do this), at least 2,000, a disproportionate quarter of whom were Swedish-speaking, went over to the German side. Joining the 27th Royal Prussian Jaeger Battalion, many of its members were to play a key role after Finland unilaterally declared herself independent of Russia on December 6, 1917, a red-letter date still commemorated today. Despite two vicious wars and economic upheavals, Finland has retained its cherished independence since that time and has gone on to become one of the world's richest and most successful countries, a model to those in both East and West.

Mixed Legacy

So perhaps all things considered, the legacy of Russian imperialism was by no means all bad, like a marriage, happy in its early years but turned miserable and unpleasant as it drew to a close. After all, as the writer, Matti Kurjensaari wrote in *A Story of Helsinki* (1962), the heart of Helsinki on the southern tip of its little peninsula still retains its essentially imperial legacy from the early nineteenth century, even if the north has different traditions as a suburb of workers:

> In the south lies Ehrenström's and Engel's Helsinki. This means a tradi-
> tional order, senators, professors, The Book about Our Country *(by
> Topelius), Doric columns, theatres, opera, posh restaurants, educational
> establishments. In the north, there are factories, workers, hubbub,
> machine oil, steam, hearth stoves, fuchsia in the windows.*

However true that may be, it is the new marriage of a royal and imperial past with a working, industrialized, and highly technological present that has made Finland the contemporary success story which it is.

CHAPTER THREE

Military Helsinki: War and Warriors

After its founding in the sixteenth century Helsinki was for centuries a garrison town, and the military long played a prominent role in its life, politically, economically and socially. As a peripheral outpost of the Kingdom of Sweden, which had ruled Finland since the thirteenth century, it was on the front line when war broke out with the Russian Empire. As a result, the Russians had been, and continued to be for many centuries, the perpetual bane of the Finnish people. During the winter of 1570-7 they had attacked the newly established town, burning much of it down and leaving the plague in their wake. It was just one of many such incursions which would continue to afflict Finland, situated as it was as a buffer zone between the two great powers Sweden and Russia.

Later, as hostilities between the two nations erupted again in 1700, another disaster overtook Helsinki, lying virtually unprotected on the Gulf of Finland, for the Swedish government had never seen fit to construct any city walls, and other fortifications were minimal, to say the least. As a result, Helsinki was almost completely destroyed during the war when on May 11-12, 1713, the Russian navy, with some 17,000 men, laid siege to the town. The governor of the province of Uusimaa, Johan Creutz; the town's mayor, Henrik Tammelin; and its military commander, Count Carl Gustaf Armfelt were all convinced that evacuation was the only response. What other choice was open to them, bearing in mind that the Finnish garrison could muster only 1,800 defenders? As so often happened during Russian wars in the region, the city was duly burnt to the ground by the defenders themselves. Those fortunate enough to succeed in leaving Helsinki then sought their way to Stockholm or hid in the countryside as best they could. Those less fortunate found themselves carted away to Russia as prisoners of war, many of whom were enslaved as serfs elsewhere in Russia, never to return. Altogether, it was a bitter blow to the town, made worse as all of the south of Finland was rapidly brought under Russian control.

As for the newly arrived Russian troops, they succeeded in rebuilding and enlarging Helsinki's fortifications, such as they were, while at the same time constructing new barracks. Only eight years later, with the Peace of Uusikaupunki of 1721, was a treaty with Sweden finally concluded by which Sweden was once again given possession of Helsinki. Not until then did many of its exiled inhabitants finally return.

But the wars with Russia were not done, and a generation later, in 1741, Sweden attacked Russia in a desperate attempt to regain its lost territories. It proved disastrous. In 1742 the so-called War of the Hats brought Russian forces once again to the environs of Helsinki and once again Russian forces seized the town, provoking the second flight of its inhabitants within a quarter of a century. This time, however, the occupation lasted only a year and the town was not destroyed, so that with the signing of the Peace of Turku in 1743 Helsinki was returned to Swedish jurisdiction and the adjusted border neared to the Finnish capital, about seventy miles away, too menacingly close for comfort.

Suomenlinna Fortress

With the fall of Viipuri and Ingria (the territory surrounding the Russian city of St. Petersburg, newly founded by Czar Peter the Great), Sweden was in greater need of a defensive bulwark than ever before, and the little town of Helsinki was now only a short distance from the frontier itself. The Russians, meanwhile, had their own impregnable island fortress, Kronstadt, protecting the entrance to St. Petersburg at the eastern end of the Gulf of Finland. So in 1748 the Swedish authorities, under Adolf Fredrik, commenced the building of Suomenlinna on a series of islands in the inner archipelago of Helsinki. Shortly before on July 20, 1747, the government had issued a promulgation making Helsinki an officially fortified town.

No fewer than 6,400 Finnish military personnel took part in the construction of the fortress, not including laborers and others who had arrived from Sweden to work on the project. When the first major phase of work was finally completed in 1758, Finland finally had its own mighty bulwark. Built to the designs of the architect and engineer, Count Augustin Ehrensvärd, who was also a Swedish field marshal, a second phase was completed under the supervision of Captain Nils Kellander (ennobled under the surname Mannerskantz) in the years after 1772. Ehrensvärd was later commemorated by the somber but majestic tomb in which he is interred, constructed in the neo-Etruscan style brought into fashion by Giovanni Battista Piranesi in Rome. It is situated in front of the commandant's residence in the heart of the fortified complex on the principal island of what was then called Gustafholm, a suitable memorial to his vital role in its establishment. But it is the imposing King's Gate (1754) by the Swedish architect Carl Håreleman that today offers the most imposing architectural insight into the military fortifications of Suomenlinna, for it boldly captures in its form and decoration the Baroque nature of the Swedish kingdom itself. There is also a museum there, dedicated to Ehrensvärd's memory, in what was formerly the commandant's residence.

The fortress of Suomenlinna was the largest architectural project undertaken in the Nordic world up to that time and indeed for a long time thereafter. Even today it is a striking feature in the rocky entrance to the city's harbor, still posed to smite any aggressor foolish enough to brave a coastal assault. But its image was more successful than the reality, as the debacle of its fall during the Napoleonic Wars in 1808 was to demonstrate. But few remember its military failure then and today, most appropriately, it is a World Heritage Site established by UNESCO in 1991. Some have compared its naval role to that of Portsmouth in Britain. Yet Suomenlinna was even larger than Portsmouth, which was in its own right one of the United Kingdom's most important naval bases in the later eighteenth and nineteenth centuries.

Geographically, the fortress is situated on seven rocky islands, several of which are connected by a series of bridges. Most of the officers lived in modest accommodation within the fortress, but at the earliest opportunity the more prosperous ones also purchased their own country houses around Helsinki. Its isolation in the sea by no means implied any social isolation, according to an Englishman, Edward Daniel Clarke, who visited Helsinki in 1799. As he wrote in his autobiographical *Travels in Various Countries of Europe, Asia and Africa, Part the Third* (1824), it was a cosmopolitan place, on occasion full of jollity:

> *Nothing can be more gay and pleasing than the scene, exhibited on the ice, from* Helsingfors (Helsinki) *to the fortress of* Sweaborg (Suomenlinna), *which is situated on an island, distant two* English *miles. The road is marked on the snow by trees, or large branches of the pine, planted in the ice. Sledges of all sizes and descriptions, open and covered, of business, burthen, or pleasure, plain or decorated, with beautiful little prancing* Finland *horses, are seen moving with the utmost rapidity, backwards and forwards, the whole way, from morning to night. Officers with their servants, ladies, soldiers, peasants, artificers, engineers, form a crowded promenade, more interesting and amusing than that of* Hyde Park *in* London, *or the* Corso *at* Rome.

Such sophistication should perhaps come as no surprise, since many of the officers who served there had also been active in The Royal Suédois Regiment, which actually had its headquarters not in Sweden but in Strasbourg in Lorraine, with military contingents in Paris itself.

Yet winter there was a trying time, with damp and cold permeating every corner. It was also a time of particular danger in wartime since the frozen waters surrounding it could be crossed by invading forces with relative ease. But as visitors commented at the time, the more than 150 pieces of cannon on view, not to mention mortars, land batteries, and other similar machinery of war, altogether to the tune of a thousand pieces, fostered an image of impregnability, even in winter.

With its good harbor, it naturally became one of Sweden's most important naval bases. Sixty sails of the line could be accommodated there, though large ships had to remain outside. It could also shelter large numbers of people, troops as well as logistical personnel and clergy. In 1805 Suomenlinna's population exceeded 4,600, making it more populous than Helsinki itself, at the time with a population of only 4,200. By 1808 there were 7,000 men stationed there.

The garrison normally stationed there consisted of three army regiments along with one naval and one infantry regiment. Additional to these were 200 artillery soldiers, not including a further thousand stationed in Helsinki itself. The officers lived with their families in comfortable accommodation, perhaps not as luxurious as that enjoyed by their colleagues on the continent but far superior to what they might expect elsewhere in Finland. It was also a sociable life, as we have seen, with balls and assemblies at which some forty "ladies of fashion" could be found dancing away.

Russian Stronghold

In March 1808 Suomenlinna's true value in military terms was tested when during the Napoleonic Wars Russian forces besieged it. It failed the test; despite his superior strength, in May of that year the Swedish Admiral Count Carl Olof Cronstedt surrendered with his garrison of 7,500 men, for reasons that were never clarified and which continue to make his name a source of contention today. At least two frigates were lost along with 3,000 kegs of gunpowder, 10,000 rounds of ammunition and 2,000 cannonballs. Still, bearing in mind that 340,000 projectiles had been lobbed at the fortress, the damage was less than might have been expected. But the galley fleet was surrendered to the Russians, with the squadron at Turku burnt by the Swedes.

Henceforth until Finland achieved its independence Suomenlinna was defended by Russian troops, on average 13,000 at any one time, and after its surrender forces of the Russian navy under Major-General

Constantin Gavro occupied it forthwith. Having now become the Russian military's most important fortress in the region after Kronstadt, it was too important a base to entrust to the newly founded Finnish forces, even under Russian control. These were relegated to the Guards Barracks at Kasarmintori, the Turku Barracks, near today's bus station, as well as elsewhere in the capital. There was also an important naval barracks at what is now Laivastokatu 22 on Katajanokka, designed by Engel among the first buildings he planned for the new capital. Over six hundred feet in length, the officers' wing to the west has a colonnaded façade, clearly influenced by the Admiralty in St. Petersburg. Interestingly, another wing was added as recently as 1987, for the complex is now used by the Foreign Ministry. The non-commissioned Russian soldiers and their families were provided with residential sites on the western side of Töölö Bay, not far from the present Glass Palace (Lasipalatsi). Only after 1860 and until 1902, when relations with Russia had seriously declined, did the Finnish Guards Regiment itself thrive as the Grand Duchy's own local army, although it had been first constituted in 1829.

Suomenlinna failed to prove itself once again during the Crimean War, which is discussed in more detail below. For that reason, a new line of defense was constructed further out in the archipelago and the fortress was given over to administrative and logistical uses, though a garrison—Russian until 1917, then Finnish—was stationed there until 1973. It was then demilitarized and given over to civilian administration and uses. Today it houses the Nordic Art Center in the old Russian barracks, designed by Pekka Helin and Tuomo Siitonen in 1985, and some artists' studios, both on the island of Susisaari (Wolf Island, in English).

The Cantonist Military School

After Russia's victory over Sweden in 1809, one of the Czar's first actions with respect to the military was to commission the construction of accommodation for his soldiers on Senate Square in an elongated building adorned by a colonnade. (The colonnade was later removed to enable a better integration of the Great Church of St. Nicholas with Senate Square by means of a vast flight of steps with flanking pavilions.)

Alexander also determined to establish a military school for orphaned Russian children, the so-called Cantonist School, which now serves as a medical clinic and part of Helsinki University. Engel made the first plans in 1820 and the school was completed in 1824, after which time it was able to accommodate some three hundred boys, sent there from all over the Grand Duchy. As such, it was just one of many such military schools established throughout the Russian Empire between 1758 and 1856. Orphaned boys over the age of eight were trained in these establishments for a military career at government expense while being educated in the basics of religion, grammar, and geometry. For those with the prerequisite skills, drawing and instruction in the playing of militarily useful musical instruments such as flutes and drums was also provided. Positioned on the top of a hill on Union Street, named in celebration of the union of Finland with Russia under the Czar, the Cantonist School's prominent position was symbolic of the important role Alexander gave to it as an institution.

While some of the boys lived in the school itself, others were housed with families in the community. Those who proved unsuitable as soldiers were nonetheless provided with ancillary occupations useful for an army or navy: cooks, tailors, boot makers—all were needed to supply Russia's vast military machine.

Engel's Military Barracks

The Czar also commissioned Engel to build a new military barracks for the capital, with an imposing square for military marching just south of the Esplanade. Adorned with a monumental Doric portico of eight columns, its principal façade, the architect felt, would be in line with traditionally classical views and provide a suitable order for a "masculine" military establishment. Its interior public rooms, meanwhile, were decorated with images of arms and armor in the customary way. Here, too, the inspiration was more St. Petersburg than ancient Rome: the resemblance to the Smolna Institute in the Russian capital by the Italian architect Giacomo Quarenghi, long in use as an elite school for girls, is especially striking.

A separate residence for the military commander of the Russian forces stationed in Helsinki was also built from 1822-5 on the south side of the Esplanade, where it can still be seen. A two-story building, the ground floor had offices and ancillary rooms for domestic duties, while the upper floor provided a residence for the commander's family, as well as their private chapel. When the office of military commander was abolished in 1840, the building was renovated to provide a new governor general's residence in place of the old one on Senate Square. Its first occupant of that standing was no less than Prince Alexander Menshikov (1787-1869), a scion of one of Russia's grandest families. Yet he rarely visited Helsinki, and it was only with the inauguration of a Finnish-born assistant governor general from Viipuri, General Alexander Amatus Thesleff, that the residence was occupied on a regular basis.

Other edifices of note were also built, such as the house on the Pohjoisesplanadi, today serving as the Helsinki City Information Center. It was designed by Pehr Gransted, who actually specialized in the construction of fortifications. He had been a prisoner of war in St. Petersburg during the summer of 1808 and had used the opportunity to carefully copy some of the architectural monuments and buildings he saw while in the Russian capital.

Military and Police

The attitude of the Czars towards Finland and Helsinki, warm as it was on the surface, remained cautious, especially when Nicholas I ascended the throne, and the Decembrist uprising broke out on 26 December 1825 in St. Petersburg against his autocratic rule. Secret police were introduced into Helsinki as early as 1829 to uncover conspiracies before they could cause any harm. Its administration was placed in the hands of the governor general of the Grand Duchy who also represented the Ministry of the Interior in the imperial capital itself.

Yet none of this prevented many Finns from entering the ranks of the Russian military. Some 3,000 of them served as officers during the long century of Russian rule, with thousands more serving as volunteer enlisted men in special Finnish units. Moreover, by the 1840s, the importance of the navy in Helsinki was indisputable and Finns enlisted in it as well. As an American by the name of Maxwell wrote in 1848:

This, the modern capital, contains one of the largest naval arsenals in the world, and is the principal recruiting station of the imperial fleet. So important is Finland to the naval marine of Russia, both in regard of men and materials, and the sailors and timber she affords, that the whole province is under the immediate control of Prince Menshikoff, Minister of Marine.

But despite this otherwise favorable impression, Maxwell also remarked that "the town of Helsingfors is not worthy of particular mentioning. It is regularly laid out and the most youthful looking town we saw in Europe." That, it seems, was no special virtue.

Though Finns were often warmly received in St. Petersburg and indeed throughout the Empire, Russians themselves, as a people, continued to be unwelcome in Finland. Only the military were granted the right of settlement in Finland, a privilege taken up by a significant number of Tartar and Jewish conscripts who established themselves in trade after their military service.

In contrast with the large military presence in and about Helsinki, during the second quarter of the nineteenth century only four policemen patrolled the streets at night in the interests of public security. This dearth of patrolmen did not mean that Helsinki was a city in which such custodians were unnecessary. On the contrary, criminality, including sexual immorality, was rife, and it was for this reason that the city fathers instituted draconian curfews on occasion. Needless to say, these were burdens that fell exclusively on the poorer classes. For example, in 1836 a city magistrate decreed that:

the rank and file of the defensive forces of the city, serving women, mechanics and apprentices, namely, all those of the lower orders, shall be forbidden to go abroad during the dark months after ten o'clock in the evening, in the city, unless they had specific gainful errands to fulfil, in which case they might be allowed to proceed.

Even internal migration was curtailed, as admission to Helsinki and the right of abode was by no means open to all. Only an official document, the so-called *papin todistus* (priest's authorization), permitted the migrant or even ordinary traveler to enter Helsinki, a regulation as rigorously applied to Finns from the provinces as to foreigners. Helsinki was not alone in having such strictly enforced restrictions on movement; even in small villages and the countryside people were not permitted to move about or take up residence as fancy moved them. Internal documentation was required of all and, with respect to those in domestic service, letters confirming completion of service from the previous employer were obligatory.

Yet for all these measures, violence and other crimes persisted. For more serious crimes against public order, a site near to the stables of the Imperial Guards afforded a flogging post and place of execution, while Suomenlinna Fortress also served as a prison for both military and criminal. That said, Finland and the Russian Empire as a whole were progressive in some respects, since the abolition of capital punishment occurred relatively early in 1825, after which time convicts were sent to Siberia.

The Crimean War

In 1854 the outbreak of the Crimean War, which pitted Britain, France and Turkey against Russia (and therefore also Finland), once again made Helsinki an important point in the protection of the imperial capital itself. For the first time since the Napoleonic Wars the fortress of Suomenlinna again became the site of a major European confrontation. About the same time, British and French forces also attacked the Åland Islands, where the imposing Bomarsund Fortress was rapidly reduced to rubble, observed by onlookers who had specially arrived from the occasion—an early instance of "war tourism".

Suomenlinna itself came under attack as the joint British-French bombardment began in August 1855. The 22nd Infantry Division provided the defense, aided by five battalions of Grenadiers. There were also cavalry detachments as well as gunners and engineers, not to mention troops of Grodnos Hussars and Cossacks, some stationed in the fortress while others were positioned in Helsinki itself. This extraordinary event on August 8, 1855, was recorded by the journalist August Schauman, who nine years later founded Helsinki's *Hufvudstadsbladet*, the Swedish-Finnish newspaper:

> *I rushed alone from my lodgings directly to the knoll of Ulrikasborg (Ullanlinna). There can hardly, ever, have been a better vantage point*

for a theatre of war. All the fortified islands of Sveaborg lie, as is well known, in a long chain before one's eyes. And the entire row was blazing in one great flame, a helpless target for the enemy's bombs and shells. On the right, between Rönnskär (Pihlajasaari) and Gråhara (Harmaja), were the ranks of the English and French navies, and in front of those great ships, in constant motion, small mortar vessels, continually hurling their ammunition. We could follow with our eyes the back-and-forth motion of all those little craft; we could, if we wished, follow the great arc of each bomb from the moment when it left the mortar to when, exploding, it reached its target, and at the same time each spluttering Congreve's rocket on its lower trajectory...

Not all the imagery resulting from the bombardment, as captured by Schauman, was necessarily fearsome; in fact, some smacked of the absurd. He related his experiences during the course of the following day when local residents had fled their homes for their safety and encamped in the city's spacious parks:

... we jolly boys found ourselves able... in the Henriksgatan Street (Henrikinkatu Street, now Mannerheimintie Road) park, to stop to gaze at a matrimonial bed in which both spouses rested, with their natural retinue of children's beds and cradles in which their little angels were sleeping; over there was an old bachelor sleeping on his leather sofa; there, a couple of ladies keeping themselves awake with sips of coffee and talking about the imminent end of the world and their hope of coming by some more coffee; there again, a couple of drinking companions who had fallen asleep on the lawn, with the bottle forming the third member of the group between them.

Helsinki had escaped lightly this time, but the Russian authorities, always insecure when defense was at stake, arranged for the construction of new military installations after the conclusion of the Crimean War during the 1860s and 1870s. These included a new barracks by the coast as well as a so-called Russian port at Iso Mustasaari, by Suomenlinna.

General Strike

With the outbreak of revolution in St. Petersburg in 1905, revolutionary activity in Helsinki also escalated, aggravated by the constant attempts of the Russian authorities to integrate Finland more fully into the increasingly centralized imperial administrative system. A general strike was called, with which, as elsewhere in Russia, the authorities dealt heavy-handedly. When the Cossack troops arrived to preserve order, the image of them sweeping up the steps of the Great Church of St. Nicholas while crushing the strike left a permanent scar on Russian-Finnish relations. People who had formerly taken a more neutral position now found themselves firmly rooted in the anti-Russian camp which wanted autonomy, even independence, for Finland. There was even a revolt of Russian forces stationed at the fortress on Suomenlinna. Yet it should be remembered that even at this time of crisis many Finnish officers continued loyally to serve the Russian Czar, not least in the Russian-Japanese War of 1904-5. Perhaps the leading example in this regard was Gustaf Mannerheim himself, later to become the supreme commander of Finnish forces after independence.

The First World War, Independence and the Civil War

With the outbreak of the First World War, the Russian government attempted to strengthen its forces in Helsinki, and 25,000 land-based troops were stationed in the city. Many of these belonged to the 427th and 428th Infantry Regiments, though large numbers of the Field Artillery and Don Cossack Regiments were also present. The navy, Russia's Baltic fleet, also had a strong base there, including the usual forces of cruiser brigades as well as a submarine flotilla and mine-laying vessels. In fact, a large part of the Russian fleet remained in Helsinki's harbor throughout the war, where it largely escaped any military confrontation. This was also the case with the Peter the Great Fortress, built to protect Helsinki as well as St. Petersburg and Tallinn from a sea-borne attack. This was not one single conventional fortification but a series of defenses on either side of the Gulf of Finland, erected on various islands with all the latest military innovations.

Yet at this stage the real threat was more from within than without the body politic. By the autumn of 1917 revolutionary elements among

Finnish workers had led a general strike. Then, on December 6, 1917, Finland issued its unilateral declaration of independence from Russia, a date later given religious overtones by the custom of lighting candles by graves, both civilian and military.

Almost immediately a new specter of political violence haunted the new nation: civil war. Finnish socialists, the so-called "Reds", began to seize power in towns and cities in several parts of Finland, also targeting individual landowners, industrialists and others seen as enemies of their cause. Their political opponents, the "Whites", responded by quickly organizing their own defensive units under the leadership of General Mannerheim, who had returned to Finland following the collapse of imperial authority in Russia.

Full-scale civil war then erupted in Finland in late January 1918. The Whites, assisted by a division of German troops led by a German general, engaged in some of the bitterest fighting the country had ever known. Already in January, the Reds, both Russian and Finnish, had briefly seized the military port of Hanko (Hangö) where many Russian troops were still present and established a pro-Bolshevik government there. The Whites' new national government of independence meanwhile re-established itself in Ostrobothnia, while the Reds occupied Helsinki. The outcome was a foregone conclusion given the better leadership of the Whites. And while initially the Reds had the greater number of weapons, matters changed during the course of the war, especially as the Whites began to receive armaments from the Germans. Another crucial advantage was the war experience of their officers in the Russian army, that of their soldiers and NCOs in the German army, and the expertise of their German allies. By April 1918 the Reds had been effectively defeated. A monument from 1921 in the gardens of Liisanpuistikko in Kruununhaka by Gunnar Finne and Armas Lindgren commemorates soldiers of the Pellinki expedition who died during that war, eighty miles east of Helsinki, in a battle against the Reds. These were, of course, not the only deaths in the conflict. Some 10,000 died on the Red side, mainly of starvation and illness while kept in the prison camps of the Whites. Thus, the ratio of Red to White deaths was in the region of twelve to one.

The Bolshevik connection with the Finnish capital was nothing new. Years before, in 1905, 1906 and 1907 Lenin had already spent considerable time in Helsinki and he had first met Stalin in the Finnish industrial city of Tampere. Even then, he and his fellow revolutionaries enjoyed some private Finnish support. For example, a wine merchant and erstwhile gardener, Valter Sjöberg, allowed his shop at Erottaja 3 to be used as a base by Russian revolutionary couriers. Similarly minded revolutionary soldiers who had participated in the rebellion at Suomenlinna but had been fortunate enough to escape had also been taken in at Sjöberg's private residence at Pietarinkatu 18. Later, in 1917, Lenin once again arrived back in the Finnish capital for an extended stay on his return journey to Russia in 1917. On this occasion he took up residence in Hakaniemi opposite the market hall at Sörnäisten Rantatie 1, near the 1908 Trade Unions Hall, where the table at which he took his after-dinner drinks is still to be seen. Nearby at Hakaniemi Square is the Friendship Monument by the Russian sculptor O. S. Kiryuhin, a gift of the city of Moscow in 1990.

Gustaf Mannerheim

The rapid successes of the revolutionaries in Helsinki were not to last, for their progress was suddenly blocked by the arrival of the Imperial German Baltic Division, which the German government had ordered from Estonia where they had been stationed to assist the anti-revolutionary Whites. The real hero of the occasion was General Baron Gustaf Mannerheim (1867-1951), who was to prove the most important Finnish figure in this, as in so many military events of the first half of the twentieth century.

Mannerheim, born into an aristocratic family with roots in the Netherlands, but an ancestral seat at Louhisaari in the southwest of Finland, had attended school in Helsinki. There he was expelled for unruly behavior, after which he was obliged to pursue his studies at the austere Hamina Military College in the southeast of the country. He was expelled from there, too, his unwillingness to follow rules seemingly unremitting. More successful was his career at the Nicholas Cavalry School, in St. Petersburg, where he matriculated in 1887 and from where he entered the Russian imperial Chevalier Guard upon graduation in 1889. Not long afterwards he married an aristocratic Russian lady, further integrating himself into Russian society, while his military training in the capital was to serve him in good stead after he volunteered to fight for the Russian Empire in the Russo-Japanese War of 1904-5. Successful on the front lines, he was soon promoted to the rank of colonel and in the years 1906-8 undertook an important military expedition to Turkistan and China on behalf of the Imperial Russian General Staff. Ultimately commissioned as a general, Mannerheim later served on the Polish front during the First World War from 1914 to 1917, when Finnish independence was declared. Success such as this, though, was by no means extraordinary for Finnish officers in the Russian military: even as far back as the mid-1850s one in five Finnish aristocrats had been imperial officers. Yet after the declaration of Finnish independence Mannerheim resigned his commission in the Russian army, taking up the cause of the defense of his beloved Finland.

No friend of the Germans, Mannerheim had been keen to free Finland from revolutionaries without foreign intervention, and although he had taken Tampere, Helsinki and other pockets remained under revolutionary control. With reluctance, he had to content himself with the arrival at Hanko of German troops under General Count von der Goltz. These forces rapidly proceeded towards Helsinki, as revolutionary Russian troops and their Finnish Bolshevik sympathizers retreated towards Russia. Between April 12 and 14 German forces, supported by a naval squadron, took Helsinki, to the general popular acclaim of its residents. The Turku Barracks, on the site of the present-day Glass Palace, where Russian troops had been stationed, were destroyed, except for a small part of what is now the bus station ticket office. Otherwise, except for bomb damage to the Borgström Tobacco Factory, which revolutionary women had vainly seized as a stronghold, the capital remained intact.

Mannerheim was not so jubilant at the growing German influence in Finland, when, on May 16, 1918, he led the victory parade. As a gesture of Finnish national identity, the march paused at the monument to the national poet Johan Ludvig Runeberg (1804-77) on the Esplanade. Mannerheim then went into exile from Finland, only to return after the Germans had departed later that year. In the meantime, some of the ugliest events in modern Finnish history took place, not least the establishment of concentration camps such as that at

Suomenlinna for pro-Bolshevik prisoners, where executions, starvation and disease took an enormous toll.

The poet Eino Leino (1878-1926), a native of Paltamo in the northern province of Kainuu, has provided us with arguably the most insightful imagery of the horrors of the 1918 Finnish Civil War, as he saw them in Helsinki itself. Perhaps such memories played a part in his slow death by alcoholism. Yet what most violently attracted his opprobrium were the women who rallied to the Red battalions, in league with the Russian Bolsheviks over the border. Here, he describes them, as German troops, called to assist the Whites, are about to enter the city in April 1918:

As soon as it was noon a terrible hullabaloo began, rising at times to the infernal: a hellish music accompanied by enormous whumpings of artillery in the distance.

The streets were empty except for the march of some Red guard patrol—or some rabid women's battalion, irresponsibly toying with their guns, poking them in windows, and stopping you looking through, at least for the time being.

This was the first time I'd seen so many of them gathered together, and I have to confess, in the name of truth, I've never at any other time witnessed such human savagery, bestial frenzy, mental derangement and physical disfigurement.

A couple of them had on occasion passed me by in the street, in Aleksanterinkatu Street, during daylight. But then they were gunless and embarrassed by people's glances, which seemed to be bypassing their blameless male attire and derisively weighing up their over-buxom figures. Nor did they endure this high street promenade for long: with uneasy looks and a swing of the hips they made a hasty escape into some side street. Now, in a troop, and particularly driving motorised vehicles, they looked like outright Furies.

Happily, by 1918 the Civil War had come to an end and General Mannerheim, now regent, ratified the country's new constitution the following year; Finland could now begin to pick up the pieces and sort itself out. This inter-war period was a time of sullen peace, and Helsinki, along with the rest of Finland, enjoyed a period of relative tranquillity only occasionally broken by an outburst of revolutionary activity, such as the trade union demonstration on the so-called Red Day, August 1, 1929, which was broken up by the police.

The Winter War

As war clouds gathered in the Baltic, Stalin's foreign minister Vyacheslav Mikhaylovich Molotov—after whom the famous explosive cocktail was named—approached the Finnish government in October 1939 with a proposed deal. He offered some territory in the hope of coercing Finland into allowing Soviet troops to occupy, ostensibly for defensive purposes, parts of the Karelian Isthmus, Hanko and a number of islands in the Gulf of Finland. Ministers Paasikivi and Tanner both traveled to Moscow for the negotiations. When these broke down on November 14, the Finnish government immediately sent its White Guard Regiment to the Isthmus and the 4th Division from Helsinki to Hanko. In the meantime, a voluntary evacuation of Helsinki had already been carried out.

It was just as well. Two weeks later, the Finnish-Soviet Non-Aggression Pact was rejected by Stalin. Finnish forces were mobilized. Then, on November 30, 1939, the Soviet Union attacked Finland, fulfilling the worst fears of the Finnish people, not least those in Helsinki. Volunteers then rushed to the young nation's defense, including 350 Finnish-American volunteers, several Japanese and one native Jamaican. Hundreds of Scandinavians and Italians also joined in. A Finnish Legion, an international brigade, was also established in London under the auspices of the American Kermit Roosevelt, President Theodore Roosevelt's son.

That same day Helsinki fell victim to heavy bombing, which commenced just after 9 am. Fortunately, bomb shelters had already been built in the final months of 1939. The first of these, in fact, had already been incorporated into the cellars of Stockmann's Department Store on the North Esplanade.

This first attack, the worst of the entire war, was to last for two days. The central bus station and the Technical High School were the first important buildings to be destroyed, while aerial machine guns massacred people fleeing through the streets. Fortunately, the weather sided with Finland; wintry storms provided a protective screen, enabling a general evacuation of Helsinki and improvements in its defense system to be completed. Yet the war continued and indeed was to last 105 days until March 13, 1940; the several hundred bombs reckoned to have fallen in and around Helsinki took the lives of 91 people, leaving almost 250 wounded. But it was the military, of course, who paid the highest price: more than 1,700 soldiers from the Helsinki area lost their lives in the Winter War. Many had come from the latterly created 12th Division, which drew its troops from Helsinki, but these were transferred, under their leader Colonel E. A. Vihma, to near Miehikkälä on the Karelian front in 1941.

As for the political effects of the bombardment, dramatic changes occurred. Firstly, civilian President Kallio immediately relinquished his command to Mannerheim, made a Field Marshal in 1933, while the central command, after a brief stay in Helsinki, moved its headquarters to the interior of Finland at Mikkeli, where it remained for the war's duration. Much of the government itself, though, stayed in Helsinki, where the Hotel Kämp was used to hold presidential receptions, with the strong-room of Finland's National Bank providing the venue for cabinet meetings. The president's residence was moved to the suburbs of Helsinki at Kuusisaari, as was that of the defense minister to an underground bunker from the First World War in Meilahti. Parliament itself was transported far away from the seat of war to Kauhajoki in Ostrobothnia. In the meantime everyone in Helsinki eagerly listened to the broadcasts of Olavi Paavolainen (1903-64), who ever since the outbreak of war, though a native of Karelia, reported on the latest military events and their effects in Helsinki.

Finns could take the greatest pride from their victory at Suomussalmi in January 1940, when two Russian divisions were surrounded and then annihilated by limited Finnish forces. The tactics they used have since become legendary and even today form part of military history courses taught at West Point. This offensive or *motti* takes its name from the Finnish word for a pile of chopped logs, secured by stakes, intended for use as firewood. In the Winter War the term meant that the Finnish military dealt with the invading Russian forces as if they were *motti*, for they were literally surrounded as blocks and chopped to pieces in the battlefields just north of Lake Ladoga and in the almost Arctic reaches by Sala far to the north.

Nonetheless, for all the military prowess and daring of the Finns, sheer superiority in terms of numbers and military equipment gave ultimate victory to the Russians. Only with the greatest reluctance did President Kallio finally consent to submit to the draconian conditions of peace laid down by Moscow. A famous anecdote relates that as the sorrowful president put his signature to the hated treaty, he exclaimed, "May the hand that has been compelled to sign such a document wither!" Whatever the truth of this story, it is a fact that several months later Kallio suffered a severe stroke that left his right arm paralyzed. On March 13, 1940, Finland, too, was paralyzed, as the treaty took effect, leaving huge chunks of Finnish Karelia as well as Hanko in Russian hands.

In desperate straits, the Finns turned to Germany for assistance as help from the British, French and others in the League of Nations failed to materialize. Finland thus found itself forced to accept assistance from the only source open to it, despite the deep reservations of Mannerheim, who disliked Finland's new co-belligerent. The Nazis' ominous presence in the capital was felt in a variety of ways. Some five hundred Jews were rounded up for deportation onto a ship in Helsinki harbor, but a timely intervention by Mannerheim forced their release. It was said that a Gestapo headquarters was maintained in Helsinki in the Swedish Club, situated at the southwestern corner of Liisanpuitikko.

The Continuation War

After a brief and uneasy period of peace after the conclusion of the Winter War, Helsinki waited with bated breath. Then, on June 17, 1941, Finnish troops in the south of the country were once more mobilized. With the renewed outbreak of hostilities, Helsinki was in a much better position to defend itself and withstand an aerial assault. For one thing, the city now had seven heavy anti-aircraft batteries defending it, as well as two anti-aircraft platoons and six others specializing in searchlight units. The tactic of deceptive lighting to mislead the enemy into bombing empty fields would also be deployed later. Meanwhile, President Risto Ryti and his wife sought refuge at the Villa Kallio in Tamminiemi, where a bunker had recently been installed.

Matters also improved for the Finns with the fall of Estonia to the Germans, when the presence of any threatening Soviet air bases and, to a lesser degree, submarine bases there was suddenly eliminated. The flames of optimism were further fanned in September 1941 not only by the retaking of the Isthmus of Karelia but much of Russian eastern Karelia, as far east as Petrozavodsk during the autumn, as well as territory historically part of Russia. Since after 1943 the Germans provided a significant quantity of anti-aircraft material, the most important of which was radar, the aerial defenses of the capital were further strengthened. In any case, the pressure by this time was slightly off Helsinki, since the presence of German forces on the Eastern Front by Leningrad demanded the attention of Soviet forces elsewhere. The home guard was also mobilized, with all men between the ages of sixteen and sixty, 30,000 in total, called upon to provide civil defense duties between dusk and dawn. Still, bombardments continued, to one of which the University of Helsinki itself fell victim. The worst were in 1944. Although more than 100,000 had been evacuated, a further 88 people died at this time, with hundreds more wounded. As for the fabric of the capital itself, more than 250 buildings were destroyed or heavily damaged.

The short-story writer and essayist Leena Krohn looked back in her novel, *Gold of Ophir* (1987) on stories related in her family from life in Helsinki during the Continuation War:

Bang! It was a German naphtha ship which was blown up into tiny pieces of an autumn night on the North Shore, Helsinki. Burning naphtha flew as far as Katajanokka, there was smoke in the streets and the windows in Kauppiaankatu street rattled until they broke. The brilliance of the sabotage dazzled the entire peninsula. Fragments were hurled into dark rooms where people slept in all positions of slumber. My parents' bed was on the ground floor, under high windows; suddenly they noticed that they were lying under a crackling blanket of glass. But they weren't even scratched; it was their wedding night.

My grandmother, whom everyone called Mamma, wore an aluminium saucepan on her head when she walked in the town. On top of that she had succeeded in fixing a leather flying cap. With the help of these accoutrements she felt she would survive both the Winter War and the Continuation War, and she did.

For many ordinary women, it was not writing but the Women's Auxiliary Defense Organization, Lotta Svärd (named after an altruistic folk heroine from the Napoleonic Wars) into which they channeled their constructive energies. There they carried out many jobs in transport, munitions production and logistics, the refitting of captured enemy aircraft, not to mention nursing, both at the front and in war-torn Helsinki itself. A museum dedicated to the memory of Lotta Svärd is located at Tuusula, just north of Helsinki.

Peace and Resettlement
Finally, on September 19, 1944, a cease-fire was achieved, as more refugees flooded in from the old Finnish territories now ceded to the Soviet Union, swelling their numbers since 1939 to more than 425,000. Relations with Germany were concurrently broken off and the Lapland War ensued, ravaging that region and leaving most buildings destroyed in its wake (the Germans attempted to prevent their use in harboring the enemy). Meanwhile, 30,000 people fled to Helsinki, 20,000 from the port city of Viipuri alone. Many of these, along with other refugees, were resettled in accordance with the 1945 Land Acquisition Act, whereby some 11,000 people were each given 300 hectares of farmland, while 100-hectare building plots were allocated for almost 3,000 single family homes, along with about fifty blocks of flats. This was a major accomplishment that no other European country at the time could equal. This is especially true if one bears in mind that of those who sought refuge in Helsinki—which in any case had grown by more than 83,000 new residents, half of whom were refugees—some 85 percent were women, many of whose men were still at the front or had fallen on the battlefield.

After the conclusion of the Continuation War, a Soviet Administration of War Reparations arrived in Finland to negotiate and supervise the process. It would remain for eight years in the Hotel Karelia, where up to 200 members lived and worked until 1952. It was during this period that a large number of Finland's naval and merchant vessels were transferred to the Soviet authorities as reparations, dealing a blow to the Finnish economy and that of Helsinki in particular. Across the street from the Soviet administration, its opposite number, the Finnish War Reparation Office established itself on the top four floors of the Sokos Building. It enjoyed a degree of independence and authority of which the Soviet side could but dream, for without continuous consultation with Moscow little could be negotiated by the Soviet representatives.

In the meantime, from September 1944, the Allied Control Commission, composed of both Russians and British members, established itself in the Hotel Torni, where it was to remain until September 1947. By the end of that year all parties had signed the peace treaty at a special ceremony held in Paris. As treaties went with a former Axis ally, it was relatively lenient. Yet the cost of the war had been significant, even if compared to the losses in several other European countries including the UK, the price paid by Finland was relatively low—1,566 women were left widows, along with 1,693 orphaned children. Moreover, a significant refugee population still had to be housed, given that during the four years between 1946 and 1950 over 24,000 people had migrated to Helsinki, 9,000 of these moving from Karelia alone.

Post-war Retrenchment and Reconstruction

The post-war years were a difficult time, and Finland looked towards its old hero, always there in its need, for leadership. Thus, from 1944-6, Field Marshal Mannerheim, with his enormous prestige, assumed the office of President of Finland. Rather than take up his principal residence in the presidential palace in the center of Helsinki, he also preferred to live at the Villa Kallio, at Tamminiemi. Two years earlier, that heavily traveled urban artery, known as Heikinkatu, along with its extension Turuntie, had already been re-christened Mannerheimintie, in celebration of the hero's seventy-fifth birthday. Appropriately, it was the principal thoroughfare to Tamminiemi.

The field marshal fulfilled his task admirably and when he finally died, in 1951, almost ninety years old, he was interred in a military grave at Helsinki's Hietaniemi Cemetery, a site that has since assumed an almost cult-like atmosphere of commemoration for Finland's greatest figure. Later, a statue of the field marshal by Aimo Tukiainen

was erected opposite the House of Parliament in 1960, paid for by public subscription, the first of many of Finland's presidents to be commemorated by statues including Paasikivi, Svinhufvud, Ståhlberg, Kallio, Ryti and Relander.

Many school boys upon graduation continue to come to Mannerheim's grave, wearing their white student caps, to pay their respects, later going to meander around the tombs of so many other soldiers killed during the Winter, Continuation and Lapland Wars. Fittingly, a day of remembrance has been officially established, the third Sunday in May. Then, all Finnish soldiers fallen in war are commemorated and flags fly throughout the land. Although there is no official tomb for an unknown soldier, as elsewhere in the world, the event still offers a focus for honoring the dead, as many people visit the city's cemeteries while the government lays a wreath on the grave of a particularly heroic soldier from one of the three wars.

Although there is no unknown soldier, it is the third novel of Väinö Linna, *The Unknown Soldier* (1954)—turned into film and drama in several versions over the last half century—that stands as a monument to Finland's experience of these wars and the many who died in them. Its author from Urjala, in central Finland, where he grew up in a working-class milieu, the novel captured the hearts of millions of Finns and by 1990 had sold over half a million copies. Yet it is no provincial tale of the woes of war; rather, it provides a wide canvas of epic proportions, more influenced by the heroic aspects of Tolstoy's *War and Peace* than the mournful pessimism of Remarque's *All Quiet on the Western Front.* The most recent film version of *The Unknown Soldier* is that by Rauni Mollberg, first shown in 1985.

Later, the advent of President Urho Kekkonen (1900-86) as the most powerful man in Finland and a "True Finn" of unquestionable commitment to his country ensured that a middle road would be taken, less positively known in the world beyond Finland's borders as Finlandization. According to its tenets, Finland was to the tread the thin tightrope of political independence while carefully avoiding any act or statement that posed a perceived threat to the Soviet Union. Yet political scars were not the only ones to remain from Finland's wars, for they would be visible for years in many ways. As Kjell Westö put it in *Kites over Helsinki* (1996):

> *I now began to understand that the Helsinki I was getting to know still had its bomb scars, that it remained a post-war city.*
>
> *For my city had been full of holes and gaps, wastelands.*
>
> *There was the area around Tilkka where Sammy and Robbi and I hung about and got into fights with any Finnish speaking Finns who appeared there. It was a nothing place, just a watery swamp. The hodgepodge of buildings there bore no resemblance to Lill-Hoplaks, that postmodern suburb.*

Since the 1940s the military, though strong and supported by national conscription, has not been called to any active defense, even if it has been involved in United Nations and European Union peacekeeping operations. Yet the Finnish trait of *sisu*, a word signifying incredible guts in the face of adversity, remains imbedded within it, a resource that could once again be called upon, should the need to arms arise. The Finnish military's long history, dating back to the seventeenth century, can be explored at the Military Museum situated in old red-brick barracks at the corner of Maurinkatu and Liisankatu. A visit to the Public Swimming Baths at Yrjönkatu is also revealing as the visitor will encounter elderly war veterans from the Winter, Continuation and Lapland Wars, who, despite the fact that their limbs may have been blown away, still make their regular visits to the sauna. Here they continue to share reminiscences, though in rapidly declining numbers.

CHAPTER FOUR

Ethnic Helsinki: Language, Identity and Community

Helsinki's ethnic mix, with a generous respect for minority rights since the Second World War, has an interesting history, which, for all its pitfalls, should serve as inspiration for the troubled cities of the Balkans and elsewhere. Each part of the city can be said to possess its own peculiar characteristics in ethnic and social terms, but the sum of the parts seems to function as a cohesive whole of mutual enrichment. The presence of a variety of ethnic communities spread across the city has also served to break down a homogenous identity.

Since the nineteenth century, Helsinki's population, like Finland's as a whole, has contained six principal minority communities: Swedish-speaking Finns (the easternmost variety of the five Swedish linguistic variants), German speakers, Romany Gypsies, Jews, Russians and Tartars. More recently in the past few decades Somalis, Croats and Saami (Lapps), among others, have also formed communities.

While those speaking Swedish as their native tongue form less than six percent of the entire population of Finland today (about 300,000 individuals), in Helsinki the proportion is considerably higher. Still, the Finns—and indeed the citizens of Helsinki—are not a loquacious folk, and one should perhaps remember Bertolt Brecht's comment on the true linguistic nature of the Finns, namely that they are "silent in two languages".

Early Ethnic Composition
In the sixteenth century Swedish, Finnish and German were already spoken in Helsinki, even if only the first two were permitted as official

languages of the town council. It was not only the "Swedish-speaking better folk", as they are still sometimes called by some in Finland with perhaps a certain irony, who spoke that language, but large segments of the working classes with a presence in the city going back hundreds of years. Certainly by the 1780s not only merchants, but artisans and others who lived by their handiwork were also Swedish-speaking. Many of these also spoke Finnish, albeit as a second language, since members of both linguistic groups often worked side by side. It has been said that in Helsinki a working-class milieu had come into being in which people were totally bilingual, both at work and at home. These circumstances were further reinforced in the nineteenth century when at least a fifth of marriages in Helsinki involved partners from both linguistic groups.

Such distinctions did not only relate to the Swedish-Finnish language divide. For both Finnish-speaking Swedes and Finns had their own linguistic differences relating to geographical and social distinctions. For example, working-class Swedish speakers and those who worked in the fishing industry generally spoke their own dialects while aristocratic and other privileged Swedish speakers adopted a language more closely related to that traditionally spoken in Sweden, albeit of a more antiquated variety. (It is said that modern Finnish-Swedish resembles that spoken in Sweden in the eighteenth century.) And even within the Helsinki region, clear linguistic distinctions can be noted, as in the Swedish spoken in the area between Espoo (Esbo) in the west and Vantaa (Vanda) in the east.

Similarly, well-educated Finns often spoke quite at variance to their fellow countrymen of more humble origins and employment, especially if they had originally come from the provinces. Regional dialectical distinctions were and remain very considerable, while local slang and colloquialisms also differ significantly from written Finnish.

Whatever the linguistic distinctions, one can hardly speak of two different ethnic groups, since over the past few hundred years, many Swedish speakers adopted Finnish and many Finnish speakers Swedish as their preferred language of communication. This was also true of Jews, Germans, Tartars and others who arrived later as part of the Russian military forces in the Grand Duchy. And even within mono-linguistic communities there is a much greater ethnic diversity, in a genetic sense, than might at first glance be imagined. Many elite Swedish-speaking families, especially those of aristocratic background, for instance, are not of Swedish or Finnish ethnic ancestry, but of German, Russian and even Scottish backgrounds. It should be stressed, then, that the ethnic and linguistic dimensions of identities based upon the use of Swedish or Finnish as a mother tongue is complex; to speak of a clearly demarcated Swedish or Finnish ethnic identity based solely upon language is inappropriate. Culture, material and genetic factors must also be taken into account.

Swedish and Russian

Swedish-speaking Finns form the most significant ethnic minority community in Helsinki. Their coastal presence in the vicinity goes back centuries, even if their presence further inland only dates from around 1610. It is estimated that Finland as a whole had about 87,000 in the 1750s, perhaps one-fifth of its total population. By 1815, these numbers had almost doubled, in relative balance with a similar increase in the population of the country as a whole, but most of these Finnish-Swedes lived near Helsinki, Turku and Vaasa. Thereafter a period of equilibrium ensued.

When Faddei Bulgarin visited Finland, in the early nineteenth century he found "that the Russian is not looked down on, but is honored, and even many ladies of noble family know Russian and have respect for the good things in our literature." A society existed, the Friends of the Russian Word, where Russian literature was read and discussed in the company of Russian officers and traders.

Certainly, in linguistic terms, Russian influence on Finnish and Swedish remained very limited. Swedish continued, as it had always been, the official language of administration. In higher education and the civil service knowledge of it was indispensable and many Finnish-speaking Finns acquired proficiency.

Needless to say, many Russian government officials were not happy with this state of affairs and some even sought to undermine Swedish's role in the official and social life of the nation. To this end, while aware that the widespread introduction of Russian was hardly viable in Helsinki, much less Finland as a whole, a number of Russian administrators sought to encourage a sense of Finnish identity, focused around the Finnish language. This could serve as a means of severing the age-old political and cultural ties with Sweden.

The Finnish Folk Revival

Both with and without Russian support, the Finnish folk revival, which permeated all segments of the Finnish population in the course of the nineteenth century, took on a life and vitality of its own. The literary revival that occurred, especially among well-educated Finnish- and Swedish-speaking Finns in the 1830s and 1840s, was especially significant. Its flagship was the monumental epic, the *Kalevala*, based on Karelian stories handed down by word of mouth, but compiled and reworked into a coherent form by Elias Lönnrot (1802-84). Born into a Finnish-speaking family, he only learnt Swedish as a child in order to be able to attend school. In the 1820s, while still a student, Lönnrot had joined the growing band of enthusiasts who were collecting traditional Finnish poetry both from old records and publications and from surviving singers in Finland. Lönnrot was one of first to extend his search for old Finnish poetry across the Russian frontier into Karelia with several trips between 1828 and 1833, the year he was appointed a district medical officer in Kajaani. The outcome was the so-called *Old Kalevala*, published in 1835 and later expanded and revised for a new edition in 1849.

This book inflamed Finnish cultural and political consciousness and struck a note of alarm in Russian governmental circles. Within a year the Russian authorities, troubled by the uprisings in several European cities in 1848, had banned all but religious and economic writings in Finnish. But it was too late to arrest this growing literary development and the prohibition was soon rescinded. Nonetheless, the fact that a chair in the Finnish language was established in 1851 at Helsinki's Alexander University, named in honor of its founder Czar Alexander I, indicated the importance attached by the authorities to the use of Finnish.

Johan Vilhelm Snellman (1806-81) was another figure of immense importance for the development of Finnish national identity. He was deeply influenced by the nationalistic and cultural philosophical concepts of the German philosopher Hegel, protested against any attempts to integrate the Grand Duchy more closely into the Russian

Empire, and vociferously advocated the so-called Finnicization of public life and government in Helsinki. Large numbers of the educated classes, both Swedish- and Finnish-speaking, rallied to his call and saw in Finnish culture and literary production the creation of the nation on both sides of the divide, which, in linguistic terms, seemed to be widening by virtue of Snellman and his supporters.

Snellman was later commemorated on May 12 (a day also known as Finnish Day), a tradition that continues up to the present. On that occasion the Association of Finnish Culture and Identity lays a wreath at his statue, situated outside the central offices of the Bank of Finland in the city center, to remember this great hero of Finnish national identity.

Snellman's role in Finland's nation-building was essentially interactive, for he took as much from his contemporaries as he provided. His main contribution was the politicization of his contemporaries' ideas of national identity, and an important part of that was as a facilitator of the so-called *Lauantai-seura*, or Saturday Society, which supported many of his goals. This discussion group was founded in the 1830s by a number of graduates of Helsinki University, including, along with Snellman, Lönnrot, the poet Johan Ludvig Runeberg, and Johan Jacob Nervander, whose early experiments with electricity had earned him considerable acclaim. Carl Niklas Keckman also played a key role as the principal organizer. But it was Runeberg, who as Finland's national poet was later most prominently commemorated. Not only was his birthday, February 5, made into a day of public festivity, but in the 1840s a sponge cake, smothered in jam, was even named in his honor.

Not surprisingly, a political dimension soon followed in the wake of these developments. When in 1863 the Finnish Diet was convened for the first time since the Napoleonic period, Snellman was appointed director of the Department of Finance within the Senate, an important position that enabled him to propagate his "Finnicizing" vision. Not only was the censorship of Finnish literary materials curtailed, but the language itself became an official medium of government, alongside Swedish. Moreover, to encourage its usage more widely in educated circles, the first Finnish-based high school opened in 1869. The result was a new generation of *Fennomans* in Helsinki, many of whom joined the newly established Finnish Party, the first modern political party of its type in Finland. Yet for all its cultural novelty, it was hardly a radical party; deeply Lutheran and economically conservative, it soon predominated in two of the four estates: that of the clergy and that of the small farmers.

With a power base such as this, it was soon possible to introduce new measures securing the centrality of the Finnish language and culture in both Helsinki and the nation as a whole. In 1883 Finnish became an official language of the lower courts, while the rights of Finns to use the Finnish language in legal matters were extended. Most importantly, an imperial decree of Czar Alexander II, whose image is forevermore embedded in Finnish cultural consciousness as a defender of national identity and independence, made the majority language of the respective municipalities also the language of the local administration.

Awakening of Swedish-Finnish Identity

As the 1850s passed, a new resurgence of feeling made itself felt with respect to the identity of some Finns who saw their roots more in terms of Swedish culture and language than Finnish. Such an interest was soon to take on significant political overtones in Helsinki under the guidance of Axel Olof Freudental (1836-1911), who led the Swedish national movement, a body which envisioned Finland as an integral part of a new pan-Scandinavian union of nations. Later that decade, a growing wave of support from the Alexander University joined in the call for a new awareness of the historical Swedish role in Finland's history, so that throughout the 1860s and 1870s a greater sense of Swedish-Finnish cultural identity gained momentum in the intellectual circles of the capital. One of the most radical of these groups, though perhaps one of the least academic, took delight in calling themselves Vikings. Strongly antagonized by Snellman, these largely middle-class Finnish-Swedes held the view that they were a nation in their own right, distinct from their Finnish-speaking compatriots.

Their views soon found political expression during the 1880s, when the Swedish Party was established within the Finnish Diet. But the ethnocentric ideals of the so-called Vikings were hardly those with which their more elite compatriots would sympathize, given that many of them were married into Russian, German or other continental European noble families. For them such concepts of race smacked of the herd. Not surprisingly, they preferred to follow a more inclusive political vision. They saw themselves rather as representatives of a "cultured Swedishness", seeing their more strident fellow Swedish speakers as representatives of a "rural Swedishness", even when this made its appearance in Helsinki, as immigration from the countryside gradually increased. Thus, the forty percent of Helsinki residents who spoke Swedish as their mother tongue as the nineteenth century came to its end were from quite varied backgrounds. In any case, on a social level, a greater cosmopolitanism reigned amongst these Helsinki patricians, who gathered for grand social occasions at the House of the

Nobility, than those of the more linguistically preoccupied segments of the middle classes.

For many foreign visitors to the Finnish capital, the ethnic mix was quite stimulating, and some, like the French scientist Marmier, found it positively fascinating. He wrote:

The salons of the Helsingfors aristocracy are as elegant as the finest Paris salons, and the society that frequents them, Finnish at heart, Russian through circumstance, French in wit and manners, presents the foreigner with a curious assemblage of ideas, sympathies, ancient traditions, new hopes and various languages.

Finnish-Russian Relations

By the early 1890s the emergence of a new cultural and political organization, the Young Finns, helped somewhat paradoxically to achieve a new consolidation of both Swedish- and Finnish-speaking Finns. This was in part a reaction to the growth of Pan-Slavism within the Russian Empire from the 1880s onwards. It also reflected anxiety in the face of the growing desire of almost all western nations to achieve a greater centralization of political power and a more homogenous and unified nation state, in which what was considered the dominant and superior culture would come to permeate and supersede the others. The Finns were unwilling to accommodate themselves to this new hegemonic political and cultural vision. Their vision of Finland was one purified of foreign influences.

Yet during the middle of the nineteenth century these influences had nonetheless been growing, as a significant number of Russian merchants established themselves in Helsinki. Some, with names like Sinebrychoff, Kiseleff, Kudrakoff, Uschaoff and Koroleff, would become household names of Finnish industry later in the century, completely integrating themselves within the Finnish upper classes. The advent of a Russian secondary school, established through the initiative of the Czar in 1870, also furthered Russian interests in the capital.

But in wider terms social interaction between Finns and Russians in Helsinki was by no means a happy picture. During the later 1890s, Mrs. Tweedie presented a bleak view, based on her own experiences:

"Do you mix much with the Russians?" we asked one of our new friends.
"Hardly at all; they have conquered us, they rule us, they plant whole regiments among us, and they don't even take the trouble to understand us, or to learn our language. No, we keep to ourselves, and they keep to themselves; our temperaments are so different we could never mix."

Lower down the social scale, many Russians active as street traders, in glassware or other commodities, were coming into contact with Finns on a regular basis. Nonetheless, as was noted at the time, they also kept themselves to themselves, even if they were hardly the only minority involved in such trade who maintained their ethnic identity. While a total of fifty-five of them were active in 1874 in trade, twelve Germans, eight Scandinavians and even one Briton were also similarly employed.

Cultural Divide

Antagonism between Russians and Finns was growing, but so too was that between the Finns themselves, along their own Swedish-Finnish divide. In 1902, as if in symbolic unison against the Russian political and cultural threat, Swedish and Finnish were finally placed on linguistic parity. But with the abolition of the Assembly of the Estates and the establishment of a unicameral Finnish parliament or *Euduskunta* in 1906 (it still functions today), the Finns now achieved a numerical majority in representation and so could encourage the enactment of laws favoring the Finnish-speaking majority. In reaction, many Swedish-speaking Finns from all social backgrounds came together to form their own Swedish People's Party, to further their political, cultural and linguistic interests. In any case, during the early years of the twentieth century, indeed at least until the First World War, Swedish-speaking Finns, exercised an influence out of all proportion to their numbers. Yet that said, many Finnish-speaking Finns were certainly making their way in the world. In 1906, when Snellman's birth centenary was celebrated, 35,000 Finns with Swedish surnames registered and published in the national press new Finnish ones in their place. As Professor Max Engman of the Åbo Akademi has pointed out, names are by no means an indication of Swedish or Finnish ethnic identity.

A small group of activists, however, saw matters differently. Plans were also emanating from the Swedish People's Party, to organize Swedish-speaking cantons along the lines of the monolingual cantons of Switzerland. This stood in sharp contrast to the policy of many Swedish-speaking Finns a few decades before, when Swedish speakers enjoyed significant political influence. When the newly founded Swedish Assembly convened for the first time in 1919, a new lobbying organization appeared to defend Finnish-Swedish interests in the new political climate.

That same year a new constitution was promulgated for Finland, in which formal parity was established for both Finnish and Swedish. Three years later, a new law came into force—it is still in force today— by which all Finnish municipalities and other administrative districts became legally monolingual or bilingual, according to the size of their respective linguistic populations, whether Finnish or Swedish (but not Saami).

Such minority accommodations notwithstanding, the Finnicization of Helsinki itself continued unabated. This process was further aided by the foundation of a new Finnish-speaking nationalist movement, the *Aitosuomalaisuus* or True Finns. Drawn largely from Finnish-speaking middle-class families or those from rural areas with small landholdings, their ethnic perspective was limited and fiercely xenophobic. They were keen to purge their new nation from anything that smacked of the foreign, even including the rights of Swedish-speaking Finns to use Swedish as a language of tuition at Helsinki University. Yet their political base remained limited and they failed to win political power to carry out their visions for a homogenous Finnish-speaking polity. Instead, they served as a source of opposition to such new radical Swedish groups as those who supported the concept of "Eastern Swedishness", advocating the incorporation of Finland's Swedish-speaking areas into Sweden. But like their opposite number, their expectations of forming a political party proved unrealistic. Both were obliged to act as lobbying groups, pursuing the advancement of their linguistic communities in education and local politics.

The late 1930s, marked by the growing threat of Stalinist power on Finland's eastern borders, witnessed a respite in Finnish-Swedish ethnic and linguistic hostilities. The rise of the *Lapua* movement, drawing its members from both sides of the linguistic divide (though largely from a middle-class constituency and therefore firmly on the right of the political spectrum), helped foster unity among Finnish people. Even the great divide between conservatives and socialists, which festered throughout the 1920s and 1930s, was fading away in the confrontation against the Soviet Union. But the increasingly violent profile of parts of the organization, especially against the political left, seemed to many in government to endanger the democratic basis of the Finnish state itself. In the spring of 1932 it was prohibited. Its conservative and nationalistic mantle was then carried by the new political organization, the Patriotic People's Movement (IKL), a fascist organization based on Hitler's brownshirts. Its policy favored the Finnish-speaking population over the Swedish-speaking, drawing its ruling members from the True Finnish movement after its election to Parliament in 1933. This, in turn, led to such a deterioration of relations between the two communities that considerable violence broke out on the streets of Helsinki. Fortunately, no one actually died as a result of these ethnic hostilities, but only after the Winter War in 1940 was this turbulent period of confrontation finally laid to rest.

German Speakers

While Finnish- and Swedish-speaking Finns were the two largest ethnic groups, German-speaking ones formed a significant minority, especially among the rising middle classes. They had a long and respectable connection with the capital. Many had arrived from the various German states during the 1830s and 1840s, seeking employment as craftsmen (the guilds of the city were still thriving), bookkeepers or in shops. Others came from German-speaking communities in the Baltic, Russian Empire and elsewhere in Eastern Europe. Few, however, became successful independent merchants, for in 1842 only three were officially registered as such. Many of those actually born in Germany migrated to Helsinki from the northern ports, significant numbers from the old Hansa city of Lübeck, with its trading connections to the Baltic.

To serve the needs of this German-speaking community in Helsinki, a German-language girls' school had opened in 1862; yet so fashionable and successful did it become that by 1875 seventy percent of its students were from prosperous Swedish-speaking rather than German-speaking backgrounds. It later expanded to accept boys and soon boasted one of Finland's most important collections of German books in its large library.

The city in Finland with the largest number of German-speaking residents in the late nineteenth century was Viipuri. But Helsinki also attracted many of their compatriots, some of these immigrants becoming household names over the decades as merchants because of the high quality of the goods and services they provided. The name Paulig, for example, became synonymous with coffee, as Fazer did with chocolate. Kämp established Helsinki's leading hotel and König a noted restaurant. Similarly, Stockmann is today not only the most famous department store in Finland, but has recently opened a subsidiary in St. Petersburg on Nevsky Prospect. Other names form a veritable litany of Finnish trade and retailing: Bargum, Knief and Kleineh, Osberg, Schröder, Staudinger and Wulff all brought their expertise from Germany.

War and Reconciliation
War can be a great unifier. So it was with Finland during the Second World War. Though war with the Soviet Union brought much misery, death and destruction, it did achieve one beneficial effect, cementing both Swedish- and Finnish-speaking Finns into a single nation. This nation had a common goal and a common enemy, and the war helped to start the healing process between right- and left-wing Finnish-speaking Finns, evident in the film *Tuntematon sotilas* (The Unknown Soldier). No other event in Finnish history has been so successful in forging the unity of the Finnish people, and this was as true in Helsinki as anywhere else in the country. Both Swedish-speaking and Finnish-speaking Finns joined together in the defense of their country. The Swedish-speaking reservists generally served with Infantry Regiment 11, taking the letter "S" as their symbol, which led them to be known among their Finnish-speaking compatriots as the *Ässä-rykmentti* or S Regiment. Even the integration within Finland of 400,000 people from territories lost to the Soviet Union under emergency legislation initiated by President J. K. Paasikivi, failed to undermine the new-found harmony.

Yet there were other difficulties, fraught with ethnic dangers. The rapid industrialization of Finland in the 1950s and 1960s led to a dramatic increase in urbanization and nowhere was this more apparent than in Helsinki. With the vast influx of Finnish-speaking Finns from elsewhere in the country desperately needed to provide labor, many previously Swedish-speaking areas felt themselves linguistically and culturally eroded. To assuage their anxieties, a new amendment to the Language Act was carried out in 1962, under which the presence of a certain number of Swedish speakers in a district assured the continuation of its bilingualism, even if in proportional terms it had sharply diminished. The rights of the Swedish-speaking minority were thereby preserved and enhanced.

Literary Expressions
The poet Gunnar Björling (1887-1960), a native of Helsinki, spent decades exploring Finnish-Swedish identity in his poetry. His first collection of poems, *Resting Day* (1922), was followed by some twenty more, the last with the strange title of *You Go the Words*, first published in 1955. With their eccentric and esoteric form and substance, they appear to be more linguistic archaeological remains—literary fragments devoid of punctuation—than a coherent poetical expression. Perhaps they should be seen as linguistic jokes, a continuation of the Dadaism that Björling, as its only Finnish literary exponent, had advocated as far back as the 1920s. Yet his works are by no means mere word games. Rather, they are infused with moral and ethical pre-occupations and reflect in no uncertain term the focus given to such issues by the Finnish sociologist and professor at the London School of Economics in London, Edward Westermarck, whom Björling greatly admired.

Another prominent Finnish-Swedish poet and author is Bo Carpelan, deemed by many to be the most important of his generation. Less esoteric than Björling, his earlier works introduced a more accessible version of Swedish modernism to a Finnish public. His most noted work in recent years is the novel *Axel* (1986), in which an extremely eccentric relative of the composer Jean Sibelius is the anti-hero.

The Swedish Finn Kjell Westö captures in a much more contemporary idiom the problems that could confront a member of that linguistic minority growing up in a largely Finnish-speaking area. A short story, reflecting life in Helsinki during the 1970s features a bully called Melba:

I don't know why he was called Melba; there was certainly nothing peach-like about him...

Melba didn't have to try very hard to find fault with me. It was enough to open the door and see the nameplate on Entry F. It was enough to discover that the only Finnish I could really understand was "Give me the ball!" "Pass!" "Shoot!" "Cover him!"

Melba had many opinions about Finland-Swedes, none of them flattering. Quickly he dubbed me Håkan. It was from him that I learned the intimate connection between the Swedish language and pantyhose: according to him anybody who spoke Swedish was a faggot, a Homo-Håkan, a pantyhose-model.

In late 1960s Helsinki, gangs were sharply divided along ethnic and linguistic lines. Westö wrote in his novel *Kites over Helsinki* (1996) about one character's gang, under the leadership of a certain Jacke Petterson, which hung about in the vicinity of Köpis and Riikinkukko near Munkkiniemi: "Jacke's gang consists of tough guys, who don't give a damn for the Finnish ones who think they're something special, giving them as good as they get, fighting back, with great success." This is, however, clearly a youthful confrontation, which recedes as they grow older. For then, "They start to listen to the Cream and Hendrix and Jefferson Airplane or get motorbikes..."

Such an attitude was not merely restricted to immature teenagers, and even the elderly were affected. The grandmother in the novel has a particular horror for the linguistic inroads of Finnish in her family. As Westö expresses it through the lips of his character:

I remember how uptight Father always became before she arrived for her Christmastime visit. How each time, just before he went to the station to collect her, he laid down the holiday rules of conduct for us, how we had to use Swedish, no sloppy expressions borrowed from Finnish or swear words.

In contrast, more upbeat and positive views of relations between Swedish- and Finnish-speaking Finns were given in the nineteenth century by Karl August Tavaststjerna in his novels, and then in the early twentieth by Edith Södergran, with her visionary, even ethereal poetry. In our own times, the novelist Christer Kihlman, the satirist Henrik Tikkanen, his wife the dramatist, poet and novelist Märta Tikkanen and the poet and dramatist Claes Andersson have also presented happier scenarios of such relations, many examples of which have been published in English and other translations.

Language and Legislation

With such attitudes prevalent, it is not surprising that national and local government implemented measures to reduce friction between Finnish and Swedish speakers. Between 1972-7 the provision of obligatory courses in both languages was introduced in public primary schools. Since this was an approach supported by President Urho Kekkonen, a "true Finn", its success was assured.

As for the legal system and governmental regulations, these were, in any case, promulgated in both languages. In education, the Swedish School of Economics and Business Administration, based in Helsinki, achieved fame as the most important institute of its kind in Finland and also attracted many Finnish speakers to its lecture halls. The University of Helsinki has also continued to provide education in both languages. Indeed, in some departments such as law and medicine special quotas were provided, making it easier for Finnish Swedish speakers to gain admission to their courses than Finnish speakers, an area of positive discrimination that has caused some controversy.

Roma and Saami Peoples

An amendment to the Finnish constitution in 1995 extended further linguistic rights to the Roma, many of whom live in Helsinki. The constitution provides for the preservation of their culture as well as the variant of the Roma language in Finland, a fascinating tongue composed of Finnish, Swedish and Hindi elements. In any school in which four or more Roma children are enrolled, education in the language is also provided, if they so wish.

Many of the ancestors of these Roma arrived in Finland by way of Sweden during the course of the sixteenth century. Today Finland has the largest Roma population of any Nordic country, with about 10,000 spread out over the country but a large proportion settled in the periphery of Helsinki.

These rights also apply to the Saami peoples in the far north of Finland, some of whom now also live in the capital. The Saami language itself (in reality several different but related languages, each with its own dialects), is commonly known as Lappish, a word today often taken by Saami people in a pejorative sense. It was first recorded in the mid-sixteenth century, but for years its usage was circumscribed, even suppressed. Today, however, Saami have the right to receive official communications, education and other important information in their native tongue, a hard-won privilege for the 1,712 Saami who speak it as their mother tongue, according to the 1996 census. A Saami Assembly is now also elected, with its base in the far north of the country.

Helsinki's Jews

Such linguistic variety also has its expression within Helsinki's ecclesiastical world, where all major churches—Lutheran, Orthodox, Roman Catholic and the Free Churches—provide services and catechism in both Finnish and Swedish. The Swedish-speaking minority has therefore been seen as one of the most privileged in a world otherwise plagued by ethnic dissension and violence.

Jews number about 1,500 in Finland today, but the country, unlike its eastern European neighbors, has happily suffered little in the way of anti-Semitic discrimination. Many of their ancestors came to Finland from the 1830s when they served as conscripts in the Russian military. By the 1870s such notable Jewish families as Drisin, Rung, Skurnik and Stiller had established themselves in Helsinki. They organized the establishment of a Jewish school, adjacent to the synagogue and still functioning today, on a site freely provided by the municipal government. A later scion of the Stiller family, Mauritz, achieved notability for having launched the Swedish diva Greta Garbo into the world of Hollywood. He was not the only Jewish Finn active in the world of the cinema; the Rung brothers played a key role in

developing Helsinki's film industry during the second decade of the twentieth century.

Many of the more modest Jews carried out their trade at Narinkka, the so-called Jewish square of Helsinki (a derivative of the Russian-Yiddish term for square, i.e. *na rynke*), situated in the vicinity of Simonkatu. Many were second-hand clothes dealers. Later in the second half of the twentieth century some of these and their descendants had prospered and set up a number of the largest and leading fashion shops in the capital. Of these, the majority until the 1930s were Swedish-speaking, especially in Helsinki. Thereafter, like their non-Jewish compatriots, most spoke Finnish as their first language.

With the advent of the Continuation War and Finland's connection with Nazi Germany as a co-belligerent, the horizon looked ominous for Finnish Jewry. Despite the fact that some farsighted Finns saw the risks involved by joining forces with the Germans, others, it must be admitted, sympathized with them unreservedly. Yet as far as Finnish Jews were concerned, their rights remained fully respected. They suffered no official discrimination and many served proudly in the Finnish military. Of the approximately 200 Jews who fought for

Finland, 23 sacrificed their lives for their country. But for Jewish refugees, especially those from central Europe or the Soviet Union, the situation was less rosy. Some were initially sent to labor camps in the north of the country, in Sala, and on Gogland, in the Gulf of Finland, but most ultimately were released and granted Finnish citizenship. When the Nazis requested the deportation of some Jewish refugees in Finland to concentration camps in German-controlled territories, the Finnish authorities did initially round up a number of them. But at the last minute, Mannerheim, in conjunction with President Rytti, both of whom were only now made aware of this situation, intervened and ordered their immediate release. Nonetheless, a small number of non-Finnish, Eastern European Jewish refugees, alleged to be criminal, were deported to Birkenau, of whom only one survived.

Russians in Helsinki

Today the Finnish Parliament comprises 200 members, of whom over the last few decades about eight to ten percent have been Swedish-speaking. Of these many belong to bilingual political parties, even if the Swedish Party continues to use Swedish more or less exclusively in its political activities. The Swedish Assembly also continues to represent the interests of Finnish Swedish speakers.

The one ethnic group that remains somewhat apart, as it has done through Finnish history, is the Russians. Most Russians who settled in Finland except for the odd aristocrat arrived after 1809, the year Finland was ceded to Russia as an autonomous Grand Duchy. Except for those in the military, their numbers were strictly limited and only in 1917, the year of the Russian Revolution and Finland's unilateral declaration of independence, did a major influx occur. As more than two and a half million Russians fled their homeland, 15,000 made their way to Finland by 1919, many of whom settled, if temporarily, in Helsinki.

Such a major influx stirred up a xenophobic reaction among certain segments of the population and a political movement arose seeking to curb the perceived flood of aliens. Its xenophobia was also fed by the general dearth of food and housing in the capital. These circumstances encouraged Bruno Jalander, the governor of Uusimaa province, to oppose their arrival and settlement to such a degree that, ultimately, only a few thousand Russians dared remain. Most preferred to seek refuge from the revolution in more welcoming western European countries.

In contrast, the descendants of the Tartars who migrated to Finland from Nizhnii Novgorod in northwestern Russia during the last two decades of the nineteenth century, have been recently granted similar cultural and linguistic rights to the Saami people. Many were traditionally involved in fur trading and carpet dealing, activities still thriving in Helsinki today despite the animal rights lobby that has tried to prevent the fur trade in most other European capitals. They are generally Muslims and just under a thousand in number.

Latter-day Refugees
The next political refugees to arrive after the Russians were left-wing Chileans who had supported the socialist president, Salvador Allende. Fleeing the repressive regime of General Augusto Pinochet, they came from 1973 onwards. They were followed in the 1980s by a small number of Vietnamese, escaping from civil war in their homeland.

During the 1990s a number of other communities sought refuge or economic betterment in Finland, including Somalis fleeing the civil war and anarchy in their home country. Altogether 1,500 people arrived in Helsinki at this time, coming from a total of 28 different countries including the former Yugoslavia. Nowadays, refugees living in Helsinki total well over 3,000, and their numbers continue to grow, even if it cannot be said that Helsinki is as welcoming to political refugees, in terms of numbers, as a number of other western European countries.

Over the past decade since the collapse of the Soviet Union, over 60,000 Russians have come to settle in Finland, approximately 25,000 of whom live in Helsinki, making them the largest single ethnic minority to arrive recently in the country. They not only have their own Russian-language magazine, *Vestnik*, serving their community since 1993 (first established in Helsinki back in 1845), but the benefits of a Finnish-Russian school that has operated for forty years at Kaarelankuja 2. Yet neither their language nor culture has any official status, a surprising fact considering their numbers, but understandable when Finland's historically troubled relationship with Russia is taken into consideration, as well as the fact that they are not refugees, but voluntary economic migrants, who can return home whenever they wish.

The Contemporary Scene

Today 4.2 percent of Helsinki's population is comprised of foreign nationals. Of those who are Finnish, Finnish-speaking Finns account for 87.6 percent, Swedish speakers 6.4 percent and those of other languages six percent. In 2000 a mere seven percent of Helsinki people still had Swedish as their mother tongue.

Swedish-speaking children are now obliged to learn Finnish in secondary schools, but so too must Finnish-speaking children study Swedish, as they have done for decades. All, however, are keen to learn English. For although in the autumn semester of 2001, only 6,000 foreign students came to study in Finland, many of these came to Helsinki and so English has become the *lingua franca* for foreigners in their contacts with Finns, whatever their national background may be.

Perhaps in these times of change, ethnic, cultural and linguistic, one should recall the poetry of Arvo Turtiainen (1904-80), a native of Helsinki, where his father was a tailor. He focused upon life among the city's working class in many of his poems, which seem to hark back to the medieval troubadour tradition. At other times, he would write nostalgically, using the local *Stadi* slang, about his beloved Punavuori, as in "A Farewell to the Rööperi of My Childhood":

> *How many years—more than fifty, now*
> *since I first walked these streets...*
> *was Mother holding my hand then*
> *as mothers hold their children's hands today*
> *on these same streets?*

Today's Helsinki may be a city in flux, but there is a welcoming continuity as well, which crosses ethnic and cultural divides.

CHAPTER FIVE

God and Helsinki: Churches, Faiths and Religious Diversity

As any visitor who arrives by sea will see, the skyline of Helsinki is dominated by the great dome of St. Nicholas' Church, towering above the magnificent buildings designed by Engel laid out below it. As such, it is one of the most imposing, integrated pieces of urban planning in northern Europe and its classically inspired architecture seems to link Helsinki with other ancient Christian capitals.

Yet Helsinki, of all the European capitals, is one of the most recently Christianized. Where Rome was brought into the fold in the fourth century and London, conclusively, about three centuries later, Helsinki—or that part of southern Finland on which it is now situated—was only Christianized around the year 1200. And this process would only really be completed successfully by the following century. Only the Baltic regions of Europe, occupied by Latvians, Lithuanians and Estonians, whose ruling classes, both Polish-speaking and German-speaking had been converted to Christianity in the later Middle Ages were Christianized at a later date. Moreover, features of non-Christian beliefs and practices would long continue in the south of Finland, and even longer among the Saami people, in the north.

In the non-Christian religious practices that prevailed when paganism reigned in Finland, Midsummer's Eve was one of the most important festive occasions, on which the light and zenith of nature's life-giving forces were celebrated. Christianized as the Feast Day of St. John the Baptist, it nonetheless continues to express the same vitality and luminosity, as any visitor to the city's elegant central avenue, Esplanaadi, with its leafy gardens thronged with people, can witness on

Midsummer's Eve around the summer's solstice. At the same time, new, modern political associations have also been married to Midsummer's Eve, so that it has become in modern times Finland's Flag Day, a celebration of national identity and unity. Still, many vestigial aspects of the pagan celebrations remain; the bonfire or *kokko*, for example, is still a key element, and the emphasis on light and fertility is unmistakable. This is especially evident when, surrounded by carousers around Midsummer's evening, a plethora of fires illuminate the luminous sky as the sun barely sets below the horizon.

Early Churches

Helsinki was first founded under the aegis of the Swedish king Gustaf Vasa in 1550, so the oldest churches in the vicinity were not built for the city itself, but predate it. This is true of the so-called Helsinki Parish Church (1494) at Kirkkotie 45, a stone church of three aisles, dedicated to St. Lawrence, which served the needs of rural Uusimaa, the province in which Helsinki is situated. Unfortunately, the church was devastated by fire in 1893, after which it was heavily restored. More authentic is another very ancient house of worship, the Espoo Parish Church, built in the late fifteenth century in what is now a western suburb of the city. With its rectangular nave, also of three aisles, gray stone walls, and brick tympanum, it is typical of Finnish churches of this period.

Yet Helsinki's first house of worship proper was the Christina Church, a stone edifice built to honor the Swedish Queen Christina, of Greta Garbo's film fame. (One of the most acclaimed films of 1933, *Queen Christina* was shocking not only for its steamy eroticism, but for the bisexuality evinced by the eponymous heroine, Queen Christina, portrayed by Garbo, herself a Swede whose real name was Greta Lovisa Gustafsson.) The church was built in 1643 on land donated by the Crown for the re-founding of the city on a more salubrious and beneficial site, at least with respect to trading possibilities. Unfortunately, a fire (always the bane of cities and towns in Finland) destroyed it in 1654.

Not long after, the Church of the Holy Spirit replaced it. Constructed of wood in the interest of economy, it fared little better and also burned down during the general and deliberate conflagration in the town in 1713, when Russian troops were threatening the city with imminent occupation. Yet almost immediately, with the arrival of occupying Russian troops and accompanying merchants, a new little Orthodox church was erected.

When peace finally returned and the city reverted to Swedish authority, one of the first important buildings to be constructed was the Ulrika Eleonora Church, named after the Swedish queen of that time and completed in 1727 on the western edge of the Market Square by what is now Senate House Square, where its outline is marked out. Cruciform in plane and painted a red ochre, it could accommodate more than 700 parishioners, making it one of the largest churches in Finland until its demolition in the early nineteenth century. At this time Helsinki formed a part of a vast diocese including such widely spread cities as Viipuri, now in Russia, Porvoo, and Tampere.

The Old Church
It was in the early nineteenth century that the ecclesiastical architecture of Helsinki really achieved its greatest flourishing. After Finland had been ceded to the Russian Czar Alexander I in 1809 as a Grand Duchy, its ruler, respectful of the established Church in his new domains, decided to erect a splendid Lutheran church on Senate House Square, the centre piece of his architectural vision for imperial Helsinki. This was not to be a rapid undertaking and so in the interim a much smaller wooden church was also built as a substitute for the Ulrika Eleonora Church, which was torn down on Senate House Square in the process of redevelopment. The site chosen, adjacent to what would become the Bulevardi, was then on the outskirts of the city. But it was by no means as small as might be imagined for a "temporary" building; in fact, it also became what was one of the largest wooden buildings in Finland at that time. This new house of worship, now known (as its older "sisters" disappeared) as the Old Church, was designed in 1824 by Carl Ludvig Engel.

Completed two years later, the Old Church is based on a Greek cross pattern, more characteristic of Orthodox than Lutheran churches, surmounted by a tunnel vault. But its external appearance is playfully deceptive; from the outside it would seem to be a typical Latin cross

Protestant church. Be that as it may, it commemorated the earlier church by incorporating various objects, ecclesiastical and architectural, salvaged from the old structure into its fabric. The austere and rustic Tuscan order, suitable for its somewhat rural location, adorns its façade. Engel also added an adjacent funerary chapel to serve as an architectural foil in a similarly Spartan neoclassical style. Though intended to be a temporary structure, the Old Church is still with us today. There is also a discreet German war memorial in the adjacent cemetery, erected in the twentieth century to commemorate fallen German soldiers in 1918. It stands not far from where victims of the devastating plague of 1710 are also remembered.

The Great Church of St. Nicholas
Without doubt, the most important church in Finland today, not just in Helsinki, is Carl Ludvig Engel's Great Church of St. Nicholas. It has long been the mother church of the capital, that is, the most important church in Helsinki with ecclesiastical precedence, even if it only became a cathedral and seat of a bishop in the twentieth century. Indeed, the archiepiscopal seat of the Lutheran primate of Finland was and continues to be in Turku.

Commissioned by Alexander I, who took a keen interest in the construction of a new and imposing church—an important symbol of his *largesse*—Engel had already commenced making a variety of designs for the church in the early months of 1819. But it was not until 1822 that the Czar chose the design that pleased him most, to the considerable disgruntlement of Engel who had himself preferred another. Construction first commenced in 1830, on the tercentenary of the proclamation of the Augsburg Confession, the basic confession of the Lutheran Church presented to the Holy Roman Emperor Charles V, in 1530. For financial and other practical reasons, the process of building took decades to complete and only in 1850, during the reign of Alexander I's brother Nicholas I, was the church finally consecrated.

From an architectural point of view, for all its neoclassicism, it is an eclectically inspired building, the inspiration for which can be traced back to both Roman and Renaissance values. Yet in terms of its practical construction, it is a very modern nineteenth-century edifice, benefiting from the latest technical innovations. Here a Greek cross

plan was also used, not because Engel particularly admired that arrangement, but because it enabled a great cupola to crown the whole, providing a focal point from miles around. On the other hand, Engel did appreciate the Orthodox use of the iconostasis, or screen of wood or stone which separates the sanctuary containing the altar from the nave, which he felt exerted a strong emotional appeal. Nonetheless, inconsistent as this architectural feature was with the theology of a Lutheran church, this Byzantine-inspired partition was never built.

To ease the church's integration into Senate House Square, with its other important buildings, the Guards' Barracks was removed from its base and a huge flight of steps constructed in its place. These are more reminiscent of Eisenstein's famous film *The Battleship Potemkin* than anything Nordic, despite the chapel pavilions erected at the top on either end.

In terms of technical innovations, it was provided with the latest system of central heating, utilizing cast-iron stoves situated in the cellars below, from which pipes carried hot air into the church. To better withstand the humidity, a special type of calk was used to line the walls of the edifice, later renovated in the course of time by more modern and weather-resistant forms of cement. Even the columns and their capitals were specially treated with a special concoction of acid oil in order to preserve them against the cold and damp of the climate. The bases of these columns themselves were made of cast iron or granite, but brick was employed for the joists and tympanum as means of saving money. Even an imperial purse had its limits, it seems, and with workers laboring fourteen hours a day, the enterprise was one of the most costly ever carried out in Finland until that time. Still, it was money well spent, for even today, after a major restoration that took place during the 1960s, the church towers over the center of Helsinki, a perpetual reminder of imperial munificence.

For some Finnish nationalists in the following decades, its symbolism was less positive; the Finnish-Swedish author and poet Zacharias Topelius (1818-98), best known for his tales *Fältskärns berättelser* (The Surgeon's Stories, 1851-66), complained with considerable scorn that St. Nicholas Church looked like "a chicken, in possession of neither wings nor a tail", the "bourgeois" architectural expression of a mediocre imperial aesthetic. Fortunately, this jaundiced viewpoint is not shared by many admirers of Helsinki today.

Spiritual Diversity

Though the Lutheran Church was the established church of Finland both under the Swedish kings and Russian Czars, its position masked an ever growing range of ethnic, indeed, spiritual, diversity in Helsinki. Many priests were of Finnish-Swedish extraction (a minority now, but in the early days of Helsinki an overwhelming majority), and most were obliged to speak both Swedish and Finnish in the Helsinki region in order to effectively serve their linguistically differentiated flocks, united by a common religion. Indeed, even today, priests within the diocese of Helsinki preach in both languages, a growing luxury, albeit a civilized one, for a city with an ever-dwindling community of Swedish speakers, now about six percent of the population.

There were also the new arrivals of Orthodox Christians, Jews and Moslems who came to settle in Finland during the Russian period from 1809 until 1917. Many of these had arrived as military conscripts— one of the few channels open to immigrants to Finland—since they were entitled to settle in that part of the Russian Empire in which they carried out their service. Otherwise, the established Lutheran Church of Finland acted as a filter to foreign integration, preventing the entry and settlement of non-military personnel or higher administrators since Finnish law excluded most non-Lutherans from settling there. Orthodox members of the military were, however, provided for. Today the little Orthodox church at Hietaniemi still functions and continues to use the old Russian calendar, a vestige of this early relatively tolerant multi-ethnic and increasingly multi-religious period.

For all the growing toleration, though, it should not be forgotten that the role of an established church also had important political overtones. For one thing, it was still the Lutheran clergy who exerted a primary influence on the various ethnic and religious minorities, not only on the spiritual and moral welfare of their flocks, both willing and unwilling, but even on their physical movements as well. For example, documents from a parishioner's local priest were required for any internal migration and resettlement the individual might wish to undertake, even when the individual concerned was not a practicing Lutheran! That said, the role of the Lutheran Church was by no means oppressive compared to the role of established churches elsewhere. Moreover, the Orthodox Church also enjoyed a position of considerable power and freedom, supported as it was by the Czar's own deeply-held Orthodox faith.

Holy Trinity Church

The first architectural expression of support for Orthodoxy in Helsinki was the construction of the Holy Trinity Church, near Senate House Square. At first, it catered primarily to the needs of Russian military officers, government administrators and others, although today its congregation is composed of Finns who are Orthodox. Built in 1826, it too was designed by Engel. It is situated to the north, behind the Great Church of St. Nicholas, and opposite the Cantonist School, where military training for orphans was provided. Though Orthodox, the use of a Latin long nave gives it a very Lutheran appearance. It also has a certain Baroque affinity to the famous Admiralty Building in St. Petersburg (1806-23) by the Russian architect Andreyan Dimitrievich Zakharov by virtue of its bold pilasters. The wooden tower with which it was once crowned has since made way for a stone one, added in 1898, while the small cylindrical tower to the west is clearly derived from the Peter and Paul Church at the eponymous fortress in St. Petersburg by Domenico Trezzini. There were originally two small pavilions on either side of the steps leading up from the street, but these have long since disappeared.

Military Chapel

With the outbreak of the Crimean War, the eighteenth-century fortress of Suomenlinna took on new importance. During the course of the war, especially during the bombardment in August 1855, the little Russian Orthodox regimental church in the fortress, on the island of Iso Mustasaari (Great Black Island), only dedicated the previous year, seemed to symbolize survival for the beleaguered troops. Known as the Alexander Nevsky Church, it was dedicated to St. Alexander Nevsky. Nevsky was the thirteenth-century patron saint of Russia who had defended the principality against the Swedes and Germans and so was a suitable patron for a Russian military chapel. As August Schauman, a journalist of considerable repute and founder of Helsinki's leading Swedish-language newspaper, *Hufvudstadsbladet*, wrote shortly after the bombardment:

> *From the new Greek church of the fortress, whose cupola had evidently been pierced by gunshot but was otherwise intact, its bells call the devout to evening prayer; amidst the flames we could see men crawling out of their shelters, whilst others quietly and devoutly made their way to the house of worship.*

Schauman was the descendant of an aristocratic Livonian family, long resident in Finland. If he at the time was a staunch supporter of Russia, his relation, Eugene Schauman, was later (in 1904) to assassinate Helsinki's Russian governor general Bobrikov. But for the time being the loyalties of Schauman and most Finns remained with the Russian Empire and Czar Nicholas I. As such, the survival of the Orthodox church on Suomenlinna remained a positive symbol of Finnish loyalty, rather than a reminder of an alien religion, as it later became.

In the 1920s, after independence, this centrally planned church, the cruciform shape of which was highly popular in the Russian Orthodox world, was converted to a Lutheran house of worship and lost its onion domes.

The Uspensky Cathedral

Within a decade of the Crimean War, the building of a new major Orthodox church was begun in 1862, and four years later the grand Uspensky Cathedral was completed on Katajanokka Island, providing the city's most prominent Orthodox counter pole to the Lutheran Great Church. Of warm red brick carried by ship from the Bomarsund fortress on the Åland Islands, destroyed during the Crimean War in 1854, it still boasts twenty-two carat gold domes, the central one of which is supported by four massive pillars of granite, as well as a further twelve smaller ones, symbolizing Christ and the Apostles, respectively. As such, it is the largest Orthodox church, not only in Finland, but in all of western and central Europe. Designed by the Russian architects Aleksei M. Gornostaev and Ivan Varnek, it was subsumed into the Orthodox diocese of Viipuri of which it remained a part until the conclusion of war in 1944 and the cession of that city to Russia. Among its most important patrons can be numbered members of the Sinebrychoff family, of brewing fame, who established themselves as some of Helsinki's most prominent citizens in the course of the nineteenth century.

Aside from the numerous chapels within the body of the cathedral itself, there is also another little chapel in connection to the Uspensky Cathedral, hidden away within the ecclesiastical residence of the Orthodox Church in Helsinki. Located in Liisankatu, a street named after the Orthodox Czarina Elisabeth, wife of Alexander I, it was actually built through the financial *largesse* of General Bobrikov, otherwise castigated in history as a brutal suppressor of Finnish political and cultural rights.

Unfortunately, the old Peace Chapel, erected to the front of the cathedral in 1913 and with a richly decorated interior, had to be torn down when its steatite façade, made of a dense aggregate of talc, was attacked in 1919 by vandals hostile to any Russian symbolic presence in independent Finland's capital (it commemorated the Peace of Hamina, which gave Finland to Russia, during the Napoleonic Wars).

Orthodox Autonomy

As the Orthodox Church in Finland gained strength in the course of Russian rule, albeit in a modest fashion, the Grand Duchy was eventually granted its own independent Orthodox diocese, based in Helsinki, by the Russian Orthodox ecclesiastical authorities. Previously Helsinki, and indeed the rest of Finland and Karelia, had been under the authority of the metropolitan of St. Petersburg. Nonetheless, these new autonomous arrangements in no way eliminated controversy; the degree to which Finnish diocesan independence could be maintained and the question of whether the language of liturgy would be Finnish or Old Church Slovonic (the latter now only a liturgical language in use in Orthodox churches) remained a source of contention until well after the declaration of Finnish independence in 1917, finally ratified in 1918.

The Russian Revolution and the establishment of the Soviet Union exerted their own influences on the Russian-speaking Orthodox community in Finland. Most importantly, its size increased dramatically as refugees flooded in, causing such a burgeoning of the Russian Orthodox population that the old parish of Helsinki city split into two during the second half of the 1920s. Meanwhile in 1923 the higher Finnish Orthodox ecclesiastical authorities transferred their allegiance to the patriarchate of Constantinople. Then, the Finnish Orthodox Church, centered in Helsinki, became an autonomous Orthodox archbishopric, shorn of any further ties to St. Petersburg. In 1970, moreover, it was granted legal parity with the Finnish Lutheran Church. Today's Orthodox adherents number some 57,000 in Finland as a whole, but a significant number reside in Helsinki. With Russian-speaking adherents totaling more than 1,000 parishioners, the Church has assumed its most important role in the religious life of Helsinki since Czarist times, as the impact of post-Soviet Russian migration into Finland has made itself felt. On occasions such as the Orthodox Day of Ascension its profile becomes even higher, as the traditional procession of priests and laity winds its way behind the cross to the harbor—an event culminating in the blessing of the water in the presence of large crowds of onlookers of various faiths.

This multi-religious aspect of contemporary Helsinki is most obvious at the cemetery of Hietaniemi, where Christians of all denominations, Jews and Moslems all find their final resting place in a complicated but harmonious legal arrangement of jurisdictions, in which each confessional community looks after its own graves. Interestingly, the little Orthodox chapel, which by a juridical anomaly is under the ecclesiastical authority of the Patriarch of Moscow, is situated cheek by jowl with the Jewish cemetery, all at Hietaniemi.

The Jewish Community

The arrival of Jews in Finland has been a relatively recent event, for throughout Finnish history, including the period of Swedish hegemony, Jews were prohibited from settling, a prohibition that continued well into the Russian period. Under the Czars, however, an exception to the rule was made: Jews serving as soldiers in the Russian military in Finland were permitted to remain there after their period of service. This option was taken up by significant numbers of those entitled to do so. For not only was Finland a place where pogroms were unknown—after all, there were no Jews there and therefore no history of hostility—but the prospects for trade were also highly promising. Some Jews, indeed, had already arrived from Sweden and Russia and, having converted to Lutheranism or Orthodoxy, became active from the 1810s in trade, running hostelries and eating-houses. But it was during the course of the middle decades of the nineteenth century that much larger numbers of Jews arrived in Finland, where they settled predominantly in Helsinki and Turku.

A large proportion of these were from families of Russian military conscripts, who had previously served in Finland, taking advantage of a new law that enabled ever greater numbers of former soldiers and their dependents to remain in Finland, especially after 1869 when the law was liberalized. From 1870 they were permitted to sell second-hand goods, and a very lively market in old clothes and other items soon developed. This took place at Narinkka, the Russian market located until the twentieth century at Simonkatu, not far from where a synagogue would later be built. But a draconian law of 1876 forbade Jews from trading or carrying out a craft anywhere outside their places of residence. Moreover, Jews formerly living in Finland, if conscripted to Russia itself, were not permitted to return. Also, the children of those permitted to take up residence in Finland were themselves in no way entitled to similar freedoms. On the contrary, once they left the parental home or married, they, too, were obliged to leave. Nonetheless, the number of Jews in the capital continued to grow: no fewer than 1,000 lived in the Grand Duchy as a whole, and most of these in Helsinki.

For all the prohibitions, Jews in Helsinki enjoyed a greater freedom of lifestyle than anywhere else in the Russian Empire at this time, and the prosperity of many increased. In 1906 the largely Orthodox Ashkenazi community commissioned the construction of the Helsinki synagogue, at Malminkatu, not far from today's central bus station. The building was designed by the Finnish-Swedish architect Jakob Ahrenberg in 1906 and remains to this day an important center of Jewish life in the capital, complemented by a school for Jewish children and with a kosher butcher's shop nearby. Various Jewish organizations are also connected to it, including a youth group, founded in 1969, and a Makkabi (Maccabee) Sports Club, established as far back as 1906, the oldest of its type in Europe. Its eclectic architecture is typical of its period in that it draws inspiration from a variety of sources, superimposed upon which are a number of decorative features inspired by the Orient, especially its crowning dome. Especially interesting within the interior are the figures of lions guarding the tablets that are visible in the large central lunette above the *bimah*, made by Jewish soldiers stationed at Suomenlinna.

Within a few weeks of the declaration of independence, on December 22, 1917, Jews were granted civil rights by parliament, and a law promulgated on January 12, 1918 gave them full citizenship. During the following years so many Jews from the Soviet Union flocked to Finland as a refuge that by the beginning of the Winter War their numbers had more than doubled. After this war against the Soviet Union had broken out, and later during the Continuation War, Jews rushed to the defense of Finland, even though Finland's co-belligerent was Nazi Germany. Yet despite German political pressure, to Finland's great credit, no racial laws were ever instituted against Finnish-Jewish nationals and those who enlisted served their country well. Today their bravery is commemorated by a memorial in the synagogue, first celebrated on December 6, 1944 (Finnish Independence Day) in the presence of Marshal Mannerheim, president of the country between 1944-6 and himself a great friend of the Jews of Finland.

During the post-war years the Jewish community continued to thrive, entering all walks of life. In 1979 the first Jewish Member of Parliament, Ben Zyskowicz, was elected and Max Jakobson became Finland's first ambassador to the United Nations. Others from the community were active in the arts: Simon Parmet, for example, became a noted composer and conductor, while the painter Sam Vanni was made a member of the Finnish Academy. Nonetheless, assimilation took its toll and some Jews emigrated abroad. By the mid-1990s their numbers in Helsinki had diminished to 1,200 out of a total population of 1,500 Finnish Jews, some of whom were Israelis who had married Finnish wives.

The Catholic Minority

With respect to the other major Christian denominations, historically much more curtailed in Finland than even Judaism, adherents of Roman Catholicism were only able to practice their religion openly as the eighteenth century drew to a close. It was then that their first church, St. Hyacinth, situated in what was then Russian Viipuri (Vyborg), was founded in 1799, becoming the first Catholic church to serve the community in Finland since the Reformation. Even after Finland was transferred to Russian sovereignty, it remained the only Catholic church in Finland until 1856, excluding the military chapels established at Suomenlinna, Tusby, Turku and Bomarsund, which had long served the needs of Polish and Lithuanian soldiers within the Russian military. After the Crimean War, however, Helsinki was finally granted leave to have its own Catholic house of worship. This is St. Henrik's Church, designed by the German architect Ernst Bernhard Lohrmann and constructed near Kaivopuisto in the center of Helsinki. Opening in 1860 and consecrated to Finland's medieval eponymous saint, it served some 3,000 Catholics in Helsinki. Perhaps its greatest bulwark at the time was Governor General Berg, whose own Italian-born wife was a devout Catholic. Yet the Catholic Church in Helsinki, indeed in Finland as a whole, was marginal, a fact recognized by the ecclesiastical authorities in Rome: only in 1955 was Finland granted leave by the Vatican to have its own resident bishop, today a Polish cleric.

Muslim Helsinki

As with the Jews, the role of Muslims in Helsinki, and Finland, began after incorporation into the Russian Empire. The first official record of any significant numbers in Helsinki was in 1853, but the establishment of a Muslim cemetery for Russian military personnel during the 1830s indicates that there were already some living in or near Helsinki a generation before that date. Even so, their numbers remained small; in fact, in 1870 there were only 46 Muslims recorded in the city. Most if not all of them had arrived in Helsinki as Russian soldiers of Tartar extraction, but had remained in Finland after their period of military service ended. In general they earned their livelihood as merchants, often in the fur trade, and their numbers remained small. Towards the end of the century, many others arrived from Nizhnii Novgorod, in northwestern Russia. Today, their descendants total about a thousand and they maintain a strong ethnic and religious identity. They continue to practice their faith and have their own houses of worship, but their burial grounds, while self-contained, are ecumenically adjacent to their fellow Christian and Jewish Finns. The first mosque was constructed in 1960 at the corner of Fredrikinkatu and Uudenmaankatu after well over a century of Muslim presence in Finland.

Only in the final quarter of the twentieth century did large numbers of other Muslims arrive in the capital, as civil war and various upheavals drove members of other ethnic groups, including Somalis, North Africans and Arabs, to seek refuge in Finland. Most preferred to reside in cosmopolitan Helsinki, where economic and social opportunities were greatest. Some of these migrants have been so numerous that in recent years they have formed their own religious communities, established along ethnic lines. There are around 10,000 members of the Muslim community in present-day Finland, most in Helsinki.

Religious Freedoms

It should also not be forgotten that even within the Lutheran fold of the established Church, a number of ethnic groups were granted the right to establish their own churches, with the liturgy said in their native languages. This was especially true for the Swedes, the Germans, and the British. The Swedes, for example, have their own Lutheran house of worship, the Olaus Petri Church, situated in Apollonkatu. Interestingly, it enjoys the rare privilege of having church bells that are regularly rung, a tradition otherwise forbidden in modern noise-conscious Helsinki.

German-speaking people, meanwhile, have formed a significant minority in Helsinki since its foundation, and during the period of Russian hegemony many higher administrators frequently came from aristocratic Baltic German families, who were also permitted their own forms and house of worship. As a result, German services were held from 1838. Twenty years later, in 1858, a German Lutheran parish was established, which also included in its congregation those German merchants who were active not only in the capital, but also in the outlying regions. The German church itself was built later in 1864 at Ulrikaporinvuori, known today as Tähtitorninvuori.

With respect to those of the Anglican-Episcopalian Church, there is a chapel in the corner pavilion to the right of the Great Church of St. Nicholas that belongs to the complex of St Nicholas itself. Under the ecclesiastical authority of the Bishop of Stepney in England, whose jurisdiction strangely includes Finland, British, Americans, Canadians and others from the world-wide Anglican Communion come to worship here from miles around every Sunday. By a concord of both the Anglican and Lutheran Churches, adherents of both are also entitled to take communion in one another's houses of worship and to otherwise feel a part of the larger Christian community to which both adhere.

Despite such multiculturalism, it is difficult today to appreciate that complete legal religious toleration only came into effect in 1923, when Finns were first granted total freedom to adhere to the religion of their own choice. And it was only in the final quarter of the twentieth century that the two principal religions of Finland both attained official recognition as established Churches: the Lutheran and the Orthodox. This development was perhaps assisted by the growing flood of Orthodox Finnish refugees arriving from Karelia, which was incorporated into Russia after the Continuation War. Many of these established themselves in Helsinki. As a result, the city's ancient cemetery at Hietaniemi, the oldest still in use in the capital, has found its Orthodox burials considerably augmented in number.

The more fringe Protestant denominations only became firmly established in Finland in the twentieth century. The Pentecostalists were among the first, establishing themselves in Helsinki during the 1910s and now numbering around 50,000 adherents in Finland as a whole. They were followed by the Seventh Day Adventists, who founded their first church in 1923, only registering themselves as a community in 1943 during the Second World War. Despite the rise of such movements, the more evangelical wing of the established Lutheran Church did not lose its impetus and it, too, continued to proselytize, not only in Finland but abroad as well. It is this aspect of religious life that the Mission Museum at Tähtitorninkatu 18 (Observatoriegatan) focuses upon, particularly with respect to missionary activity in Asia and Africa in the nineteenth and early twentieth centuries. The Salvation Army Museum at Uudenmaankatu 40, meanwhile, considers the role of that body in Finnish religious and social life since its foundation in 1889. As for the Jehovah Witnesses, their numbers in the country have increased startlingly in recent years to about 17,000 today, many of whom live in Helsinki.

Other Religions

Along with mainstream faiths, there has also been a growth of fringe religions and cults in Helsinki. This is in part a result of increased religious toleration and a loosening of the grip of the established Lutheran Church, but also a symptom of connections with old established Oriental religions and sometimes strange Messianic cults emanating from California and elsewhere. Some of these began to flourish in Helsinki during the course of the early twentieth century. This was the case with the eccentric evangelical movement of Maria Åkerblom, an erstwhile convict who had established her cult's headquarters in the 1930s at the splendid Villa Toivola at Tamminiemi, originally built by the stalwart, if improbable-sounding, Lieutenant W. Tunzelman von Adlerflug.

But most cults have been products of the last few decades, first arriving in the wake of the hippie flowering of West Coast America. More recently, New Age religions have also made inroads, though these tend to congregate at informal meeting halls and private homes. Buddhism, in particular, has seen a growing following, a trend heightened by a visit to Helsinki in the early 1990s by the Dalai Lama, when hundreds came to the auditorium of the main building of Helsinki University to hear his talks on the religion and values of old Tibet.

New Churches

Today Helsinki is clearly a city with adherents of a multiplicity of religions. Even among the older Christian traditions it can boast three bishops, one Lutheran, one Catholic and one Orthodox. Despite the radical reduction in those attending church and the rise of other religions and cults, certain high holidays still continue to be observed as they traditionally have been. At Hietaniemi Cemetery, for example, a sea of candles illuminates the graves every Christmas Eve and All Souls Day, two days of the church calendar which embody symbolism relating to the passage of humanity from spiritual darkness into light. The city's recent expansion, with the rise of new suburbs, has also meant that new church building has been in demand. Already in the first half of twentieth century the construction of new churches had begun in response to Helsinki's growing population.

Kallio Parish Church remains the most prominent of these on the Helsinki skyline today. Situated at Itäinen Papinkatu, it was built in 1912 to the designs of Lars Sonck in the form of a traditional Latin cross, with a broad nave, surmounted by a barrel vault. Typical of the period, the exterior is of gray granite and the whole is dominated by a massive tower. When seen from the opposite end of Unioninkatu, positioned as it is at the far end of a little garden square, it appears deceptively high, more like an American skyscraper than a church. Yet its bells are undeniably Finnish; they play a medley by the composer Jean Sibelius.

Another important new house of worship is the Töölö Parish Church at Topeliuksenkatu 4, built in 1930 by Hilding Ekelund. It is a monumental block-like building, over which Romanesque and Baroque features have been imposed on what is otherwise a rather typical "1920s classical" building. A similar edifice is the Luther Church at Fredrikinkatu 42, built in 1931 also to the designs of Ekelund, later one of the principal architects of Helsinki's Olympic Village. Really an enlargement of an old prayer hall, with an earlier neo-Gothic brick façade from the 1890s by the Finnish-Swedish architect Karl August Wrede, it is an elongated building, surmounted by a barrel vault and in part illuminated by natural light from an adjacent internal courtyard. Also worthy of mention is the Mikael Agricola Church at Tehtaankatu 23, built in 1935 by Sonck, but with a basilica form crowned by a gable tower of red brick that recedes towards the top. Its interior is surmounted by a cross vault, while in an adjacent complex there are flats as well as the usual parish offices. For all its ecclesiastical functions, from the outside it looks more like a 1930s skyscraper than any church in the traditional sense.

During the post-war years a spate of other churches were built as the suburbs of Helsinki continued to burgeon. Lauttasaari Church at Myllykalliorinne 1 was constructed in 1958 to the modernist designs of Keijo Petäjä. Situated on the slopes of Myllykallio Hill, its belfry features prominently on the little island suburb's skyline, adjacent to a small military cemetery. Of sandblasted white concrete both inside and outside, it serves a Swedish-speaking congregation, symbolic of the age in which it was built and one in which the latest techniques were employed.

Yet the most innovative and noteworthy of Helsinki's post-war modern churches is doubtless the famous Temppeliaukio Church at Lutherinkatu 3 by the architect pair Timo and Tuomo Suomalainen. Known colloquially as the Rock Church, it is internationally renowned for the innovative style in which it was constructed in 1969. Competitions for the commission had been held as far back as the early 1930s, and an early design by the architect Pauli E. Blomstedt had already envisioned a church built into the granite rocks. But it was only in the post-war period that the undertaking was finally commenced. With only its copper cupola visible above ground, the entire edifice is embedded within the very rock upon which it sits. Its most striking entrance is from Fredrikinkatu, from which a subterranean tunnel leads into the church. With walls of bedrock or quarried stone, it has excellent acoustics, making it an even more popular as a musical venue than as a church.

Of special interest during the last twenty years is Myyrmäki Church, with its parish center, which opened in Vantaa in 1984, designed by the architect Juha Leiviskä. Although situated by a railway line, it is actually towards a wooded setting of lofty birches that it opens out, incorporating a rhythmic sequence of spaces in which carefully designed lighting and appropriate textiles play a major role. With a growing international clientele and renown, Leiviskä was awarded the prestigious Carlsberg Prize for Architecture by Queen Margarete of Denmark in 1995, a clear indication that ecclesiastical architecture in Helsinki is in no danger of becoming a dull affair.

CHAPTER SIX

Helsinki and Nature: Weather, Sports and Public Health

Almost uniquely among European capitals, Helsinki is situated in a most splendid natural setting. Also uniquely, a considerable number of its inhabitants can, if they so wish, ski directly from their doors to work in the winter. With an immense amount of nature woven into its urban fabric, Helsinki provides a spectacular example of how green a modern and vibrant city can be. With average temperatures varying between -12°C, in February, and +20°C in August, there is a rich range of Nordic nature in and around the city, not least some 1,725 hectares of parks.

Yet Helsinki has also known the harshness of nature, not just in its long dark winters but also in natural disasters and epidemics. The drastic improvements in public health that have made modern Helsinki one of the healthiest capitals in the world are paralleled by the city's proud record in sports, crowned by the 1952 Olympic Games.

The city is surrounded by woods and water, but it is perhaps the granite stone upon which and with which so much of its core is built that is Helsinki's most significant natural hallmark. As Leena Krohn put it in her short story, *Doña Quixote and other Citizens* (1983):

> *It was everywhere, carved and uncarved, rough and polished until it shone. It was used to cover the surfaces of the squares and edge the narrow pavements; it was used to build steps and pedestals of statues and grandiose memorials to great men…It was this place's plinth and raw material, it was the city's seal and destiny, like the sand of Rotterdam, the mud of Venice or the oil-shale of Pittsburgh.*

Landscaping the New Helsinki

As part of his grand plan for the redevelopment of Helsinki into Finland's capital, Engel had envisioned the creation of two tree-lined avenues. One of these, the Esplanade, situated slightly to the south of Senate Square, is in reality two avenues, with a central garden in between. It was laid out on what had been a water meadow before being enclosed and formed a demarcation between the civil buildings around Senate Square to the north and the military ones to the south. It was planted with trees and extensive lawns in 1824, and a number of grand residences soon lined the avenue. Those of wood gradually disappeared over the years, some already in Engel's time, making way for brick, stone and other materials.

Then Engel carried out the laying out of a second broad avenue, this one to the west and adjacent to the Old Church, which became known as the Boulevard. Here, too, trees were planted to line the street. It was also the Boulevard that provided the location for the architect's own home, itself long departed from the scene as the avenue's semi-rural character became urbanized. Engel's house, placed in a large garden, had been adorned with the unusual feature of a greenhouse for growing flowers and vegetables, rare commodities during the colder months in one of Europe's most northerly capitals.

In some respects, Russian planning regulations assisted in the spacious layout of Helsinki and its many green spaces. For one thing, as a measure against the spread of fires in this largely wooden city, principal streets had to be laid out with a width of about ninety feet, while even ordinary ones had to be over fifty feet wide. Stipulations concerning construction and the boundaries of plots also provided considerable space for the layout of gardens. The 1856 Town Building Act also encouraged generous urban planning, so that small orchards, kitchen gardens and other such amenities became characteristic of many parts of Helsinki even into the twentieth century.

Engel had imagined Helsinki endowed with a city garden four to five times the size of the Lustgarten (Pleasure Garden) in his native Berlin and crowned by the astronomical observatory. In what became Kaivopuisto Park, later created by the German-born gardener Holm, rich Russians enjoyed festivities during the heady days of the 1840s. Adjacent to the Pump Room, there was also an English garden, an unusual feature in Finland at this time. The prime ingredient, however, was the sea itself and its health-giving properties. As the visitor and bather Bulgarin commented after his visit in 1838:

> *Here there are no valleys, no marshes, no downy woodlands to spoil with their own exhalations, so effective in the treatment of many illnesses. Nothing is exhaled from Helsinki granite, and the fine sea mist that settles on the rocks morning and evening is a genuine elixir of life.*

The park's location by the sea could also offer a novel vantage point, as later the citizens of Helsinki watched with a mixture of amazement and horror the bombardment of the fortress of Suomenlinna by British and French troops during the height of the Crimean War in August 1855.

Botanical Gardens
Other gardens were also in the making despite the rigors of the city's climate. As Anders Ramsay, a Finnish nobleman of Scottish descent, noted in his memoirs, published in the first decade of the twentieth century, the sapling maples that had been planted in the center of town were constantly succumbing to the waterlogged soil. Mosquitoes were also a serious inconvenience, not to mention health risk in the central

area of Kluuvi, especially during the early years of the nineteenth century. This had been a marshy region of the city, infested by insects during the summer months. On the other hand, in the winter it became an ideal place for ice-skating.

It was in precisely this vicinity that Helsinki's most important garden was about to be built. For with the establishment of Helsinki's Alexander University came the establishment of the Botanical Gardens in 1829, based on those of the Imperial Botanical Gardens in St. Petersburg, designed by Franz Falerman in the 1830s. They are still situated in the heart of Kaisaniemi, less than half a mile from the Central Railway Station, and here tropical greenhouses, splendid herbaceous borders, as well as a variety of temperate, arctic and sub-arctic plants and flowers all rub shoulders. The first greenhouse was built in 1835. Then in 1884 Finland's first rock garden was established, followed in 1889 by the so-called Palm House, by Gustaf Nyström, a structure of particular interest built to replace Engel's earlier greenhouse. Its skeletal structure is of wrought iron, but cast iron has been used for the staircases and surrounding balconies in a fashion typical of the time. Nyström also built a Botanical Institute and Botanical Museum here in 1903. Thirty years later, when the centenary of the garden's opening was celebrated, it could boast some 5,000 different varieties of plants. During the Second World War the greenhouses were destroyed by bombing, but in 1948 they reopened once again with 1,600 different plant types.

More recently in 1990 three early nineteenth-century wooden houses from Punavuori were moved to this site for preservation, one of which has become a charming café. A major refurbishment of the greenhouses followed a few years later.

Planting the Esplanade

It was Svante Olsson, the Swedish son of a *torpare* (a variety of crofter) who left the greatest imprint on the Esplanade. He had already carried out important landscape designs in Sweden, first at the great aristocratic estates of Tullgarn and Säfstaholm, then at royal properties at Stockholm's Palace and Haga. When he arrived in Helsinki, aged thirty-three, to become the city's first landscape gardener, a huge task lay before him and he was to remain here for over fifty years. The

Esplanade had previously served as a grazing ground for horses, and it was not one urban entity, but three—namely, the Kappeli Esplanadi, the Runeberg Esplanadi and the Theatre Esplanadi, focused as they were around their most significant features. But the landscaping activities of Olsson gave them a new "green" unity. In 1889 he radically altered this area, one of the city's four so-called green spaces, by laying out trees, shrubs and flowerbeds throughout the park. He also encouraged the development of other green spaces, so that by the 1920s the city had at least thirty-two. He then redeveloped the hilltop upon which Engel's Observatory is situated into one of Helsinki's most charming parks, a project that took fifteen years to complete. Yet, at the time, he faced considerable opposition, and at one stage, an important and ungrateful government official revoked his free pass on the city's trams. Despite this slight, he preferred to remain in Helsinki rather than take up the position of Head Gardener to the City of Stockholm.

Kaisaniemi Park

Kaisaniemi Park, the plebeian alternative to patrician Kaivopuisto, also had its charms. Originally designed by Fredrik Granatenhjelm, a Freemason whose grave (1784) was ultimately placed there, its links with the watering hole of Mrs. Kajsa Wahlund and her successor, Emelia Myhrmann, made it a much sought-after venue for summer outings, even after a terrible storm in 1890 uprooted many of its trees. What it lost in exterior charm in winter it made up for in the conviviality of the Kaisaniemi tavern, full of students and the intelligentsia of the capital, ardently discussing the latest political and social events over coffee, beer or vodka. This café had originally started life as a kiosk in 1837 before Mrs Wahlund and the butcher Salomon Jansson had a building erected there in 1839.

Later in the early years of the twentieth century, the new residential area of Töölö, with its avenue-like streets lined with lindens, also became a recherché area of the capital in which to live. Kaisaniemi Park also remains unique for a European capital, since even today by a careful choice of route one can go from city center to the countryside, apart from crossing the odd road, through a wholly rural environment.

Attractions of Nature

In the first quarter of the twentieth century the city administration saw to it that new parks were established throughout Helsinki, in part under the influence of the developing philosophy of the garden city emanating from England. These included the Deer Park, the park at Töölö Bay, the Grejus woods, and the city's own central park. Later, the garden city theme was taken up during the course of the twentieth century in both Käpylä and Tapiola. In any case, during the early years of the century many homes in Helsinki still maintained a village atmosphere: many had gardens of relatively large size on which not only some crops but also farmyard animals, like chickens and cows, could be maintained.

One influence on the garden city movement in Finland was the British social reformer Ebenezer Howard, whose *Tomorrow. A Peaceful Path to Real Reform*, published in 1898, was of seminal importance. It was in the wake of such ideas that various private initiatives were taken in Helsinki and Espoo during the years 1905-8 to create garden suburbs for the prosperous working and middle classes, which combined the blessings of the countryside with the benefits of the city.

But, for all the beauteous parks, squares and tree-lined avenues of Helsinki, the allure of the surrounding countryside remained great. Especially in the warmer months many residents of Helsinki took advantage of the long days to retire to the countryside. As Mrs. Tweedie wrote in the late nineteenth century:

> *Life in* Helsingfors *is very pleasant for strangers in the summer, but for the natives it has no attraction. Accustomed to a long and ice-bound winter, the moment May comes every family, possessed of any means, flits to the country for three or four months. All the schools close for twelve weeks, and the children, who have worked hard during the long dark winter, thoroughly enjoy their holiday. Summer comes suddenly and goes swiftly. The days are long, as the nights are short... and even in* Helsingfors, *during June, [the sun] does not set till about eleven, consequently it remains light all night—that strange weird sort of light that we English folk only know as appertaining to very early morning.*

Perhaps the *tunnelma* (*stämning* in Swedish), that is the mood or atmosphere of the ominous approach of evening, has best been captured in visual imagery by the writer Tove Jansson, not dissimilarly to the way her father, the sculptor Viktor Jansson, captured it in an image of more abstract form. She looks back over her childhood among the writhing forms of the Art Nouveau buildings that surrounded her in Katajanokka:

As soon as twilight comes a great big creature creeps over the harbor. It has no face but has got very distinct hands, which cover one island after another as it creeps forward. When there are no more islands left it stretches its arm out over the water, a very long arm that trembles a little and begins to grope its way towards Skatudden. Its fingers reach the Russian Church and touch the rock—oh! Such a great big grey hand!

For the Swedish-speaking author Bo Carpelan, it was the wind that most characterized Helsinki, especially as experienced in his childhood district of Kruununhaka, where, as he put it in the novel *Benjamin* (1997), it seemed as if, "My city is built of winds, and after him, silence." Sometimes man's relationship with nature is one of disharmony, as in Carpelan's little poem of compacted lines reminiscent of the Nobel Prize-winning Norwegian Knut Hamsun's *Pan*:

There was a tree in the backyard.
It stood looking anxious most of the time.
On blowy spring days its last year's leaves still rattled along the walls.
Now that I see it perhaps more as a tree
Than as the upright-standing broom we took it for...

Winter in Helsinki

It is in winter that Helsinki's unique geographical characteristics with respect to nature most clearly come to the fore. As the Swedish-speaking Finn Kjell Westö wrote in *Kites over Helsinki*, childhood displeasure in winter became transformed through time into an appreciation of it: "Previously, I hated the winter in Helsinki. People seemed to become grey and withdrawn. Darkness overwhelms everything. The city is eternally windy and raw. And slushy, for there never seems to be enough snow." But with the passing of the years, this view gradually turned into an appreciation of the city's more positive characteristics:

> *It was an icy cold winter, week after week the cold kept its grip on the city. Nonetheless, I began to learn to like winter and darkness; for I could then see people. I saw that winter was a duty demanded both by nature and ourselves, a duty to sleep, dream, bide one's time. And I learned that there are people who cast a glance which, so to speak, is full of light, their eyes glow in deep colours, in violet, brick red and ochre...*

The natural pleasures of a wintry Helsinki were not only to be found outdoors: the city's Winter Garden, complete with rockeries and greenhouses, had been set up by the Finnish Horticultural Society in 1893 in the midst of Eläintarha Park. A bust by the sculptor Walter Runeberg to the businessman J. J. Lindfors, who had financed the greenhouses, can be seen there not far from C. E. Sjöstrand's National Romantic sculpture, *Kullervo Addresses his Sword* (1868), inspired by the epic *Kalevala*.

Rus in Urbe

If a garden city movement emanated from England, a more academic approach came from Germany. Gardening, long studied as an academic subject in Germany, was introduced into Helsinki's primary school curriculum in 1912. This included a strong practical element by which children were allocated garden patches where they could grow plants, both useful and decorative, according to the latest methods. Some of the most important Finnish architects tried to incorporate some of these lessons into their landscape designs. This is true of the architectural triumvirate of Saarinen, Gesellius and Lindgren whose utopian scheme of 1915 for the development of Munkkiniemi on the periphery of Helsinki incorporated gardens into the courtyards of urban blocks and more spacious terraced villas.

During the interwar years there was a growing preoccupation with the establishment of green spaces within Helsinki. One extraordinary creation during these somewhat troubled times deserves mention: the Roof Garden of the Savoy Restaurant, on the South Esplanade, from 1937. It was laid out in three sections—Scandinavian, Mediterranean and Japanese—and provided an exotic milieu of landscape poetry to a city still attempting to recover from the great Depression.

Less lyrical but perhaps of greater utility for large numbers of people was the development at about the same time of private garden allotments. This increased the ruralization of Helsinki not only by providing green areas scattered throughout the city, but, most importantly, by making the diets of many residents healthier. One of the most typical schemes from this period was at Hietaniemi, laid out in 1934. There were 182 allotments, 250 feet square, on each of which a little cabin was entitled to be built, all according to the most "scientific principles". Some of these were also to be applied in the very architectural shapes incorporated into new buildings. When, for example new blocks of apartments like Käärmetalo (The Snake House, 1951) were erected, they rejected the angularity of functionalism, preferring to look towards the world of nature for inspiration. Instead of utilizing a strictly functionalist intellectual approach, the architect Yrjö Lindgren preferred to derive inspiration from curved, organically inspired shapes in his buildings and their decorative features and layouts.

The integration of the countryside in an urban setting was arguably most successful in the new town of Tapiola, which acquired international acclaim in the 1960s and 1970s as the modern answer to the need for a new type of garden city in the orbit of Helsinki. Today green spaces in and around Helsinki have become so ubiquitous that it is hard to recognize the seminal role that Tapiola played. For those who wish to explore the relation of Helsinki to its natural environment, the Natural History Museum at Pohjoinen Rautatiekatu 13, in what was the grammar school for Russian boys, provides the geographical context with respect to the region's flora and fauna. There is also an interesting zoo on the nearby island of Korkeasaari. Further afield, the arboretum at Meilahti, established in 1967, boasts not only a wide range of trees but rare varieties of local roses.

Epidemics

Nature could also be less kind to Helsinki. For many years after its founding hygiene was at a minimum, and the city suffered severely from the visitations of epidemics. Its situation in the cold and remote far northeastern corner of Europe offered no protection. On the contrary, its relative isolation frequently meant that when diseases did arrive, there was little natural immunity. Moreover, on the trading crossroads of east and west, epidemics arrived with devastating frequency from either direction. During the winter of 1570-71 bubonic plague broke out after the arrival of refugees from a Russian attack in nearby areas, and hundreds died.

Epidemics continued to occur in the course of the following century. That of 1695-6 was so bad that regulations demanded that the victims be buried within the cemetery at Kamppi within twelve hours. But this was nothing compared to the disaster wrought by the plague of late summer 1710, which followed an influx of smitten refugees from the Great Northern War. No less than half the population of Helsinki expired from the contagion.

Severe outbreaks of smallpox occurred in 1754, 1763 and 1771, despite the somewhat haphazard introduction of inoculation. Vaccination was more successful, and by 1820 Helsinki in particular and Finland in general, enjoyed the highest percentage of vaccinated inhabitants in the world. It was also about this time and slightly later that numerous hospitals came to be built, the most important at Lapinlahti, designed by the imperial architect Engel himself. He was also instrumental in the construction of the Clinic for Internal Medicine, built in 1823 at Unioninkatu 38, originally intended as the Cantonist School for Orphaned Children. Its façade is decorated with massive double columns of the Tuscan order, and it was converted into a military hospital in 1831. The Old Clinic, built in 1833, was situated just next door at Unioninkatu 37 and served as the university hospital. The Lapinlahti Hospital was finally completed in 1841 to the designs of Engel. An austere two-story building of two longer wings, connected by a foreshortened center block, it stands in a park at Lapinlahdentie, where it functions today as a psychiatric hospital.

With innovations such as these and growing improvements in hygiene, the Finnish capital was becoming a salubrious place. The Helsinki Deaconess Institute Museum, at Alppikatu 2, gives an insight into the care of patients in the late nineteenth and early twentieth centuries in a former hospital and chapel founded by the aristocrat Aurora Karamzin.

The Olympics

As public health improved, so there was a growing appreciation of the need to keep healthy and avoid illness though the careful "maintenance" of the human body. This found its clearest expression in a new interest in gymnastics and the body beautiful. The number of gymnastics clubs for both men and women mushroomed, reaching a zenith during the 1920s and 1930s, as it did elsewhere in Europe. Curiously, the interest in naturalism typical of the gymnastics movement never made inroads in Finland, as it did in Sweden, Germany and Estonia. But a cult of physical activity certainly encouraged the local variant of the Olympic movement, established in 1896.

It had long been a dream of many Finns, even in the years before independence, to stage the Olympic Games in Helsinki. In 1912 Erik von Frenckell, later to become an important administrator in the city government, had proposed the idea. Later, after independence, support to host the Olympic Games grew among a wider section of the city fathers, keen to display a symbol of the country's newly achieved statehood and equality with other nations, old and new.

In 1920 the first initiative was taken to build a stadium and place a tender for the games. This culminated in 1927 with the foundation of an official body, the Oy Stadion AB. Then in 1932 a formal application was made with respect to the 1936 Summer Olympics, though these were, of course, ultimately held in Berlin. Tokyo had at first won the ballot for the 1940 Summer Olympics, but military incursions in China in 1937 ultimately delivered the selection to Finland. Tickets went on sale in both New York and Paris. By 1938 the designs for the stadium by Yrjö Lindegren and Toivo Jäntti had been carried out, utilizing the latest technology in record time, and an Olympic village was also constructed. A rowing stadium was also built, at the tip of Toivo Kuula Park. But the long-awaited Olympics were canceled just three months before the appointed time, with the outbreak of the Winter War.

Even the advent of war left some hopes that the event would take place unextinguished. During the Soviet bombing of Helsinki the Finnish Olympic Committee continued to meet in a bomb shelter, from where it proceeded to organize a competition for the opening fanfare. But as the war took its toll, the grim reality became all too obvious and the committee dissolved itself. So the Olympic village at Käpylä, designed by Hilding Ekelund and Martti Välikangas, with its 426 apartments, was allocated to Karelian refugees who had fled to the capital as a desperately needed haven.

In 1952, twelve years after they were originally to have taken place, the Olympics were finally held in Helsinki. Not only did the Finnish capital become the smallest city ever to host the Summer Olympics, but Finland too became the smallest country to do so.

Most appropriately, it was Paavo Nurmi, the so-called "Flying Finn" of the Olympic Games of the 1920s and 1930s who carried the torch into the Olympic Stadium, an event glorified by Paavo Sysimetsä's poster. Nurmi had achieved special success at the 1924 Paris Olympics, having won not only the 1,500-meter race but the 5,000-meter competition as well, and both on the same day. Altogether in his career as a runner he won nine gold medals. Today a sculpture by Wäinö Aaltonen commemorating him is to be found near the Olympic Stadium in the adjacent park. Nearby is a statue of another famous runner, Lasse Viren, by Terho Sakki.

No fewer than 4,800 athletes from around the world participated in the 1952 Olympics, a significantly larger number than the 3,200 who had been originally registered in 1940. They were cheered on by more than 140,000 foreign visitors between July 19 and August 3 in what was the greatest overseas influx the city had ever witnessed. Helsinki also enjoyed worldwide coverage, with 1,848 journalists and other media personalities from 69 countries. Sweden alone sent 124.

The Olympics were not the only sporting events at which Finns excelled in the post-war years. In the 1951 Milan Triennale, for example, Finns succeeded in winning six grand prizes, seven gold medals, as well as eight silvers, a winning streak that continued well into the late 1960s.

While running may have ceased to be a Finnish specialty, other sports have come to the fore. In 1995 Finland's national ice hockey team won the world championship, an event celebrated by 100,000 supporters on Market Square, while in skiing and other winter sports Finns, many from Helsinki, feature prominently. The Helsinki Marathon, for its part, has attracted visitors not only from Helsinki, but from all around Finland and neighboring countries, as well.

Contemporary figures have also made their mark in the realms of rally racing. Tommi Mäkinen and Marcus Grönholm, the current world champion, are of great note, while Formula-1 drivers Kimi Räikkönen and Mika Häkkinen, now retired, achieved great fame. Finally, it is worth mentioning the high profile of football in Helsinki, from where a number of players have gone on to achieve international success, especially Sami Hyypiä, Liverpool's captain, Jari Litmanen formerly at Liverpool, and goalkeeper Antti Niemi at Southampton.

CHAPTER SEVEN

Helsinki and Romanticism: Myth, Epic and Architecture

From the first half of the nineteenth century until today, the *Kalevala*, the Finnish national epic, together with the National Romantic idiom in art, architecture and other aspects of culture, have played a major role in the emergent identity of the Finnish nation. This cultural reassessment was one national component in a pan-European trend to turn back to traditional roots, just at a time when growing industrialization and migration were changing the nature of society and identity. The presence of the National Romantic is apparent not only in the realms of governmental commissions, but even in a plethora of commercial and domestic buildings constructed in and around Helsinki. At the same time, the Finnish national epic and the oral traditions on which it was based have given expression to splendid literature, art and "folk" architecture.

Runeberg and Lönnrot

In order to understand the origins of the National Romantic idiom in Finland's culture, it is necessary to go back to the works of two writers: Johan Ludvig Runeberg, who wrote in Swedish and is one of Finland's greatest poets, and Elias Lönnrot, a cultural polymath who wrote primarily in Finnish but also in Swedish. Like so many of their contemporaries in Finland and other parts of Europe, both men were influenced by the thinking of scholars such as Johann Gottfried von Herder about the national significance of folk poetry and song. Of particular importance were German translations of the Serbian tradition, as collected and translated by Vuk Stefanović Karadžić, which circulated widely in Europe in the 1810s. Runeberg himself published a selection of Karadžić's work in Swedish in 1830, *Serviska folksånger* (Serbian Folksongs) and two years later in his rhapsodic *Elgskyttarne* (The Elk Hunters) introduced Finnish readers to the Karelian bardic tradition at the same time as his colleague Lönnrot was collecting materials for his *Kalevala*.

Runeberg's two volumes of *Fänrik Ståls Sägner* (Tales of Ensign Stål, 1848, 1860) marked an important step in the shaping of Finnish identity. The poems present a concept of nationality linked to statehood, in which duty to one's own people and to the state comes before everything else. While the poems illustrate this theme in an account of the heroism of Finnish soldiers during the Swedish-Russian war of 1808-9, fought in Finland, Runeberg also includes poems about civilians and gives equal weight to the sacrifice of Russian soldiers who bravely fight for their ruler and country. A statue of the poet by his son Walter Runeberg, dated 1885, is to be found in the midst of the Esplanade.

As for the bardic tradition itself, it continued well into the twentieth century. On the edge of Tapiolapuisto near Aalto's Finlandia House a statue by Alpo Sailo from 1949 commemorates Larin Paraske (1833-1904), a leading Karelian rune singer. Such runes, sung in the ancient oral traditions of the bards of Karelia, were based upon ancient Finnic mythology and formed the basis of the creative compilations that went into the production of the *Kalevala*. To acquire precise details of their compositions and an experience of how they were sung from memory, Lönnrot made extensive journeys over the border into Russian Karelia, where it seemed to him the tradition had been more authentically preserved than on the Finnish side.

The *Kalevala*

Having begun in 1828 to collect his materials first from eastern Finland and then from 1832 from Archangel and Olonets Karelia (historically in Russia), Lönnrot merged them into one great compilation, the *Kalevala*, which won international acclaim as one of the world's most significant epic poems. It was published in two versions, a shorter one in 1835 (12,078 lines arranged in thrity-two poems), and a longer one in 1849 (22,795 lines in fifty poems). Eventually translated into more than fifty languages, it served directly as a model for the Estonian national epic *Kalevipoeg* (1857-61), compiled by the Baltic German Friedrich

Reinhold Kreutzwald and based on similar themes. The Estonians, living in what was than an integral part of the Russian Empire, were a sister people linguistically and ethnically to the Finns, and shared the common runic tradition based upon ancient Finnic mythology. William Longfellow also used a German translation (1852) of the *Kalevala* for his own romantic poem *Song of Hiawatha* (1855), based on a compilation of American Indian songs and legends, adopting both themes and the traditional Finnish trochaic tetrameters. It is worth comparing the two. The *Song of Hiawatha* opens with:

> *Should you ask me,*
> *whence these stories?*
> *Whence these legends and traditions,*
> *With the odors of the forest*
> *With the dew and damp of meadows,*
> *With the curling smoke of wigwams,*
> *With the rushing of great rivers,*
> *With their frequent repetitions,*
> *And their wild reverberations*
> *As of thunder in the mountains?*
> *   I should answer, I should tell you,*
> *"From the forests and the prairies,*
> *From the great lakes of the Northland,*
> *From the land of the Ojibways,*
> *From the land of the Dacotahs..."*

The *Kalevala* begins:

> *I am driven by my longing,*
> *And my understanding urges*
> *That I should commence my singing,*
> *And begin my recitation.*
> *I will sing the people's legends,*
> *And the ballads of the nation.*
> *To my mouth the words are flowing,*
> *And the words are gently falling,*

Quickly as my tongue can shape them,
And between my teeth emerging.
  Dearest friend, and much-loved brother,
Best beloved of all companions!
Come and let us sing together,
Let us now begin our converse,
Since at length we meet together,
From two widely sundered regions.
Rarely can we meet together,
Rarely one can meet the other,
In these dismal Northern regions,
In the dreary land of Pohja.

During the 1830s, then, a Finnish national identity was already in the process of formation, building on the efforts of scholars since the late eighteenth century. Finns were faithful to their obligations as subjects of the Russian Czar, but they were also increasingly aware of their own political, social and ethnographic roots. This found expression, above all, in the study of language and oral poetry and underlined the need for a public forum in which ideas could be discussed and developed, especially in the field of literature. That forum was provided by the establishment of the Finnish Literature Society in 1831, more or less at the same time as revolts were breaking out in Poland, now forcibly integrated into the Russian Empire.

The National Romantic did not find expression, of course, only in the field of high culture. It was also expressed in a whole range of other contexts, even including transport. The first locomotive to pull a train in Finland, from Helsinki to Hämeenlinna in 1862, was called Lemminkäinen, after the Adonis-like youthful hero from the *Kalevala* who traveled to the Kingdom of Death and back. Later his exploits would provide the inspiration for Jean Sibelius' *Lemminkäinen Suite* of 1885.

Aleksis Kivi

While Runeberg and Lönnrot, along with the statesman and philosopher of nationalism Johan Vilhelm Snellman, were important in the forming national identity, Aleksis Kivi (1834-72) was the author of one of the first novels ever written in Finnish, *Seven Brothers*, published by the Finnish Literature Society in 1870.

Born in Nurmijärvi, a little to the north of Helsinki, it is local life that he mirrors, with its own cultural and ethnic characteristics. His first work, *Kullervo* (1864), was a tragic piece based upon the character from the *Kalevala*, though the plays of Shakespeare also exerted a major influence on his work. This was followed by the dramatic comedy, *The Heath Cobblers* (1864), in which a rather simple-minded son of a cobbler has the leading role, confounded by complications in his marriage plans. But it is *Seven Brothers* that remains his most important work, a bitter-sweet novel characterized by the picaresque and epic influence of *Don Quixote*. As in Cervantes' work, the principal characters survive a series of madcap adventures on their travels, in flight from their previous settled lives and in pursuit of idealist values that are constantly confronted by harsh realities.

So important has Kivi been perceived in the development of Finnish literary culture (not least for political reasons after his death) that he has been given his own commemorative day celebrated annually on October 10, now called appropriately both Aleksis Kivi Day and Finnish Literature Day. It is then that his statue, completed in 1939 by Wäinö Aaltonen on the north side of the Railway Station Square, becomes a focus for celebrations. Perhaps the most colorful is that of the students from the University of Helsinki who bedeck it with flowers, while others similarly honor his grave at Tuusula, his old homestead in a village not far from the outskirts of Helsinki.

Akseli Gallen-Kallela and Karelia

In the early 1890s the growing interest in Karelia in all branches of the arts had reached its zenith. Akseli Gallen-Kallela (1865-1931), the most prominent of the artists so fascinated by the region, went there on his honeymoon in 1890, as did Jean Sibelius. The quaint wooden buildings with their rich carvings that he saw there inspired much of Gallen-Kallela's imagery. Although a Swedish-speaking Finn, he had changed his name from Axel Gallén in order to emphasize his Finnish identity. While at the art school of Adolf von Becker in Helsinki, he had illustrated temperance tracts as a means of earning extra money. Later he studied at the Académie Julian in Paris before moving on to that of Cormon. Yet it was Bastien-Lepage's *plein air* school that exerted the most profound effect upon his style and subject matter, with its emphasis upon an unflinching realism. No longer was it enough to paint landscapes full of Romantic charm or human figures according to the classical ideal. Rather, Gallen-Kallela began to paint genuine Finnish people with their un-Mediterranean features, warts and all, as in *Boy with a Crow* (1884) or *Old Woman and a Cat* (1885).

Once back in Finland, Gallen-Kallela sought out typical, unadulterated images of what he perceived to be the real country, which he married to images from the *Kalevala*. Its influence on him was immense and he used much of its subject matter for his paintings. The images are frequently overt, but sometimes they are more indirect, as with his *Waterfall at Mäntykoski* (1892-4), combining both a National Romantic appreciation of Finnish nature with musical elements. In this work a musical scale is superimposed over the picture in such a way as to stress the aural aspects of the Finnish woods and waters. At about the same time, this musical mode found its blossoming in some works by the great Swedish-speaking Finnish composer Sibelius. Sibelius drew upon a vast range of National Romantic themes from the *Kalevala* for such musical compositions as *Lemminkäinen Suite*, from which *The Swan of Tuonela* (1893) is the most famous piece.

Yet Gallen-Kallela was not only influenced by the romance of Karelia. He also looked westwards, especially towards London, where he traveled in 1895 in order to visit the Victoria and Albert Museum and other collections of the arts and crafts movement. There he came into contact with the decorative designs, especially on fabrics, of William Morris, to which he applied a Finnish dimension. Many of Gallen-Kallela's values in this respect are expressed in the house-cum-studio he had built at Tarvaspää on the outskirts of Helsinki, today a museum.

William Morris had a profound impact on the development not only of interior decoration and pictorial images, but of all aspects of architecture, both exterior and interior, in the closing years of the nineteenth century. As one of the greatest Finnish architects of the early twentieth century, Eliel Saarinen (1873-1950), later noted, the birth of the new National Romantic style can be traced to the middle years of the

1890s. Certainly, it is true that Morris' hand can be seen in the displays of the Iris factory, an enterprise that opened in 1899. In its showrooms in the Tallberg building opposite Stockmann's Department Store, the latest textiles and lamps were displayed in an *art nouveau* style suitable for the domestic interiors of Helsinki's prosperous citizenry. Many of these were based on designs to be found at Liberty's Department Store in London's Regent Street, a company for which the Swedish Count Louis Sparre af Söfdeborg, himself a designer, was an agent.

Saarinen and National Romantic Architecture

The German-inspired *Jugendstil* interpretation of *art nouveau* was also beginning to exert its influence at this time. As a result, a uniquely Finnish response to *Jugendstil* was blossoming, closely linked to architectural fashions in sway throughout the rest of Scandinavia and central Europe—yet with its own specific accent and decorative motifs. Perhaps its leading domestic example, in the heart of Helsinki, is the Villa Johanna, designed by the architect Selim A. Lindqvist in 1905. A detached house, with a large garden at Laivurinkatu 25, it was commissioned by a local businessman Uno Staudinger, after whose wife it was christened. An idiosyncratic building, full of curves, sharp angles and eccentric juxtapositions of shapes in a National Romantic idiom, its surface textures vary dramatically from smooth red-brick, Mondrian-like geometric blocks and cement to heavy rusticated granite, bands of rounded stones, and inlayed mosaic tiles. It remained in private hands until the late 1970s. Nearby, other houses of the period, also influenced by *Jugendstil*, still line the Boulevard.

Even larger and certainly more famous, though situated on the periphery of Helsinki at Kirkkonummi on the shores of Lake Hvitträsk, is Saarinen's own mansion, Hvitträsk, which he built in 1902-3 in conjunction with his colleagues Herman Gesellius (1874-1916) and Armas Lindgren (1874-1929). There all three staked out their living and artistic spaces, providing the mansion complex with their own idiosyncratic interpretation. It was a veritable icon of Finnish National Romanticism, local timber and granite were used throughout, but with interior decorative features drawing upon the Scottish prototypes of Charles Rennie Mackintosh. As such, it was a *Gesamtkunstwerk* or "complete work of art" in which all aspects of the house, its interior

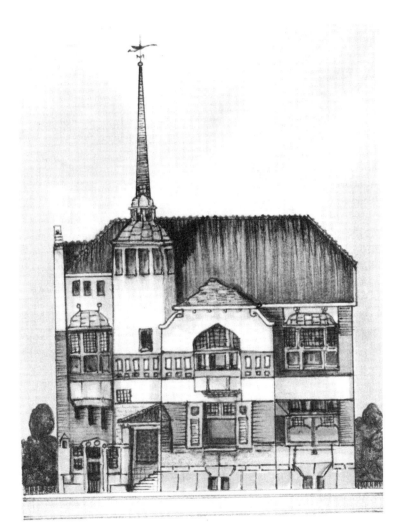

decoration and landscaping were produced by the triumvirate in a fully integrated style. It was an eclectic castellated mix, rather as if a richly decorated Karelian peasant's dwelling had married an austere Scottish castle and Hvitträsk had been its offspring. The bulk of the designs were carried out by Saarinen, who continued to live in the mansion long after his colleagues had departed. But he, too, was eventually to leave it when he went for an extended visit to the United States in 1923, one year after a fire had destroyed the north wing of the main block, thereby eliminating the overweening log tower that had loomed so large over the compound-like edifice. The surrounding forest also serves today as a fitting resting place for the remains of both Saarinen and Gesellius. In 1971 Hvitträsk opened as a museum, a popular destination for ever-larger numbers of visitors interested in the architecture of the period.

Two other important architects, Sigurd Frosterus and Gustaf Strengell, also carried out work in a National Romantic style at the Villa Nissen at Tammisaari in 1903, but this building is infused with a certain rationalism based on the design of machines. Later to become the official residence of President Kekkonen, it was a large villa, almost 5,000 square feet in size. With its spacious central salon and principal entrance to the east into the hall, it drew its inspiration from a Baroque palace of the early eighteenth century. But its exterior was pure *Jugendstil*, with five picture windows inserted on the front of the first-floor façade within an architecturally framed bow. On the second floor, by contrast, a balcony had been appended with a door, also crowned by a bow, intended to symbolize the setting sun. In the interior, *art nouveau* decorations abounded, including water lilies in the entrance hall. Various stoves were also installed, dressed with appropriate tiles, at least one of which had been designed by Strengell himself and made in the Andstén's factory in Helsinki to designs by Saarinen and Lindgren also. Sadly, in 1956 they were deemed unfashionable, removed and re-employed in the debased service of reinforcing the villa's waterside embankment.

Katajanokka
It was not only images from the Finnish epic that inspired Saarinen, but also a negative perception of the staleness of the classical;

contemporary needs and aesthetics demanded a new language of architecture. In this spirit, together with his partners Gesellius and Lindgren, he built just after the turn of the century a block of apartments and offices in Katajanokka with castellated but asymmetrical façades of pastel rendering, incorporating the bay windows and towers so fashionable all over Europe at this time. The first of many projects commissioned by the entrepreneur Julius Tallberg, it gave a unified appearance to this newly redeveloped part of the old city, formerly an impoverished and unhealthy area of ramshackle dwellings.

It was here that the sculptor-father of the Finnish author Tove Jansson, and her mother, a graphic designer, settled and where she herself grew up. It proved a fertile ground to find inspiration for her Moomintroll stories for children, rich as they are in fantasies inspired by Finland's past. Jansson had trained at art school, becoming an important illustrator of children's books. Then in the 1940s she devoted herself to writing her famous Moomin stories, tales about the magical world and inhabitants of Moomin Valley. Perhaps her most famous book in this series was *Comet in Moomin*, published in 1946, in which a sense of community and emotional interdependence of characters is emphasized. Katajanokka also had a magical atmosphere and a sense of community that inspired Jansson in her writings.

The Pohjola Insurance Company

Among other commercial buildings built by Saarinen, Gesellius and Lindgren in the National Romantic style is the Pohjola Insurance Company headquarters, on Aleksanterinkatu, still today the most striking façade in the area. Constructed of granite blocks and soapstone, the building boasts grotesque faces, while the company's emblem, a Finnish bear, is richly carved on the exterior, hovering above the entrance among a thicket of fir branches (itself a Finnish symbol), a tiny jewel of the period.

Saarinen and his colleagues also devoted themselves to larger urban planning. One such design included a utopian plan for the development of Munkkiniemi, commissioned in 1915. Here continental urban planning inspired Saarinen to design large blocks with interior courtyards, as found in Copenhagen or Berlin, but these courtyards were given a garden-like appearance and towards the outskirts of the city British-inspired terraced houses were also envisaged, with spacious gardens incorporated into the plan. Yet despite the scheme's favorable financial prospects, nothing of it was ever built.

The Helsinki Railway Station

Splendid as these designs are, though, it is the Helsinki Railway Station that has really made the reputation of this architectural triumvirate. For Len Deighton, the British author of espionage novels, the station may have looked like a 1930s radio set, but its more pervasive inspiration is derived from the *Kalevala*. That said, the building, taking fifteen years to complete between 1904 and 1919, was less marked by National Romanticism than was originally intended. Its initial form was very much inspired by medieval church architecture, but the criticisms of fellow architects Frosterus and Strengell, that it was too historicist and lacked the simplifying form appropriate to the modern age prompted a radical change in Saarinen's vision. As Saarinen expressed it after his conversion:

> *We in Finland no longer gain our livelihood from hunting and fishing; thus the plant ornamentation and bears—not to speak of other animals—are hardly suitable symbols for the present time based on the use of steam and electricity.*

As a result, the decorative features of National Romanticism were abandoned in favor of a more streamlined modernistic approach. Its massively geometric central tower seems to anticipate later skyscraper design, and its flanking wings look back to the German architect Karl Friedrich Schinkel in their simplified portico-like form. With the principal semi-circularly arched entrance flanked by four massive statues like some great cathedral portal, its appearance remains a striking mixture of the old and the new.

Yet even before this change of veneer, these National Romantic buildings were not as old-fashioned as they seemed: in reality, they were structures in which the latest architectural techniques had been employed, with rigid steel frames beneath the soft contours of what

only seemed to be a more old-fashioned architecture. A work such as the Helsinki Railway Station did heed Frosterus and Strengell when they exhorted architects in their pamphlet "Architecture, an Argument Dedicated to Those Opposed to Us" (1904) to take as their motto: "hjärn och järnstil", a Swedish play on words signifying the use of one's brain to develop new architectural solutions.

Gustav Nyström and Lars Sonck

Gustav Nyström was another important architect to carry out work in a National Romantic idiom. The National Archives of Finland (1890) at Rauhankatu 17 was his first major public building in the capital. Decorated by a monumental series of Corinthian pilasters, it is, of course, classical in inspiration, but its use of iron as an element of construction is innovative.

In terms of commercial architecture, the Telephone Company (1905) by Lars Sonck also deserves special mention, situated at Korkeavuorenkatu 35-37. Here both *art nouveau* and traditional Finnish decorative elements join forces in a mix that rejects many elements of the classical tradition over the previous several hundred years.

Seurasaari Open Air Museum

The foundation of Seurasaari, the open-air museum, must also be seen as part of the National Romantic revival. Opened in 1891, it presented an accumulation of historic Finnish churches, houses and farmsteads to a nostalgic public, in what was the countryside but is now the northwestern suburb of Tamminiemi. It was modeled on the Skansen on Djurgården at Stockholm, where a similar panoply of historic vernacular houses were on view. The wooden church of Karuna, from 1686, is preserved here. Almost all the other buildings exhibited are from homesteads, mainly from the eighteenth and nineteenth centuries. Some of those exhibited include the Antti Farmstead from Säkylä, Niemelä croft from Konginkangas, and the Pertinotsa House from Suojärvi in Karelia, with elaborately carved wooden balconies and filigree work. Given a rural setting, they provide a fascinating insight into life in a Finland that has long since disappeared.

Joined to the mainland by a bridge built the following year, a nearby "watering hole" in the so-called Early Nordic style by the architect Frithiof W. A. Mieritz provided ample liquid refreshment for visitors. Perhaps the style here was also Early Nordic, for many visitors, under the influence of drink, behaved in a way with which the Vikings would have felt at home. As a result, the authorities cracked down and attempted to develop its familial appeal as a museum rather than its notoriety as a venue for the prowling young. Certainly, farmsteads like that from Niemelä heightened its interest among the more educated classes when they were dismantled and re-erected there in 1909 as an historical theme park.

The Twentieth-Century *Kalevala* Revival

Although the inspiration of the *Kalevala* and National Romanticism diminished in the post-war years of the 1920s, another revival occurred in the following decade. It reached its peak in 1935, when the Helsinki Fair Hall (Messuhalli) opened in celebration of the centenary of the publication of the *Kalevala*. The event took place in the presence of 30,000 participants, though twice that number later came to visit the exhibition. Nor did interest abate after the Second World War.

By the 1950s the *Kalevala* was perceived as so central to Finnish cultural identity that a new holiday was established, the so-called

Kalevala Day or Day of Finnish Culture, celebrated annually on February 28 at Saima Park. On that day the Kalevala Society, dedicated to research into and the propagation of the *Kalevala*, places a wreath at the foot of the statue of Elias Lönnrot, made by the sculptor Emil Wickström in 1902. It is a tradition that continues to this day, for the epic has an unquestioned place of honor as a symbol of Finnish cultural identity. Its status is still enormous, even if the heady days of the *Kalevala* revival during the late 1970s and 1980s, in preparation for the 150th anniversary of the 1835 edition, are now gone. Then Finns began to look again at the creative processes of Finnish-Karelian oral tradition and to pay much greater attention to the mass of material subsequently collected, but to which Lönnrot did not have access. Nowadays, two hundred years after the birth of Lönnrot, *Kalevala* specialists tend to see the composition of the epic as a process in which Lönnrot played a leading role, assisted by a number of his contemporaries.

CHAPTER EIGHT

Helsinki and Modernity: Urban Growth, Architecture and Design

The needs of modernity had never historically been a high priority in Helsinki. The seemingly countless fires that broke out in the largely wooden town—in 1570, 1654, 1701, 1713 and 1808—had forced instant renewal rather than the gradual removal of unwanted constructions. The last fire, in particular, which had broken out on November 17, 1808, was the most fateful but also the most fruitful. A young man, Gustaf Lindqvist, employed by a local trader by the name of Cadenius, knocked over a candle in a wooden shed. As a result of the rapid spread of the ensuing fire, more than a quarter of Helsinki was destroyed, as sixty-one houses were razed to the ground. Terrible as it was, it provided a splendid opportunity for the complete rebuilding, after the Napoleonic upheavals, of Finland's new capital. And this happened at a very fortuitous moment, when the needs of the Russian Czar Alexander I coincided with those of his new grand-ducal capital.

Urban Change

Considerable developments were also taking place in Helsinki with respect to urban amenities. Before 1800, the city had had no public street lighting, and private individuals had made use of hemp-seed oil lamps, hung outside their dwellings or shops. In the 1840s gas street lighting was introduced, an important innovation in a city as dark as Helsinki during the winter months. Gas used for domestic purposes was introduced in 1860, though it became more common only in the 1890s. Piped water arrived in 1876, but most people continued to avail themselves of the water provided by street hydrants for years to come.

The coming of the steamboat and train had the greatest implications of modernity, not only for the industrial life of Helsinki, but for the whole working and social life of Finland itself. As the speed of travel and communications increased dramatically time and timetables throughout the country had to be synchronized with Helsinki, which thereby became the Grand Duchy's Greenwich, the clock by which all clocks were set. Perhaps it was the historian and writer Zacharius Topelius who has best described this watershed. As he wrote in *Tant Mirabeau*:

The 17 March 1862 this broad country and its wastelands, with a sudden jump, moved from the past to the present, that same jump which the rest of the world made two or three decades before. That day has pushed one of the world's most dilatory people, who are used to having centuries to wake up to such things, by means of the striking of the clock, from the slow deliberation of months to the punctuality of a minute.

Only two years before, the politician and philosopher Johan Vilhelm Snellman had seen to it that the Finnish mails were set up, a harbinger of the railway that was about to arrive in Helsinki. The capital had entered the modern world of perpetual change.

As steam and rail links improved during the later nineteenth century, Helsinki became ever closer to the rest of Europe and the world at large. In 1867, for example, one could travel by boat to Paris, via Stockholm and Lübeck, in just over four days. Then, in 1883, the new Finnish Steamship Company inaugurated a variety of regular sailings to the north of Germany, the Low Countries and Britain. Communications were improving, especially southwards, as the train journey from Helsinki to Vienna, including stops, had now been reduced to only seventy hours, a remarkable feat. On the sea, too, innovations in steam travel were changing horizons. With the arrival of the first icebreakers in 1890 Finland's days of wintry isolation came suddenly to an end. Henceforth, Helsinki was in constant touch with the rest of the world.

The arrival of the telephone was another important innovation of modernity on the Helsinki scene. Alexander Graham Bell had invented the telephone in 1875 and within two years it had reached the Finnish capital. By 1896 the city could boast 4,000 subscribers, a far higher proportion, relatively speaking, than in the imperial capital itself where fewer than 5,000 owned telephones in 1901. Electricity also made an early arrival in Helsinki, during the 1870s. Shortly after, in 1884, D. J. Wadén opened his small electricity generating company. As a result, the late nineteenth century witnessed a burgeoning of new residential and industrial areas in Helsinki, dependent on these new amenities.

By 1868 the slums of the south shore of Katajanokka, as made notorious in the eponymous painting by Magnus von Wright of that same year (now in the Ateneum), were demolished. Along with them disappeared the ill-famed little taverns tucked away in nooks and crannies in which many an impoverished resident had thrown away his last pennies in return for a shot of Finnish vodka. In their place, a new *Jugendstil* suburb made its appearance, providing salubrious accommodation in the height of modernity.

Meanwhile, to the west, other modern buildings in an eclectic new Renaissance style were also making their appearance. One was the Grönqvist House at Pohjoisesplanadi 25-27 by the architect Carl Thomas Höijer, which, when constructed in the early 1880s, was one of the largest residential buildings in the Nordic world, its principal façade 270 feet long. The ground floor of this five-story building was reserved for shops, while the upper stories contained 193 apartments behind a richly decorated façade, surmounted by towers and other picturesque elements. Named after its owner, the great Helsinki magnate F. W. Grönqvist, who also built the Hotel Kämp, it possessed such amenities as *en suite* bathrooms and elevators.

Suburban Growth

Different types of accommodation were also required for the growing numbers of working people and their families attracted by the industrialization that electrification made possible during the 1890s. Among the resulting suburbs were Hermanni, Fredrikinvuori and Toukola, to name but a few, all of which witnessed, as in Katajanokka a generation before, the removal of many picturesque, if unhygienic, cabins and outbuildings of dilapidated wood.

These new suburbs provided many new amenities not previously available to the working classes of earlier days, but they did have their social drawbacks. For one thing, they led to a greater geographic polarization of people or an early form of ghettoization. Previously, all segments of society had lived together in the same neighborhood, even in the same houses, much as was the case in many continental countries such as Italy, where the wealthy lived on the ground and first floors while their poorer neighbors found accommodation in the cellars, attic lofts or adjacent outbuildings. The new suburbs were more rigidly defined by class and income.

Advances made in construction techniques and materials also encouraged the growth of the building trade and increased urban development in the capital. From the 1890s the fabric of Finnish buildings, largely made up of poor quality locally produced bricks, was increasingly dressed by façades adorned with local granite. Not only were these façades more weather-resistant and durable but they were also more aesthetically appropriate because of associations with ancient Finnish culture, in which the granite boulders of the landscape play such an important role in the imagination. The advent of less glamorous reinforced concrete also provided another major innovation, especially for the foundations of large buildings and their load-bearing supports.

As the twentieth century dawned, an even greater number of new suburbs continued to take shape in and around Helsinki. One of the more elegant of these, Töölö, sprang up in an area sandwiched between Töölönlahti and the city's western shores. In terms of communications it depended on the principal thoroughfares of Hämeentie and Turuntie, each of which meandered its way northwards, as they had done since seemingly time immemorial.

These new suburbs embodied the social ideals of the time: a home of one's own in a milieu combining the best aspects of town and country. Slightly later and under private initiative, the middle-class havens and dormitory towns of Haaga and Lauttasaari, Munkkiniemi and Tapanila, Kulosaari and Kauniainen followed suit, built in the rural environs of Helsinki. No less a National Romantic architect than Eliel

Saarinen devised the plans of Munkkiniemi, while Bertel Jung did so for Kulosaari. And for all their quaintly old-fashioned appearance, harking back to Finland's past, many of the National Romantic buildings of this period were technologically advanced.

These latter were principally middle-class residential areas, but new suburban developments were also undertaken in the following years for working people and their families. One of the leading developments of this ilk was Käpylä, with its charming, seemingly rustic wooden houses placed in garden settings, more reminiscent perhaps of villages in Britain and the whole garden city tradition there than of Finland. In many respects, Käpylä was the most successful of the new garden cities of the 1920s and 1930s in terms of its visual appeal and successful integration of rural elements with urban amenities. It was later complemented by its parish church (1930), the only functionalist example ever built in Helsinki, by E. J. Sutinen.

While Helsinki may have appeared to visitors as a long-established city, its inhabitants possessing an equally long-established urban identity, the reality was very different. In fact, for all its apparent modernism, the urban quality of Helsinki was in many ways an illusion. Most residents had arrived from elsewhere in Finland, and the formation of a truly urban identity would take decades to accomplish. It was a fact that only a minority of Helsinki's population in the late nineteenth and early twentieth centuries were natives of the city, when, between 1870 and 1910, as many as two-thirds of them had migrated there from the provinces.

Transport

The motorcar, perhaps the most significant symbol of modernity, first made its appearance in Helsinki in 1905. Within twenty years the numbers of motorized vehicles had grown to 2,000, and five years later there were 6,000. In 1913 the author Runar Schildt, born into the family of a military officer, had already captured in *The Victorious Eros. A New Life* the exhilarating and destructive aspects of the car's impact on Helsinki:

> *Round Kaivopuisto! Mikael shouted. We will follow you! They whistled by. Far off, in the distance, the lampposts merged together, as if a plough*

of firebirds had rushed in front of them. The pressure of the rubber tyres on the wet street made the sound of the rapid flapping of wings... On the side streets, other motorcars rushed along, like clawed dragons, with wild, flaming eyes, exuding and spitting out its poisonous breath.

It was obvious to all that the motorcar was here to stay, its spread assisted during the early years of the 1930s, by the asphalting of many public streets and a growing web of roads emanating from the capital. The Helsinki Car Museum at Munkkisaarenkatu 12, along with an interesting collection of vintage cars, sheds light upon the history of the motor car in the Finnish capital earlier in the twentieth century.

Another form of transport was also providing the citizens of Helsinki with a new and rapid means of traveling around the city. The Helsinki tram had by the second decade of the twentieth century already become a cherished part of the urban landscape for the city's busy residents. Over the following decade it was developed considerably, reaching its furthest extension finally in the years just before the advent of the Second World War. Together with the motor car, it seemed to embody Helsinki's new status as a city at the height of modernity. As the writer Hagar Olsson, a friend of the poet Edith Södergran, put it in *On the Canaan Express* (1929):

The trams jingled, the motor cars honked and braked, the wind rustled in the crowns of the trees along the Esplanade—a new self-confident wind, not the old idyllic wind which rustled amongst the trees of Kaisaniemi: hum, hum, but a wind which sang of skyscrapers and petrol stations: shell, shell, shell! The city could sense its own power, the city asserted itself, the city played hide and seek with people, propelled them hither and thither, had them run each on the heels of the next, come together and disperse, meet up and separate, all according to its own rhythm.

The Tram Museum at Töölönkatu 51A, situated in the capital's oldest tram depot, provides a fascinating insight into this aspect of the city's transport history.

In 1948 trolley buses were also introduced to Helsinki, adding a cheap, new and alternative method of transport. But it was with the arrival of the airplane that a far more important modernist innovation was to make itself felt. It first came to the Finnish capital in the post-war years after independence, but soon became a regular mode of transport. The little airport on Katajanokka was inaugurated in 1924 and continued in use until 1936. From there the seaplanes of Aero Oy took passengers both west and south respectively, to Stockholm in Sweden and Tallinn in newly independent Estonia. Most exciting was also the arrival in 1930 of the ill-fated air ship, the *Graf Zeppelin*, a thrilling if rather peculiar sight in the otherwise empty Finnish skies.

Air travel was, of course, not at the jet speed of today; even at the advent of the Second World War it was still a leisurely affair. A flight to London or Paris, for example, was obviously far more rapid than boat and train, but it still took some eleven hours to make— not the three hours of modern flights. Yet by the time the new airport opened in Seutula near Vantaa, in time for the Summer Olympic Games of 1952, times were shortened and more and more travelers arrived by plane. The following year 43,000 people traveled to Finland by air, and by 1981 that number had multiplied more than twenty-fold, to one million. By the late 1990s arrivals by plane numbered 3.2 million, with travelers using the national carrier Finnair reaching more than 7.5 million, a vastly larger number than the entire Finnish population. Today Malmi Airport serves the city of Helsinki.

Urgent Development

Even before the Second World War and its destruction, Helsinki, with its ever-increasing immigration from elsewhere in Finland, was a city desperately in need of urban development. For that reason, Taka-Töölö had been built in the 1930s, a collection of unlovely buildings in the functionalist style emanating out of Germany and the Bauhaus tradition. One of the more successful examples of this style, however, is the so-called Glass Palace (Lasipalatsi) at Mannerheimintie 22, built in 1936 by the architectural triumvirate of Niilo Kokko, Viljo Revell and Heimo Riihimäki. Erected on the site of the old Turku Barracks, this functionalist palace, with its sleek glass surfaces, accommodates shops, cafés and a cinema, the Bio Rex, where eight hundred filmgoers, many of whom arrive at the adjacent central bus station, can view the latest Finnish and foreign films.

It was admittedly a rushed development, but by 1938 Helsinki was one of Europe's most densely populated cities, with some eighty-eight people per building block, compared to seventy-six in Berlin or thirty-eight in Paris. Then, with the outbreak of war between Finland and Russia, the need for housing was further increased as large numbers of displaced people arrived in Helsinki from Karelia.

With economy, speed and efficiency the primary concerns, a temporary solution was found in Sweden's offer to provide cheap prefabricated housing. The designs for these houses were produced in Finland, but standardized parts made in Swden were used. Two hundred of these wooden residential units were distributed by the autumn of 1940, where most were reconstructed in the northeastern suburb of Pirkkola. With Finnish finances in a sorry state because of the war, Sweden provided the requisite funding.

This project was, in turn, followed by a new initiative undertaken by the Finnish Association of Architects in conjunction with the League of Farming Associations to produce a further range of prefabricated houses for Helsinki, along with other major Finnish cities such as Turku and Tampere. These new projects were funded not only through Swedish resources, but also through foundations in the United States, a nation that despite the fact that its Allies were at war with Finland, never itself entered into hostilities against it; during the Second World War. Moreover, the US also had a large and active Finnish migrant population dating back to the 1880s, with active local political lobbies keen to support Finland.

Post-war Building

After the end of the Second World War, a long-term view of new residential accommodation could be taken and completely new suburbs came to be built around Helsinki. Many of these were largely independent of existing urban development and were situated in formerly rural areas in the midst of woods or open fields. One of the leading architects of these developments after 1947 was Otto-Iivari Meurman (1890-1994), Professor of Town Planning at the Technical High School in Helsinki, who had already carried out the creation of innovative suburbs for the city of Viipuri (Vyborg) during the 1920s, in which an emphasis on hygienic amenities and single-family occupancy was paramount. But by the 1950s and 1960s, new ideals were coming to permeate the architectural world of Helsinki. The Snake House (Käärmetalo) of 1951, for example, rejected functionalist values in favor of a less angular approach. Here the architect Yrjö Lindgren gave the façade, 900 feet in length, an undulating, twisting form. Various technological innovations were also making themselves apparent in housing, just as the electronic score board had done at the 1952 Helsinki Olympics. In particular, the latest household appliances were to have a ubiquitous presence in the new Finnish suburbs, amenities few other European suburbanites at the time could expect.

Finnish Design
It was in these post-war years that Finnish design became a byword for excellence in international interior design. This was especially true of that emanating from Helsinki, which acquired an ever-higher profile during the 1950s, when designers like Tapio Wirkkala, Timo Sarpaneva and Kaj Franck achieved considerable international fame. Wirkkala's greatest contribution to design was in the area of decorative glass objects. Many of these had strong allusions to Finnish nature; the famous vase *Chantarelle* is but one example. Another by him, *Iceberg*, draws upon polar imagery for its inspiration, an alien subject for Finns, since despite the fact that its northern reaches are in Lapland, icebergs are unknown in its coastal waters.

Wirkkala's wife, Rut Bryk, also made important contributions in this field, later playing a major role in the development of ceramics at the famed Arabia Works. Trained as a graphic artist, she began designing at Arabia in 1942. From then until the 1960s, she devoted herself to the production of *chamotte* and glazed earthenware plaques, using a plethora of themes both secular and religious. Many images, like her sunflowers and butterflies, are taken from the natural world, while others such as her madonnas hark back to an older more iconic tradition. More recently, like Wirkkala, she has preferred to find her artistic inspiration in Finnish Lapland, where the fauna and flora of the far north have come to feature prominently in her designs. Meanwhile, the more abstract designs of others, like Maija Kansanen, also came into vogue.

Then, in the 1960s Antti Nurmesniemi and Eero Aarnio made their mark in modern furniture design. Their so-called Globe chair became a veritable symbol of the carefree values of the 1960s. They won such international favor that even the mod fashion figure of the 1960s, Mary Quant, placed them in her new Bond Street store in London in 1968. The chair also appeared in such films as *The Italian Job*, starring the British actor Michael Caine, not to mention the very popular television serial, *The Prisoner*.

Similarly, the textile factory Marimekko, whose principal designer was Vuokko Eskolin-Nurmesniemi, became an important exponent of Finnish modern design, its main salesrooms to be found within the Catani Building on Pohjoisesplanadi 31. While the US First Lady Jackie Kennedy regularly wore Marimekko dresses in public and before the media, especially when she was pregnant, they also appealed to more modest customers and were a huge success. Another important figure in Helsinki's textile milieu was Eva Brummer, who took her inspiration from the *ryijy* tradition of home-spun rugs that are normally hung on walls. Devoting herself to both secular and ecclesiastical textiles, her work has earned her international fame.

Without the mediating influence of the Central School of Applied Arts, under the directorship of Armas Eliel Lindgren in the 1920s, it is doubtful that Finnish design would have achieved the heights it did. Leaving aside projects such as Lindgren's own Central Railway Station (1904-19), small objects also came within the School's purview. Indeed, no item was too small to be improved upon. For example, the shock-resistant lightweight scissors, with their tell-tale orange handles, a marriage of steel and plastic designed by Olof Bäckström at Fiskars, a metalwork company first founded in 1649, made even small household objects into works of high aesthetic as well as functional quality. In 1948 fashion design would be added to the lists of subjects taught at the Central School.

Arabia

A vital area of Finnish design continues to be found at the Arabia Works in a northeastern suburb of Helsinki, not far from where the original settlement had been established in the mid-sixteenth century. Founded in 1873, it is now the oldest ceramics factory not only in Helsinki but the country as a whole. It followed in the footsteps of what was then Finland's most important ceramics factory, Suotniemi, at Käkisalmi, which had been founded in 1841-2 but was finally to go under in 1892, defeated by Arabia's competitiveness. Arabia's products were sold far and wide, most of them going to St. Petersburg, where they appealed to a much wider market than that available in Finland.

Arabia had originally produced glazed earthenware products, but this line was later extended to include porcelain, stoneware and other forms of crockery. By the 1890s the Swedish designer Thure Öberg had introduced technical innovations that gave Arabia a national name for high-quality ceramic ware. A Finnish architect, Jakob Ahrenberg, also provided an important input by introducing a range of aesthetically pleasing and very fashionably designed goods. Yet Arabia could not rest on its laurels, for competition was intense, especially after the Saviteollisuus/Kera Company was established at Kauniainen in 1917. From then Arabia had to cope with a highly successful rival that continued to threaten its place in the design market until 1958, when the closure of Saviteollisuus/Kera proved unavoidable. Thereafter, Arabia was the unquestioned queen of Finnish ceramics, which it remains to this day.

Arabia's most significant competitor, though, was the Iris Factory, founded by Count Louis Sparre af Söfdeborg in 1897. Its most important ceramics designer was Alfred William Finch, a leading figure in the Nordic arts world of British and Belgian origins. The works produced under his artistic direction took their inspiration from the British arts and crafts movement, especially the pieces of burnt red clay. Many of the pieces of furniture manufactured at the factory also came under the sway of this popular philanthropic movement.

Unfortunately, the financial acumen of Iris proved less powerful than its aesthetic and the company became bankrupt in 1902. While individuals like Nikolai Boman continued to take inspiration from Iris in their own furniture designs, Finch turned to teaching, becoming the first professor of ceramics at Helsinki's Central School of Applied Arts. The students he taught there would later spread his aesthetic values beyond the frontiers of Finland; his prize student Maija Grotell became a professor at the Cranbrook Academy in Bloomfield Hills, Michigan, in 1938, a post she would occupy until 1966. Others such as Toini Muona and Elsa Elenius remained in Helsinki, the former taking up a designing role at Arabia, the latter becoming Finch's successor at the Central School.

It was in the field of crockery that Arabia perhaps achieved greatest international recognition, when it launched a range in 1932 to appeal to a discerning and prosperous middle-class market. This success was largely due to its new director Kurt Ekholm, who increased the scope of the products offered while giving them highly modern designs. In particular, the designers Kaj Franck, whom we have already come across, and Kaarina Aho were instrumental in producing a range of new and vibrant designs from 1946, forming a creative design partnership that Ulla Procop joined two years later.

In 1948 Arabia was purchased by the Wärtsilä Company, mainly known for its shipbuilding, and in the 1950s it continued to be highly successful. Franck's Kilta crockery (first produced in 1953) and Flame (production of which began in 1958) were especially sought after for their practical qualities since these pieces were oven-proof as well as beautiful. Today the company is in the ownership of the design and technology company Hackman, which purchased it in 1991.

Modern Furniture

Furniture, whether of wood (plentiful in Finland) or metal, was another important branch of Finnish design. The department store Stockmann's Studio brand provided high-quality furniture to the accompaniment of lamps by Taito. Even more famous was Artek, the brainchild of the internationally renowned architect Alvar Aalto (1898-1976) and his wife Aino Marsio-Aalto (1894-1949). This concern began to produce a whole range of items in 1935 for the interior design market—furniture, glass, textiles and other objects—which, expensive as they were then, have become even more valuable as collectors' items. Much of the furniture that developed in the 1930s had been inspired by the tubular metal pieces that the Bauhaus in Dessau had done so much to propagate during the later 1920s. Yet the Aaltos also infused their furniture with warmer, more naturalistic elements than the more clinical Bauhaus style possessed.

Aino Aalto had already begun to collaborate with her husband as far back as 1924, but it was not merely with him but also with the designers Nils-Gustav Hahl and Maire Gullichsen that she left her greatest mark on interior decoration. Functionalism was her byword and the style that characterized Artek while she was its managing director from 1941 to 1949. This approach found its most successful application in the work she did for day-care centers and kindergartens, where cost effectiveness and efficiency were especially important. But the attention she devoted to glass design, in particular the Bolgeblick series, was also fruitful. These items of pressed glass won the prestigious competition established by the Karhula-Iittala firm in 1934; even more importantly, they found favor throughout Finland, becoming *de rigueur* in almost every household.

As for Aalto's own connection with Artek, it was his laminated wooden furniture that most appealed to a wider international public. This was certainly the case at the Milan Triennale in 1933 and at another exhibition held in London that year. As his reputation grew, Aalto was commissioned to carry out designs for the Finnish Pavilion at the Paris World Exhibition in 1937 and the 1939 World's Fair in New York. Even well into the post-war years Artek continued to thrive, receiving a fresh design impetus under Ben af Schultén, who assumed the artistic directorship in 1976.

More recently, modern industrial design has received a new burst of creativity from those like Stefan Lindfors, who have acquired an international perspective. Using the experience acquired as a student at Helsinki's University of Art and Design, his works sometimes have political overtones. This is certainly true of his "thrones" dedicated to Reagan, Gorbachev and Zhao Ziyang, three of the most powerful leaders of the day, which were exhibited at the Metaxis Exhibition at the Design Museum of Finland in 1987. That said, it was his lightweight, metal frame chairs that were most innovative in practical terms, while objects like the so-called Hippolite table (1988) introduced an almost sci-fi fantasy element into furniture design. This piece, with angular wings that seem to flap, appears to be derived more from aerospace dynamics than from any more earth-bound design prototypes. Lindfors later received the Georg Jensen Prize for Design in 1992 before moving to the US, where he took up a post at the Kansas City Art Institute from 1993 to 1996. Unfortunately, the 1970s and 1980s witnessed a decline in international appreciation of Finnish design, but during the course of the 1990s a revival occurred that continues to this day.

High-Rise Helsinki

As Helsinki's population grew relentlessly, so the homely idyll that characterized the design vision of the new suburbs came to be superseded by one which placed a greater emphasis on economy of construction while maintaining a rural ambiance, at least as a backdrop. Multi-story blocks of apartments were now built in the so-called "woods towns" such as Maunula, Herttoniemi and Roihuvuori, as well as Tapiola in Espoo which popped up as Helsinki's new suburbs. Their hallmark was the fresh air inhaled through the open windows of tower blocks and smaller buildings, as well as the ease with which the surrounding forests could be reached. Publicly financed, they rose up unevenly from the rock soil upon which they were constructed in a seemingly higgledy-piggledy fashion, creating an aggressive, uneven, and asymmetrical skyline.

Beautiful they were not, but they were functional to the needs of the middle years of the twentieth century—at least that is what the architects who built them purported. Not only did they house large numbers of new arrivals to the city, or the children of older ones now setting up their own homes, but they also contained the foci of new towns in their own right: post offices and banks, as well as all manner of shops, restaurants, and even cinemas sprang up in their environs. By

1965 urban Helsinki had become an urban metropolis of more than half a million inhabitants, but one in which there were in-built planning processes to ensure tradition and respect for the environment. The height of residential tower blocks, for example, was restricted to nine floors. There was also a requirement to ensure continuity of line with already existing buildings in established areas. Furthermore, in order to preserve old local names relating to a field, stream or the like in street names, an obligation to consult with the Helsinki University place-name archives when undertaking new building was also laid down. All this encouraged historical continuity.

Alvar Aalto

By 1962 the city of Helsinki, excluding its suburbs, had 260,000 inhabitants, its suburbs 160,000. The latter had required cheap and rapidly built accommodation and this they got, since prefabricated elements made developments such as Pihlajamäki, on one of the hills to the north of the city, economically possible. Others were built at Jakomäki and Kontula.

Yet the real architectural significance in the world of modernist Helsinki must belong to Alvar Aalto. He had begun his architectural career in 1921 and soon earned considerable acclaim for his somewhat austere, classically inspired buildings, which looked in part back to eighteenth-century Nordic models, albeit with an Italian accent. But there was also a fortuitous practical side to his success; having found favor with a rich industrialist, Harry Gullichsen, and his wife Maire, whom we have already met, a series of important commissions suddenly came his way. A new residential area for employees of the Sunila factory was built under his direction in 1936-9, one of Finland's first housing estates in the modernist context. As such, it could also take its inspiration from such nineteenth-century prototypes as Bourneville, near Birmingham, which the Quaker Cadbury family had constructed for their workers. Like Bourneville, too, it could also be seen to have a social dimension, one in which the well-being of employees could be married to a prosperous democratic vision of the good society.

Aalto's own house in Helsinki, the Villa Aalto, situated at Riihitie 20 in Munkkiniemi, was built in 1936, with a great deal of assistance from his wife. While the basic structure is supported by round steel pillars filled with concrete, bricks covered by stucco and vertical boarding decorate the façade. Inside the house, a *piano nobile*, with imposing drawing and dining rooms, takes up the first floor; there is a roof terrace above and bedrooms below, with adjacent office space. As such, it is a supreme example of Aalto's so-called Romantic Modernist phase, in which functional modernism has been somewhat tempered by a more idiosyncratic treatment.

There were soon to be more important commissions of a practical nature to preoccupy the architect after the Second World War erupted. Then the requirement of providing vital accommodation for those in desperate need of cheap housing came to dominate his work. During the war Aalto had already come to see standardized housing as the only viable solution to massive displacements. In quest of inspiration, he traveled extensively in the US, seeking efficient prototypes. Thus, when he became involved with the development of the suburb of Haaga, in the hands of a private cooperative association, prefabricated elements played a major role. This approach, with its theoretical background, he was able to popularize through the good offices of the Finnish novelist Mika Waltari, author of the world-famous novel, *The Egyptian* (1945), who assisted him in the production of a booklet on the subject. A sculpture to the memory of Waltari by Veikko Kirvimäki was erected in 1985 near the Hesperia Hospital, not far from where the novelist lived.

In 1953-5, Aalto built his famous Iron House (Rautatalo) at Keskuskatu 3A. Based upon a simple plan making efficient use of a very constricted site, shops occupy most of the building, in which Artek was formerly situated in the basement, while Marimekko opened, along with other offices, at the top. There is also a spacious interior courtyard on the first floor, containing cafés. In constructional terms, it is the first building in which Aalto made use of marble and travertine for his stepped galleries, incorporated into what is basically a structure of reinforced concrete. This was followed later in 1955 by the House of Culture, a major concert venue situated at Sturenkatu 4 in the centre of town. A five-story curvaceous building (also containing offices) faced in brick with copper elements, it includes an asymmetrical concert hall accommodating 1,500 people as well as a congress wing. That same year, Aalto also designed his own Studio Aalto at Tiilimäki

20, using brick covered in stucco and white board for the façades, with an inner courtyard and interior space that follows the slope upon which it is built, creating the impression of an amphitheater.

Then, in 1962, Aalto built the administration building of the pulp and paper company Stora Enso, with its marble cladding, just over the bridge on Katajanokka. This was followed in 1965, by his new plan for the complete redevelopment of Helsinki's center. Designed to be carried out in two stages, little of it actually ever came to fruition and his great vision, based upon the purest concepts of modernity, was never fully realized. This had consisted of a fan-shaped square, with terraced buildings, along the western shore of Töölö Bay. Only one component was finally constructed, Finlandia Hall, built in 1971, with its Congress wing completed some four years later. Perhaps Aalto had lost touch with the people of Helsinki. His polemical insistence that urbanism emanated from the architectural milieu sounded meaningless to many. For him, if not for most people, the picturesque and the domesticated were not values to be emulated. As he wrote:

In the case of Helsinki, for example, there can be no happy solution if Töölönlahti and Hesperianpuisto become a type of miniature idyll, but rather something comic, if one attempts in the absolute heart of a big city, as if in a game, to create a copy or variation of a Karelian house located in a forest.

Yet this is precisely what many of the citizens of Helsinki in later decades desired. Aalto's theoretical intellectualizing had not kept pace with the deep-seated needs and hopes of most of the population. That said, the premises he built in 1969 on the Pohjoisesplanadi, opposite Stockmann's, for the Academic Bookshop took inspiration from his much earlier work at the Library in Viipuri and has become one of Aalto's best-loved buildings in the city center.

Tapiola

Far more successful than the visionary plans of Aalto was the most important new garden city, only five miles from the city center and christened Tapiola after Tapio, the god of the forest as celebrated in the

Finnish and Karelian oral tradition and the epic *Kalevala*. Really a town in itself, it includes a large array of shops, churches and other amenities, along with residential areas integrated with enveloping gardens into a largely forested milieu.

The original idea of a new town nestling within the Finnish forest had been discussed in a pamphlet entitled "Do Our Children Need Homes or Barracks?" by Heikki von Hertzen, director of the Finnish Population and Family Welfare Federation. He had established the Residential Association, a non-profit organization that assumed responsibility for the planning and building of Tapiola. The academic and theoretical basis of the whole concept, however, can be linked to Otto I. Meurman, Finland's first professor of town planning and a key figure in the methodology of the scheme.

The center of Tapiola, surrounded by three principal residential areas, is focused around a central tower block of offices crowned by a restaurant with panoramic views. There is also a central electrical power station catering for the needs, both commercial and industrial, of the community, as well as a secondary school. Further amenities were provided by the Tapiola Church at Tapionraitti, built in 1965 to the designs of Aarno Ruusuvuori, a swimming hall by Aarne Ervi three years later, as well as a number of schools.

The residential areas themselves are of roughly equal size, but diversity has been introduced by incorporating both terraced housing and blocks of apartments, all designed by a variety of different architects. The overall density is some 120 people per hectare (two and a half acres). As for the layouts of footpaths and other amenities, a concerted attempt was made at avoiding straight angles in order to achieve a more meandering rural effect.

The Changing Face of Helsinki

The late 1960s was a period of revolutionary activity among students, just as elsewhere in Europe. Large numbers of them occupied their Student Union on the occasion of its centenary, with the banner "Revolution at the University has begun!" raised in front of the building. It proved to be a flash in the pan, like so many other revolutionary outcries of that period.

Far more lasting, though hidden in the bowels of the earth, was the Helsinki underground. It had been in the planning stage since 1954, but only in 1969 did construction begin, at about the same time that electric suburban trains were brought into general service. It was finally inaugurated on August 2, 1982, running between Railway Station Square and the shopping area of Itäkeskus. By the late 1960s heating provided by the Hanasaari power plant among others also served the needs of just under half the population of Helsinki. For many, these were aspects of the ever-changing face and infrastructure of the capital. As the Finnish-Swedish author Kjell Westö put it, with respect to one of the inner areas of the city:

> *And Kampen!*
>
> *At one time there was an empty hollow, a prefab, Alkärr and Maria hospital. And there on the other side were the facades of Malm Street, as if on parade: the German school, the synagogue, the power station company's black gas drum, to the side of which was a house with a tower in Art Nouveau style and pinnacles in the style of the 1910s.*
>
> *How I loved that view!*
>
> *But all that was gone now. In their place was the SAS Hotel, and a compact residential area with pastel colored houses had filled out the space and blocked the views.*

Still, all was not lost, as several wooden houses were re-erected at the shore of Kaisaniemi, creating a picturesque ensemble by the entrance to the contemporary Botanical Garden, as well as a charming café. There were other compensations as well, as formerly working-class areas took on new residential prestige. Punavuori and Kamppi, Kallio and Sörnäinen were now becoming highly desirable residential locations, situated as they were not far from the city center just over that formerly dramatic line of social demarcation between working and middle classes, the Pitkäsilta (Long Bridge).

As the later twentieth century wore on, the number of those arriving in the suburbs continued to increase dramatically, from 195,000 to 325,000 between 1962 and 1987. But not all new developments were in the suburbs. The new residential development of Pyöli, for example, was built in the inner city itself. Another new area was Merinhaka, built during the 1970s on land filled in from what had been part of the open harbor. This was followed during the 1980s and 1990s by further developments at Katajanokka and Ruoholahti. Many of these initiatives provided accommodation for the numerous single people now living in the center of Helsinki. (The number of single households had more than doubled over the final quarter of the twentieth century.)

Tragically, the 1960s and 1970s were also a time of destruction, for more than a thousand buildings, including the historic Hotel Kämp (except for its principal façade), were wiped off the face of Helsinki in the name of modernity. Even so, the city's growth continues to be unstoppable, and on December 31, 2001, 559,718 inhabitants were recorded. Old buildings are still often found unsuitable for modern needs, and so the quest for a successful accommodation between the old and the new remains very relevant today.

Urho Kekkonen: Modern Politics

Up to now, modernism in Helsinki has been discussed in terms of urban architecture, design and amenities. But modernity in political terms has also played a major role and no one assumed a greater importance in this regard than Urho Kaleva Kekkonen (1900-86), without doubt the greatest symbol of Finland's post-war accommodation to the modern world. He was the country's longest-serving president, from 1956 to 1981.

Kekkonen was born at Pielavesi, in the north of Finland, but became involved early on in national politics. A deeply committed democrat, his early years were marked by conflict with those Finnish patriots who opted for a more authoritarian approach. This friction was evident as far back as 1927 when Kekkonen became editor-in-chief of the student newspaper *Ylioppilaslehti.* Problems increased when he became involved with the Academic Karelian Society, whose members stood even further to the right, rooted as many were in the far-right Lappua Movement. Yet he maintained his stance, deeply committed to Finnish culture on the one hand, but democratic and tolerant on the other. As a result, he felt obliged to leave the Academic Karelian Society in 1932, publishing two years later his own apologia in a pamphlet entitled *In Defense of Democracy.*

Kekkonen entered Parliament in 1936 as an Agrarian, first as a member for Viipuri. In 1937 he was named Minister of Justice as well as assistant Minister for the Interior. Taking a belligerent position with respect to the Winter War, he voted against peace in 1940. Yet after the Continuation War, he nonetheless advocated and sought a *rapprochement* with the Soviet Union by the end of 1943, which he hoped would lead to a negotiated peace. The following year he once again assumed the role of Minister of Justice under President Juho Kusti Paasikivi (1870-1956). At the same time, he also became involved in a wide range of ministerial positions relating to finance, ultimately becoming a member of the board of Finland's Bank in the decade 1946-56.

During the 1950s Kekkonen, ever more prominent, became Prime Minister no fewer than five times under the equivalent number of governments, three times Agrarian, twice Social Democratic. This role did not hinder him from also briefly serving as Minister of the Interior in 1950-51 and Foreign Minister in 1952-53. By 1952 Kekkonen had formulated a policy of neutrality not only for Finland, but the other Nordic countries as well. Such an approach found a warm response in the Soviet Union, desperately keen to ensure that its neighbors would enter no threatening pacts. It also facilitated a more favorable Soviet approach to Finland and the resolution of unfinished business relating to the wars of the previous decade. As a result, the Soviet military base, which had been established at Porkkala, was removed and the territory was returned to Finnish sovereignty in 1955. At the same time, Finland joined both the United Nations and the Nordic Council.

Basking in the success of his foreign political negotiations, Kekkonen, the Agrarian candidate, was elected president of Finland in 1956, albeit with a small majority. Privately negotiated deals with the Soviets rather than public conferences were the hallmark of his presidential office. From his residence in the Villa Tammisaari, built to the designs of the architect Gustaf Nyström in 1889, he received a wide array of foreign leaders and other politicians who would sometimes be entertained by a swim or a visit to the sauna.

Kekkonen continued over the following decades as president, taking a particularly active role in bringing world leaders to Helsinki for the Conference on Security and Cooperation in Europe in 1973. But illness finally forced his *de facto* retirement in late 1981, and the new president, Mauno Koivisto, officially assumed his office on January 27, 1982.

The Presidential Residence at Tamminiemi

Kekkonen's official residence at Tamminiemi has arguably become the greatest monument in Helsinki to his memory. Situated on the site of what had been the Meilahti Estate, it had formerly belonged to the Russian governor general. Kekkonen had first visited the residence, which was known as the Villa Kallio, in June 1944, and twelve years later, after the presidencies of Mannerheim and Juho Paasikivi, the newly elected President Kekkonen took up residence there. It had just undergone a major restoration by the architectural firm of Kokko & Kokko, who had little respect for the work of their predecessors in what was now an alien architectural medium. As far as was possible, all traces of its original *Jugendstil* were blotted out in the interest of 1950s Finnish functionalism in all its starkness.

Yet not all aspects of the decoration were bleak. On the contrary, the colorful and exuberant textiles of Liisa Suvanto softened the sharp angles of the newly restored villa. The blinds that she incorporated and the copper threads of the windows in the staircase still remain there today, more exotic to many visitors than items from the eighteenth century. Furthermore, the keen interest Sylvi Kekkonen, the president's wife, also took in the interior decorations added a deeply personal quality to the atmosphere. Assisted by Marja-Liisa Komulainen, she acquired a whole new range of furniture to replace much of the *faux*-rococo that had previously filled the public rooms.

After the relatively early death of the president's wife in December 1974, other decorative changes occurred. The functionalist pieces of the 1950s made way for the works of Alvar Aalto, now a figure of international importance, whose architecture and light-colored furniture of birchboard gave Finland an extraordinarily high profile both east and west. Less famous but also of importance for the new décor was Professor Yrjö Kukkapuro, whose pieces of furniture covered in exotic skins became a hallmark of the period in Finland.

There Kekkonen died on August 31, 1986, and the building suitably reopened as the Urho Kekkonen Museum in the following year. Situated in its park near the Seurasaari at Seurasaarentie 15, it remains decorated in the style he knew. Among its collections are gifts received from important foreign visitors as well as notable international and Finnish works of art. Perhaps most distinctive from a purely idiosyncratic point of view are the etchings of Lapland, published in London by the British artist Thomas Rowlandson (1756-1827) in 1822. A very unusual subject matter for this very British caricaturist, they are exhibited in a bedroom, as they were in Kekkonen's time. After his death, a monument entitled *Spring* by the sculptor Pekka Jylhä was commissioned in Kekkonen's memory. It was unveiled by one of his successors, Tarja Halonen on the centenary of Kekkonen's birth on September 3, 2000.

The old presidential residence may have lost its role as an important political landmark, but the new presidential residence at Mäntyniemi is a continuing sign of the government's emphasis on modernity rather than the traditional. The architect Reima Pietilä built the concatenation of structures on the outskirts of Helsinki in such a way that their granite monumentality sits snugly and unassumingly within the sharp geographical extrusions of the rocky coast.

Women's Rights

We have seen how the role of women in terms of modernity has been a major one. But it is also useful to consider gender issues and women's rights as important aspects of modernity in Helsinki as well. Indeed, nowhere did modernity make itself more clearly felt than in the growing equality of the sexes in the capital.

There is no doubt that at the upper levels of society the presence of women at Helsinki University had started quite early, in comparison with other European institutions of higher learning. In 1870 one woman was examined for entrance to the university and was admitted, by special authorization of the Russian Czarevich, the future Alexander III. Others were less fortunate and had their authorization denied. But in the following decade some women did begin to receive degrees, and from the mid-1880s an ever-growing number matriculated despite the continued authorization that was required. A significant improvement in their position came when this restriction was abolished in 1901. In any case, at least fourteen percent of the entire student body was female by that time, making Helsinki University one of the most receptive to women students in Europe.

Yet at that time the traditional role of women persisted in tandem with the modern one, not least in domestic life. Certainly among poorer people women continued to maintain hearth and home, washing, cooking and bearing children. As the British visitor Ethel Tweedie put it in her 1897 travelogue:

> *Among the lower orders the women work like slaves, because they must. Women naturally do the washing in every land, and in the Finnish waterways there are regular platforms built out into the sea, at such a height that the laundresses can lean over the side and rinse their clothes while the actual washing is performed at wooden tables, where they scrub linen with brushes made for the purpose.*

Mrs. Tweedie also marveled at the fact that Finnish women could be found in so many jobs generally carried out by men elsewhere in Europe:

Women in Suomi *do many unusual things but none excited our surprise so much as to see half a dozen of them building a house. They were standing on scaffolding plastering the wall, while others were completing the carpentering work of a door; subsequently we learnt there are no fewer than 600 women builders and carpenters in Finland.*

All in all, then, this feisty lady was satisfied with the progress made in what to her was a peripheral and isolated land. She concluded "it is remarkable that so remote a country, so little known and so unappreciated, should thus suddenly burst forth and hold the most advanced ideas for both men and women. That endless sex question is never discussed. There is no sex in Finland, men and women are practically equals, and on that basis society is formed."

In 1906 Finland became the first European state to grant female suffrage, a right confirmed by Czar Nicholas II despite his reactionary reputation. Many women had in the meantime availed themselves of the privileges of higher education. By 1918, a year after Finland had declared its independence from Russia, 38 percent of the student body were female.

In the post-war years women demanded a still more active role in the economic life of the nation and increasingly sought employment outside the home. By the 1960s some sixty percent of women were at work, a figure doubtless even higher in Helsinki. By 1967 the number of women entering university equaled that of men. Then, the shift in proportions of the sexes in higher education went in the opposite direction, as women came to outnumber men. In any case, women were assuming an ever more prominent public role. For this reason, Miina Sillanpää, the first woman ever to sit as a minister in the Finnish Parliament, was commemorated in 1968 by Aimo Tukiainen's statue, entitled *The Torch*, situated in Kallio (Berghäll) near Eläintarhatie. By 2000, 57 percent of students were women.

CHAPTER NINE

Intellectual Helsinki: Science and Learning

For all its artistic attractions, Helsinki is also a city of science. Its almost two hundred year-old astronomical observatory seems to symbolize the scientific credentials of a country that is perhaps the most high-tech of them all. Today the capital is home to numerous Nokia offices (originally established at Nokia, to the west of Tampere but with its headquarters now in Espoo) among other international telecommunications companies. It is also home to an important technological institute, the Helsinki Polytechnic University, where the latest research is carried out. An interesting exhibition center and science park at Heureka includes a planetarium and informative presentations on a wide range of scientific issues.

The capital's history of research, practice and publishing also encompasses philosophy and its world-famous training centers for architecture, design and technology.

Early Humanism
From its early days Helsinki enjoyed at least the temporary presence of a few humanistic men of science, some of whom wrote works in the newly founded town, known in academic circles by its Latin name, Forsia. One such humanist was the Lutheran clergyman Sigfridus Aronus Forsius (c. 1560-1624), who had been employed in Tallinn as a schoolteacher. More significantly, he had explored the Arctic coast of Norway, then under Danish suzerainty, and eventually went on to become professor of astronomy at Uppsala University in Sweden before retiring as rector of Tammisaari on Finland's southern coast. Today he is noted for the geographical observations he put to paper in *Physica* (first published in the 1950s), as well as a very popular almanac. His concise book *On*

Comets (1618) also exerted an enormous influence on astronomical thought in Finland, at least until the age of Zacharius Topelius in the mid-nineteenth century. Certainly, he was an oft-quoted figure at the famous Åbo Academy in Turku, founded in 1640, where the official language of higher education was Latin (it continued to be so both there and in the Finnish gymnasia until the early nineteenth century).

Towards the end of the eighteenth century, foreigners began to come to Finland, some even to Helsinki, still a small unassuming town. In 1799, for example, the Englishman Edward Clarke, later professor of mineralogy at the University of Cambridge, was fascinated during his winter stay (when he communicated in Latin) by the heavy traffic in people and goods over the ice to and from Helsinki's island fortress of Suomenlinna. His interest focused in particular on the geology and geography of the area.

Another important visitor from the world of science was the French academic Xavier Marmier, a member of the Académie Française who came to Finland in conjunction with the French navy in 1838 to carry out scientific research in Lapland on matters relating to meteorology and biology. This was to be the first of three visits, the last in 1842. His findings were eventually published in a series of twelve volumes handsomely illustrated by his fellow Frenchmen Lauvergne and Giraud.

The Observatory

Such a scientific interest, however, was occasional. Only in the early nineteenth century did the pursuit of the sciences achieve a firm and lasting base in the new Finnish capital. A shining symbol of this is the Astronomical Observatory at the southern end of Unioninkatu, a masterpiece of the German architect Carl Ludwig Engel. In collaboration with Helsinki's professor of astronomy, Friedrich Wilhelm Argelander, who provided him with his technical requirements, Engel was able to draw inspiration from other observatories within the Russian Empire, especially that at the University of Dorpat (now Tartu), in modern-day Estonia, with its long east-west elevations. Most prominent are its three revolving towers for viewing the heavens. There are also a variety of rooms, providing accommodation for the astronomer and a lecture room.

The granite columns of the old observatory in Turku were reused within the new observatory. Its most striking feature was the burning cloth soaked in oil, raised every night at midnight high above its central tower as a measure of time for ships at sea. For sailors then, the observatory was an important symbol of Helsinki, and by extension, of the Czar himself whose keen interest it was to develop the sciences in his new capital. Gustaf Nyström added a refractory tower in 1889.

Books and Printers

It was not only the presence of foreigners that made Helsinki an intellectually stimulating place. Since the nineteenth century it had been a city with an unusually high degree of well-educated and analytically minded people, a reservoir of skilled individuals for the Russian civil and military bureaucracy. It was also a very literate city. There were a number of well-stocked bookshops with large inventories of foreign as well as local books and journals. The most prominent of these was that of Wasenius, who in 1831 supplied books to the university. It became an establishment of lasting import for the capital, the Academic Bookshop, today prominently situated on the North Esplanade opposite Stockmann's Department Store. In the twentieth century Alvar Aalto provided the design for today's premises. Its most serious contemporary rival bookshop, the Suomalainen Kirjakauppa, is to be found opposite Stockmann's, on Alexanterinkatu.

The Finnish Literature Society was also a unique establishment, still thriving today and providing a library, foundation and commercial outlet for books on Finnish literature, language, linguistics, anthropology, sociology and history. It published in 1870 one of the early and very significant Finnish language novels, *Seven Brothers* (Seitsemän veljestä) by Aleksis Kivi. Along with virtually all editions of the Kivi novel, the library also contains 200,000 other works, while its oral tradition and anthropological archives are amongst the largest in the world. All aspects of Finnish culture, society and folklore are encompassed and it encourages the undertaking of many projects that might otherwise not see the light of day.

The development of Helsinki's book culture was dependent on printers. Wasenius and other bookshops largely relied upon local printing presses for many of their books. By 1828 three presses were operating in the city, and by 1840 there were seven, two of them lithographic in production. Not only books but also musical scores and reproductions of paintings were also sold, catering for a large and highly literate urban middle class. Tilgmann's printing plant was just one of the newly prominent companies of its kind during the third quarter of the nineteenth century.

Three newspapers were also established, using Swedish as their language of communication. The first was the government-sponsored, *Finlands allmänna tidning.* Then followed, under private auspices after the advent of the university, *Tidningar ifrån Helsingfors,* and the *Helsingfors Tidningar.* These carried not only a large run of domestic columns but also many articles based on foreign sources.

Over the years other newspapers have come to the fore, making Helsinki a city in which this medium of information reaches more people relative to its size than perhaps anywhere else in the world. The recently relocated Sanoma Corporation's multistory glass building of nine floors, designed by the architects Jan Söderlund and Antti-Matti Siikala, is a symbol of its power and significance. Here, The *Helsingin Sanomat* (originally founded as the *Päivalehti*), *Ilta Sanomat* and *Taloussanomat* all have their offices, the first boasting a circulation of 450,000, making it the most popular newspaper in Finland. For those with a more historical interest in newspapers, the News Museum at Ludviginkatu 2-4 explores press history from 1889 until the present. There old issues of long-gone favorites like *Uusi Suomi* and the left-wing *Kansan Uutiset* can also be viewed. Last but not least is the nearby headquarters of *Hufvudstadsbladet* in Mannerheimintie, still the most widely read Swedish-language newspaper in Helsinki.

Schools

A well-established culture of literacy, based upon excellent schooling, was a prerequisite for this interest in books, journals and newspapers. Since the early seventeenth century and until 1831 the male youth of Helsinki had been served by the so-called Trivium School, an establishment with limited academic ambitions but in which reading and writing were of primary importance. This was especially the case as all young Finns, male and female, were taught at least to read by the local clergy as part of preparation for confirmation. Many acquired writing skills. The Trivium, to which only boys were admitted, expected its pupils to be able to read and write on arrival; it improved these skills and provided other elements of education, including Latin, to permit progress to the *gymnasium* or grammar school in a boy's early teens. Those citizens with the means and keen on a more sophisticated level of teaching sent their sons if not abroad (this was possible only for a minuscule number), then at least along the coast east to Porvoo, where there was the only *gymnasium* for miles around. Or they provided their sons with private tutors, the normal alternative to the Trivium and *gymnasium.*

In 1830, on the occasion of a visit by Czar Nicholas I, the city fathers established a new primary school for boys, based on the Bell-Lancaster method. This had been used in a similar establishment already ten years old in Turku, but had long been popular in both Sweden and Russia. It enabled the school to run on a shoestring without a large body of teachers, since the older children were used in the teaching of the younger. The following year the Helsinki Lyceum was founded, inspired by the folk high schools established by the Lutheran priest Nikolai Grundtvig in Denmark a few years earlier. These in turn were influenced by the colleges of Oxford and Cambridge, which the clergyman and hymnist so ardently admired. Swedish was the primary language of communication and teaching in both. By 1892 Helsinki could claim twelve secondary schools. While five were exclusively for boys, three were for girls and a further four were coeducational, an unusually high proportion open to girls by contemporary European standards.

With the dawn of the twentieth century, literacy in Finland was virtually complete. Indeed, ever since the Reformation, thanks to the role of the Church in propagating literacy as means of spreading the Lutheran catechism, it had been very widespread, especially among men, as no one could be confirmed without passing a literacy test. Perhaps the most memorable literary depiction of this state of affairs is to be found in Kivi's *Seven Brothers*. The brothers, with the exception of the little Eero, fail so dismally to learn their letters that two of them, Juhani and Timo, are obliged to sit in a dunce's corner. Humiliated, they break a window during the lunch period and escape into the forest, where no "civilizing" constraints confront them.

By the turn of the twentieth century, however, the situation was improving so dramatically, that, according to the census of 1910, ninety percent Helsinki's population aged fifteen or over could both read and write; by 1920 the figure had climbed to 94 percent, an extraordinary achievement for a poor and isolated country. Further information is to be found at the School Museum, located at Kalevankatu 39-43, set up in three old wooden houses from the 1830s and 1840s.

Helsinki University

Finland's first university, Åbo Akademi, had long been established in Turku, where it was founded as far back as 1640. When, in September 1827, it was destroyed by the fire that ravaged much of Turku, an opportunity presented itself to the emperor for its transfer to his new Finnish capital. This occurred in 1828 and the institution was renamed the Alexander University in honor of the Czar. Here was another occasion upon which the Emperor of All the Russias could show his wisdom and magnanimity, while also moving it nearer St Petersburg and away from Swedish influence. The new Alexander University, later re-named Helsinki University in 1917 after independence, was larger than the universities of Uppsala or Lund in Sweden. As for its student population, that was also unusually large, three hundred not to mention the forty professors and lecturers who carried out research and provided them with instruction. It joined the constellation of universities in the Russian Empire, which included Vilnius, founded in 1579, Dorpat (1632), Moscow (1775), Kazan (1804), Kharkov (1805) and, most importantly, St Petersburg (1819).

A site was chosen on the western side of Senate Square, where a governor's residence had previously been mooted. Engel produced various designs from which the Czar chose his favorite, and the building was finally inaugurated in 1832. It embodied that Apollonian symbolism with which Alexander was most keen to associate himself. Thus, the façade was given a temple-like Greek Ionic portico, modeled on those from the Erechtheum on the Acropolis in Athens. Needless to say, Engel had never visited Greece—not many architects or artists had at that time—but, like so many, he was deeply influenced by such publications as Stuart and Revett's *The Antiquities of Athens* (1762-95), in which the illustration of the Thrasyllus Monument provided the greatest inspiration. By virtue of the university's proximity to the Great Church, ceremonial processions could be held with ease, and all under the watchful eyes of the newly-built Senate House on the opposite eastern side of the square, which was given a Roman architectural style deemed more suitable for the grand ducal seat of political power.

Within its interior the university was arranged around a central axis. The large vestibule, modeled upon a Greek atrium, was approached by an external flight of steps. This, in turn, was formed by two stories of loggia-like corridors, decorated by Doric columns and friezes. The vestibule led to the university's most "sacred" space, the ceremonial hall itself, where the most important ceremonies of Helsinki University continue to be held. Its shape is basically that of an amphitheater adorned with a circular portico of Corinthian columns, the central feature a bronze bust of Alexander I by the Russian sculptor and Rector of the St Petersburg Academy of Arts and Architecture, Ivan Martos. This was not the only such Russian link; it is clear that Engel was deeply influenced by designs for Moscow University produced by the Italian Domenico Gilardi in 1817 as part of a renovation of the original building designed and constructed by the architect M. Kazakov between 1786-93.

Initially, there were four faculties at Helsinki University: Theology, Law, the Arts and Medicine. In 1852 a chair in Education and Pedagogy was added, the first such faculty established in the Nordic world. Those who were awarded university degrees could be assured, as a decree of 1809 stipulated, that they would be considered for all administrative positions in preference to those without them. This approach, according to Professor Matti Klinge, suggests that Helsinki University was seen by the Czars (both Alexander I and Nicholas I) as a training ground for reformers. Its primary purpose, therefore, was not to train academics, but rather officeholders in the Russian imperial civil service, freed of some of the intellectual constraints of St Petersburg itself. This was an approach widespread in Central and Eastern Europe, especially in the German-speaking regions.

Since then Helsinki University has undergone many changes, not least the admission of women. Its greatest notoriety perhaps came in 1968, when, as in so many European cities of the period, Helsinki University experienced its own "revolution", albeit in a much milder form. On that occasion students occupied the Old Student Union Building, to much media attention, and with cheers from many a Beatle- playing thirteen-year-old who could most easily identify with rebellious feelings towards authority.

Today Helsinki University has a total of more than 35,000 students, while another 25,000 are enrolled in other similar academic institutions of higher learning in the capital, at all of which the tuition is virtually free. Other institutions relating to the arts include the Academy of Fine Arts, the Helsinki University of Art and Design and the Theater Academy. The city also has a Military Academy, which serves as a Finnish version of the British Sandhurst or American West Point. As for the sciences, no fewer than four polytechnics also serve the city.

Helsinki Polytechnic University

When, in 1848, the Helsinki Technical School opened to provide secondary education in practical studies relating to industry, few could have guessed that it would become one of the most important institutions of higher education for the sciences in Europe and the leading one of its kind in Finland. Renamed the Helsinki Polytechnic School in 1872, it was then re-established as the Polytechnic Institute in 1879, only to be named a university in 1908. Originally situated in a vast block in the old city center to the west of the Boulevard, the university was re-established in the 1950s at Otaniemi, a post-war western suburb, seven miles from Helsinki proper. Its principal architect was Alvar Aalto who had laid out the initial designs in 1949. Over the course of the following years new buildings enlarged the campus, but the transfer of some university departments was a slow process; only in 1972 did the final ones complete their move to Otaniemi.

Today, HUT, as it is more informally known, has a student body of 10,000 undergraduates as well as a further 2,500 post-graduates. Though largely a male preserve, women nonetheless form almost a quarter of the student body. Specific subjects of focus include computer science, engineering, chemistry and forestry, as well as architecture and landscape architecture. Environmental studies have assumed an ever-growing importance for HUT, as have investigations into the study of heat and cold. In particular, the Low Temperature Laboratory, at Otaniemi, founded in the 1970s has been a pioneer, not, as one might imagine, in climatological studies, but rather into its relevance for medical research into neuromagnetic brain functions. The faculty of Architecture, one of the oldest at the Polytechnic University, is the unquestioned leader in Finland. Its eleven professors are among the most illustrious in the country, and with such internationally acclaimed figures such as Aalto having been associated with it, it has always attracted a large body of foreign students.

Educated Nation

It is now the case that an overwhelming majority of the citizens of Helsinki have enjoyed the benefits of higher education in a country that now has nineteen universities. As a report from 1997 showed, of those aged between 25 and 34 no fewer than 81 percent either attended university courses or received another former of higher training, whether in the arts, sciences or another discipline. This is confirmation of the remark made by the historian and senator Yrjö Sakari Yrjö-Koskinen (1830-1903) that the history of Finland has been a progression in which the desire to be fully integrated into the mainstream of civilization has been a driving force, both privately and in terms of the nation. It is also true to say that it is no less an indication of a more simple drive to make the most out of what can be a difficult, even hostile, geographical milieu.

Students may generally live separate lives, but when April 30 comes around, that is *Vappuatto* (May Day Eve), an important day in the university calendar, they certainly come out of the woodwork. Then thousands of students gather by the statue of Havis Amanda at the northeastern end of the Esplanade, creating a sea of white student caps, one of which is placed upon the statue's crown. The following day, amid a further sea of detritus left over from the night before, a swaying body of students, still with their white caps, can be seen lolling about the streets of the capital, wearing off the drink from the night before. But it is on Finnish Independence Day, December 6, that students attain their noblest profile, for it is then, in a snow-bound Helsinki, that they parade, torches in hand, to Senate Square where they are welcomed by the city's mayor with a solemn speech worthy of the occasion.

Libraries

Of course, a central feature of Helsinki University is its library. From the beginning it required a suitable edifice, no less imposing than the university itself. But with safety issues paramount in what was then a city largely built of wood, it was designed as a separate building to be situated on Unioninkatu. From an aesthetic point of view, this grouping of buildings was a considerable advantage, allowing for a more or less contiguous sweep of palatial façades nine hundred feet long. Engel's plan (not his favorite among the several he provided but the one of which the Czar was most fond) was completed in 1833, drawing inspiration from the Baths of Diocletian for its internal design. Two large colonnaded reading rooms were placed on either

side of a rectangular central hall, and when completed, it could house over 100,000 volumes, a number vastly exceeded now after multistory annexes have been incorporated into the building in the last few years. Its façade also drew upon Roman inspiration, which pleased the Czar in whose name it was dedicated. Practical aspects such as heating were also thoughtfully considered: stoves were installed within the cellars, the heated air from which was carried by pipes into the rooms above, an arrangement also incorporated into the university building itself.

Tragically, most of the 40,000 books contained by the university in Turku before the great fire had been destroyed, and new books had to be acquired. But educated circles in the new capital, as well as in Russia itself, replenished the shelves with generous donations. More volumes also arrived from other northern European countries, including Britain, Germany, Sweden and Denmark. As a result, within twenty years of its reconstruction the university library contained almost 100,000 volumes.

Today the University Library is the National Library of Finland, containing a vast collection of Slavic books acquired by the right of legal deposit when Finland was a Grand Duchy, as well as important manuscripts. Other collections of note have also accrued over the years. After the fall of Viipuri, the Monrepos Manor Library, formerly owned by the Nicolay family, was transferred here.

The University Library, splendid as it is, is only one of many in Helsinki. Another serving the needs of a wider community is the Helsinki City Library, recently the beneficiary of a million-dollar donation from the Bill and Melinda Gates Foundation. Originally a private library, it was acquired by the city fathers in 1876. Today it is a network of 37 branches, two of which specialize in children's literature. All contain large foreign language collections, around twenty percent of the total stock, and works in at least sixty different languages are available to readers. Although half of the non-Finnish books are in Swedish, most of the others are in English, with those in other western European languages and Russian featuring prominently. Many works in Estonian and some in Saami (Lappish), languages related to Finnish, are also included.

Exploration and Philosophy

The world of scientific exploration should not be forgotten in any intellectual history of Helsinki. In the eighteenth century Finns like Pehr Kalm, an old pupil of Carl von Linné, the Swedish botanist and taxonomist, had traveled to America to carry out botanical investigations, while Petter Forsskål had been a member of a Danish expedition which explored Arabia.

In the later nineteenth century intrepid figures like the aristocratic Adolf Erik Nordenskiöld achieved international fame by his pioneer voyage, successfully maneuvering through the famed North-East Passage by Siberia. He is commemorated by a statue created by Johanna and Heikki Häiväoja at the southern end of Kaivopuisto Park in 1985. Others, like Sakari Pälsi, G. J. Ramstedt and Johannes Gabriel Granö crossed remote Mongolia independently, where, dressed as Mongol riders, they met up like Finnish versions of Dr. Livingstone and Stanley in 1909. Taking inspiration from the eighteenth-century expedition of Eric Laxman to Siberia, Pälsi also traveled into southeastern Siberia. Altogether he wrote over forty books and took up a long-term position at Finland's National Museum.

Scholars such as Anders Johan Sjögren took a keen interest in linguistic and philological studies. He had made St. Petersburg the center of Finno-Ugric studies in the nineteenth century with the assistance of Matthias Alexander Castrén, Helsinki University's first professor of Finnish. Sjögren is commemorated by a sculpture by Alpo Sailo from 1921, situated in a little park adjacent to the Parliament Building. Meanwhile, Jakob Grot, newly arrived in the capital in 1840, had the following year become the University's first professor of Russian literature and history. Other figures of note include the astronomer, Friedrich Wilhem August Argelander, and Georg August Wallin, professor of Oriental literature and an acclaimed geographer of the Arab world.

In the realms of philosophy, too, Helsinki achieved a profile of considerable significance. This was especially true of Georg Henrik von Wright (1916-2003), descendant of an ennobled Scottish immigrant family who had arrived in Finland by way of Sweden during the eighteenth century. First appointed docent in philosophy at the University of Helsinki in 1943, he became a professor there three years later. Then in 1948 he was invited to succeed Ludwig Wittgenstein as professor of philosophy at the University of Cambridge, arguably the most eminent position of its kind in the world. But von Wright preferred his native Finland and after a brief tenure returned there in 1951, once again taking the position of professor of philosophy. He also continued to lecture throughout the western world, becoming both a leading exponent of analytical and applied logic, as well as of the philosophy of science.

The Birth of Technological Research

It was in the realm of inventive technology, however, that Helsinki was to make its name. The rapid adoption of new inventions was conspicuous early on when the recently invented bicycle proved extremely popular in the 1890s. Almost 3,000 bicycles were registered for a population of at most 70,000, and that despite the fact that ice and snow covered the roads and paths of massive cobbles for almost half the year. Yet the old and the new could be blended together in quite curious ways, as the indefatigable Mrs. Tweedie commented in her *Through Finland in Carts* (1897):

Here we pass a Russian officer who is busy pedaling along dressed in his full uniform, with his sword hanging at his side. One might imagine a sword would be in the way on a cycle; but not at all, the Finlander or Russian officer is an adept in the art, and jumps off and on as though a sword were no more hindrance than the spurs which he always wears in his boots.

This was not the only innovation this well-traveled lady observed, for she also noted that electric light was everywhere and the telephone to be found in nearly every household, at least of those in her social circle. Yet as for carriage transport, the prospects were radically different, with only the hotel boasting of one large landau; but what a sight it was.

In this splendid vehicle, with two horses and a coachman bedecked like an English church beadle, we went for a drive, and so remarkable was the appearance of our equipage that every one turned round to look at us, and, as we afterwards learned, to wonder who we could possibly be, since we looked English, spoke German, and drove out with Finlanders!

By the late nineteenth century, a growing awareness of the importance of technological development for industry was beginning to take root in Helsinki. As a result, the Institute of Material Testing was founded in 1890, linked to the Helsinki Polytechnic Institute. The Institute undertook the scientific testing of various stones, both natural and artificial, a procedure of great help to the building trade, in which stone had come to be the primary material.

Then, in the midst of the First World War, the forestry industry also followed suit. Under private initiative, the Central Laboratory (Keskuslaboratorio) of Helsinki was established, in which the material structure and beneficial uses of wood could be explored. This was to prove a considerable growth industry, as increasing attention was devoted to its scientific and technological understanding. As a result, the Forest Building, designed by Jussi Paatela in 1939, was established in Unioninkatu as a research institute specifically dedicated to the academic study of forestry.

Nor did the food industry wish to be left behind, especially as war clouds were gathering and the importance of logistics to any military undertaking could not be overestimated. Valio, then as now an important cooperative dairy company, established the Chemical-Bacteriological Laboratory in 1916, focusing upon the study of food hygiene and how food preservation could be improved. During the following decade its director Artturi Ilmari Virtanen turned it into a major center of European biochemical research, rivaling similar institutions in Sweden, Germany and Switzerland where Virtanen had previously studied. The biochemist's research on vitamins and enzymes was so successful that in 1945 he was awarded the Nobel Prize for Chemistry.

During the course of the successive wars of the 1940s, significant scientific research continued to be carried out in a variety of areas. Spurred by the refugee housing crisis, the Technical Research Centre, based in Helsinki, devoted much of its energies to looking at new ways to improve and economize on building construction. New types of brick were produced, demanding less than half of the materials previously required to obtain the same mass.

Nokia

With its historical roots in a paper mill originally founded at Nokia in 1865, the modern telecommunications giant has given Finland a high technological profile throughout the world. In 1898 the company had acquired a factory for the production of galoshes and tires. Fourteen years later it began to produce industrial cables. But the modern Nokia only came into being in 1967 when the Nokia Group of Companies was formed. It was then that its subsidiary, The Finnish Cable Company, began to develop its electronics department, along with its two other sister subsidiaries. This cable company produced Finland's first computers in the late 1970s, leading to an extension into telecommunications that has made Nokia a household name. Today the company has long since moved from Nokia into its present headquarters at Espoo.

Modern Technology

With the arrival of the computer age, Helsinki has also taken its place on the cutting edge of innovation. Formerly a student in Helsinki, Linus Torvalds lives and works in Los Angeles, where he masterminded the creation of his LINUX computer software system, a rival to Microsoft Windows, and so it is the United States which has benefited most from his enterprise.

The growth of information technology has also been boosted by the establishment of a number of corporate bodies, for example, the Viikki Infocentre Korona, which opened in 1999. Here the architects Hannu Huttunen, Markku Erhold and Pentti Kareoja, using a design from 1996, have provided a computerized information center that includes a large science library as well as a branch of the City Library.

The world's ecological needs have also not been forgotten, for the Viikki Ecological Housing Project was established here, with its awareness of the need to make the most of urban needs in a rural setting. In what is really a nature preserve in the vicinity of threatened wetlands, the amenities of a national park with observation towers for watching the migration of birds has been coupled to a high-tech village. At this site the rural idyll of Thoreau can be said to meet with the sci-fi fantasies of an Isaac Asimov. Also at Viikki, the Helsinki

Science Park has been founded on the lands of the old manor house at Lato, with an emphasis on biological and other related research.

It is important finally to mention the Biomedicum of Helsinki, a scientific institute established at the Meilahti site of the University of Helsinki, where important medical research is carried out. This university medical campus, supported by both state and private funding, accommodates 300 students of medicine and dentistry, along with over a thousand post-graduate and post-doctoral researchers. Designed by the firm of Gullichsen-Vormala under the architectural direction of Timo Vormala and completed in January 2001, it is one of the newest academic establishments of biotechnology in Europe. Its important role in research, which seeks to increase human life expectancy, makes it one of the most significant institutes of its kind in the world.

CHAPTER TEN

Helsinki and Hospitality: Hotels, Drinking and Saunas

During the early days of its history under Swedish rule, it could hardly be said that Helsinki was blessed with restaurants or cafés of any quantity or note. This is hardly surprising for it remained a small town while Turku was still the Grand Duchy's capital. But by the second post-Napoleonic decade, when Helsinki had become the capital, the city did have six restaurants, not to mention four cafés. This, too, should come as no surprise, since coffee drinking came late to Finland in the course of the eighteenth century. Only in the nineteenth did it begin to permeate through all segments of society as the Grand Duchy's most popular beverage. Indeed, during the period of Swedish rule it was a prohibited commodity no less than four times and, when it was permitted, it was generally highly taxed, bringing in much needed revenues from a drink that was disapproved of as an unnecessary luxury.

By the middle years of the nineteenth century, though, coffee had become Finland's principal import. At least one kilogram per person was consumed in 1860 alone, a figure quadrupled by 1900. Not surprisingly, within less than a quarter of a century the number of eating houses and cafés had trebled to thirty-two. As for hotels, there were none until the late 1820s and though by 1850 there were at least eight, only two were really luxury establishments suitable for continental visitors: the Hotel de Bellevue and the Seurahuone.

The Seurahuone
In 1814, before the reconstruction of Helsinki as Finland's new capital had really got under way, Czar Alexander I's architect, Carl Ludwig Engel, had designed an Assembly Hall, situated by the market at the

entrance to the harbor with premises suitable to accommodate larger social and cultural occasions. But it was in 1827 that the city commenced the building of its first hotel. Known as the Seurahuone, it was completed in 1833 and continued to function as a hub of the city's social life until the early twentieth century. Today it serves as Helsinki's City Hall and remains for many maritime visitors their first impression of the capital in all its neoclassical glory. Its severe three-story façade decorated by pilasters, with one stuccoed story above the rusticated ground floor (two further ones were planned but never built) creates an elegant image. There, within its casino gentrified guests could enjoy its restaurant, hotel accommodation and, on festive occasions, its ballroom. This could accommodate more than 1,200 guests, a significant chunk of Helsinki's population. Finally built by public subscription, it opened in 1832.

Events held at the Seurahuone generally followed strict social conventions and access was restricted to a limited elite. The festive assemblies would commence at 6:30pm with refreshments, followed by music and dancing, for which each guest paid two and half roubles, after which further refreshments would be served. Then, at 11pm carriages would arrive to take the guests home.

As such a popular venue it is not surprising that it made considerable profits. Among its shareholders were many prominent citizens of Helsinki, but none was more significant than the principal investor, Czar Nicholas I himself, who had succeeded his brother Alexander. He had acquired one quarter of the entire shares, at a value of 20,000 roubles. Yet the hotel was set up not to fill the imperial coffers but rather to support charitable purposes; the profits went to the poor relief of Helsinki, an admirable gesture by the magnanimous, if autocratic, grand duke.

Advent of the Steamship

Of key importance in the development of the tourist trade in Helsinki was the advent of the steamship. In October 1833 Czar Nicholas I and the Czarina Alexandra made their first visit by steamship on the good ship *Izhora*, the first such vessel to arrive in Helsinki. The event was commemorated by the erection of an obelisk, the so-called Stone of the Czarina, at the Market Square.

When Henrik Borgström (see below) became a shareholder in the steamboat company that he established with other businessmen from Turku, Tallinn (Reval, as it was then known) and St. Petersburg, the steamship's future was secured, not least because of the anticipated influx of visitors to his spa. The inauguration of the Stockholm-Helsinki-Tallinn-St. Petersburg route was celebrated on May 19, 1837 with great pomp, including the firing of canon at Suomenlinna. At Ullanlinna fireworks were let off, while at Katajanokka torches were lit as the Band of the Finnish Guard provided a fanfare. This was the maiden voyage from Helsinki of the *Storfurst* (Grand Prince), the first steamship in regular service from its harbor. A throng of people came to witness the historic event. Made by the British firm of Fletcher and Faernell, the majestic vessel, 223 feet in length, had just arrived from London. As the writer Zacharius Topelius, at that time editor of the popular newspaper the *Helsingfors Tidningar*, put it when he visited the ship:

> *There are not many—and those who there are I consider pompous asses—who have not been deeply impressed, as they take their first cruise upon the steamship, with the intellectual power of its inventor and who, therefore, in the innermost recesses of their hearts, give all laud and honor to him who, as if by magic, laid bear the power of steam.*

The ship's first pleasure trip into the archipelago of Helsinki was enjoyed by 250 city notables and on the following Sunday it proceeded to Tallinn with 150 passengers.

Voyages such as these followed a regular timetable but were unhurried in their progress. For one thing, they traveled only in daylight, with the ships always berthing in harbor for the night. They also traveled very slowly; a voyage from Turku to Helsinki and down to St Petersburg, with lengthy stays, took two weeks. Nonetheless, they proved very popular and by 1846 another regular service to the city of Lübeck in Germany was added. This further increased the number of visitors to Helsinki, for whereas in 1839 2,268 travelers used these steam ships, by 1850 numbers had more than trebled to 7,000. Helsinki had become a popular destination.

The Ullanlinna Spa

In the early nineteenth century the Pump Room, situated on the shore below the Observatory at the end of Unioninkatu, with the adjacent Ullanlinna Spa, was one of the most important venues for social conviviality in Helsinki during the summer months. It was popular with the nobility and prosperous middle classes as well as with visiting Russian grandees and others from the continent, and most of its guests spent at least a month enjoying its amenities. By no means all of them stayed at the spa; well over half preferred to rent accommodation in the numerous private houses that let out rooms to visitors. Moreover, the lands parceled out around it by the shareholding company even before its completion provided sites on which suitably splendid accommodation for its grander guests was constructed. Many of these had come to Helsinki as an alternative to foreign travel since they were prohibited from leaving the Russian Empire for political reasons. Of these grand residences that of Princess Yusopoff, long since demolished, was without doubt the most magnificent and remained a byword for opulence for years to come.

The spa's leading light was Henrik Borgström (1799-1883), a native of Loviisa, a coastal town to the east of Helsinki, who had spent three years in Liverpool, where his business acumen had been sharpened. A statue of him by the sculptor Walter Runeberg can be seen at the city's Winter Gardens, near the Olympic Stadium. Since the Czar himself had taken out thirty 100-rouble shares, the financial foundations of the spa were solid. Nonetheless, the investors undertook no simple task. To begin with, the rocky site had to be flattened and a park developed where previously a hostile terrain had protruded into the gulf. All in all, it took nine years to complete, even if the baths themselves opened in June 1836, designed in the neoclassical style by no less a figure than Engel. Twelve suites of dressing rooms and bathrooms were provided for ladies and gentlemen respectively, with an especially grand one of three rooms built for the Czarina herself. The spa included a balcony from which it was intended that she could greet those in the surrounding gardens, but since she never graced the establishment with her presence the suite remained merely a symbol of imperial respect.

An installation for the provision of industrially manufactured mineral waters, both hot and cold, was ready for business the following year under the watchful eye of chemistry professor P. A. von Bonsdorff and Victor Hartwall. The city's medical committee supervised everything, and the company's success proved great and lasting. Even today Hartwall remains one of Helsinki's most important purveyors of beverages.

The spa included among its many amenities a grand ballroom and a bowling green. Its culinary delights also became famous in the hands of skilled German restaurateurs, *au fait* with the jaded palates of Russian aristocrats, if not those with French tastes. Yet the cuisine was not to everyone's taste. As Bulgarin informs us, the natives dined "without soup and with sweet sauces. The Swedes and Finns use sugar and jam in nearly all their dishes." Herring, often the principal dish for dinner, was very popular. The buffet table laden with vast quantities of that blend of white wines graciously known as Carolina found favor with all.

Social festivities were also not forgotten and the dances held twice a week, on Wednesday and Sunday evenings, were among the most fashionable in the capital. While the former were elegant and aristocratic occasions, the latter were distinctly more vulgar in tone. As one sneering visitor commented, Sundays provided the opportunity for "country cousins to charm second lieutenants and for shopkeepers to make triumphs."

It was unquestionably the Pump Room, though, designed by Engel and situated down by the shore below the Observatory, which was the central feature of the entire establishment. A pump installed some distance offshore ensured the saltiness of the waters, which ultimately flowed into the seemingly countless baths enjoyed by the guests, hot, cold or tepid as they preferred. The most lavish of these was the marble bath constructed for the use of the Russian imperial family, lined by a lush red carpet and far removed from the public on its upper floor. Today only the restaurant remains. Sadly, the Russian bombardment of 1944 totally devastated the spa itself.

The delights of the ladies who frequented the spa, especially those of mixed Swedish and Russian background, particularly pleased the visiting Bulgarin, but he was not alone in appreciating the enticements of Helsinki. As the French academician Xavier Marmier exclaimed in the late 1830s, the city itself had feminine allures: "It is as erect as an armed soldier, as flirtatious and ornamental as a young woman bent on conquest." The culinary and social charms of Helsinki may have been limited for foreign visitors, but among the grand guests to the capital gambling offered a much greater attraction and the stakes could be high. The Finnish-Swedish nobleman Anders Ramsay, no stranger to the gaming table, reported that:

> during a night of bad luck a Count Kushelev gambled away a thousand of his serfs, and that the general's wife Krishchanovskaya, who had a famous cook, staked him against a large sum, and lost the dear "soul" of hers...

With the abandonment of restrictions on foreign travel in Russia during the late 1840s, such colorful figures as these diminished in Helsinki, reduced further by improvements in rail travel to the four corners of Europe and especially more southern climes. Even so, by the late 1840s Helsinki had become a city of considerable sophistication.

As Ambassador Marmier wrote of his visit there in a book published in Paris in 1848, the salons of the aristocracy compared favorably with those in the French capital, with voices recounting in a variety of European languages anecdotes from the far corners of Europe, from Lapland to Paris itself.

Kappeli

By the 1850s Helsinki was well appointed with hotels and hostelries for the discerning tourist. These included the more luxurious Society House at the Market Square, which we have already come across, and Kleineh's Hotel. Designed by Gransted as a residence for the prosperous merchant, Henrik Jakob Govinius, it is situated in a house at Pohjoisesplanadi 9. With its rounded corner and pedimented façade, it is still a handsome building, although it has not functioned as a hotel since the 1930s. Then there were the somewhat more modest Hotel de Russie in Mariankatu and the Hotel de Freden, established in the Wickman House in Helenankatu. Otherwise, there were various bed and breakfast establishments.

Altogether more sophisticated was the café and restaurant Kappeli, first built in 1837 and situated towards the harbor end of the Esplanade. It was, and remains, one of the most important attractions in Helsinki, even if it has undergone period reconstruction. The original structure lasted some thirty years, though it gave way in 1867 to a far grander edifice, adorned in 1887 by an adjacent bandstand. Especially during the luminous white nights of summer, the world of Bohemia and high society could meet in a convivial, slightly risqué atmosphere, more reminiscent of Paris than anything known in Finland at that time. Appropriately, the sculptor Walter Runeberg, son of the famous poet, provided the decorations for the pediment, the figure of an alluring woman.

But Kappeli was not the first eatery to be situated on that spot. A kiosk, in the form of a rotunda and buttressed by wooden benches, had been erected a few years before, selling lemonade and other beverages to a passing clientele. Humble as it appeared, though, its patrons were largely drawn from the higher echelons of Helsinki society. Yet as the century progressed, these patricians ceased to frequent the Esplanade's avenues. For despite the appearance of the grand new Kappeli, which replaced the kiosk, soldiers and workingmen's families had now also begun to frequent the café in increasingly large numbers, also wishing to enjoy their brief leisure under its leafy boughs. With its social tone lowered beyond repair, the magisterial families of Helsinki then looked elsewhere.

The visiting Mrs. Tweedie still found it charming in the 1890s, even if she knew married men frequented it when their wives and family were away during the summer in the countryside. She wrote:

The Kapellet is a delightful restaurant in the chief street of Helsingfors, standing among trees, under which many seats and tables are placed, and where an excellent military band plays during meal times. Strange meal times they are too, for, after early coffee and roll, every one breakfasts between ten and twelve on meats with beer or wine, not an egg and fish breakfast such as we have, but a regular solid meal. Finlanders in towns dine from two to four, and sit down to supper between eight and ten, so that they have three solid meat meals a day—probably a necessity in such a climate—and drink wines and spirits at each of these functions, which so closely resemble one another that the stranger would have difficulty in knowing which was supper and which was breakfast.

For those who frequented its salons in the evening hours, it was a palace of glittering lights and nocturnal trysts, a symbol of Helsinki's seductive charms. This was certainly the case for the character Antti Ljungberg in *To Helsinki*, a novel by Juhani Aho. Here, in naturalistic style, this sometime journalist describes the naive and provincial student Antti's exposure to the temptations of the capital embodied in Kappeli. The brilliance of the electric lights, the bustle of the guests and, of course, the drink knock this freshman only just arrived at Helsinki University off balance:

In a daze, as if swept down a foaming waterfall, Antti found himself seated for a moment on a soft sofa in a green room with a many-splendored cut-glass chandelier, paintings on the walls and a huge mirror. It was as if he'd fallen into a quietly hissing pool, but not a restful one, a frothing whirlpool that a moment later would hurl him down another waterfall, still lower, with no end in sight. He felt he was being whirled

round and round, with the blood going to his head and flushing all sense
of direction from his eyes. For a moment Antti had no idea where he had
come from and where he was going.

Today it is still one of Helsinki's most popular venues, with an extremely lively outdoor terrace open in summer, to which locals and visitors throng. There is also that long established café favored by older Helsinki residents, Café Ekberg, situated on the Boulevard, with its early twentieth-century ambiance of urban elegance.

Hotel Kämp and Other Hostelries

With the construction of the Grönqvist House in 1882, the Hotel Kämp in 1887, and then the Catani House at Pohjoisesplandi 31 in 1890 (a five-story block of offices and flats commissioned by the confectionery magnate Florio Catani), all on the North Esplanade, the architect Theodor Höijer provided the city with a central European assemblage of grandly conceived buildings inspired by Eclecticism. Of these the Hotel Kämp was, in a sense, the centerpiece. Finally Helsinki could boast of a luxury standard hotel to vie with the best in continental Europe. The days when the Society House was the only important hotel were now long past, for the Kämp could offer over 75 rooms and suites, many with views over the Esplanade. As for its French-inspired restaurant, it was the most elegant in town, with a retinue of staff imported from the imperial kitchens of St. Petersburg as well as from the other major European culinary capitals. There was

also a grand two-storied ballroom in which to while away the early morning hours. An extra story was added by Lars Sonck in 1914, but the weakness of its foundations rendered the structure perilous over the years and in 1966 it was demolished.

Who would have believed when it closed its doors in 1965, as the pianist played Sibelius' beloved aria, "I shall go back to Kämp", shortly thereafter to be torn down, that it would rise phoenix-like from the ashes? It reappeared first as the head office of a bank, the Kansallis-Osake-Pankki, which replaced the building in 1969 with a structure at least outwardly resembling the old hotel. Then, during the 1990s, it re-emerged after a thorough rebuilding as Helsinki's leading world-class hotel. It now caters for the most demanding of international travelers as well as businessmen keen to impress their guests with a taste of the nineteenth century as filtered through late twentieth-century nostalgia.

After the completion of the central railway station, two new hotels were constructed in its vicinity, Hotel Fennia and the new Society House. The former complements the Ateneum art gallery opposite in architectural terms, while the embellishment of its exterior with the names of some of Europe's most important cities suggests from which corners of the continent its guests were drawn. The latter, built in a National Romantic style with the ubiquitous rough-hewn granite blocks, blends in seamlessly with its similarly clad neighbors, the railway station and National Theater .

New hotels sprang up in the 1950s, partly to cope with the crowds of visitors expected for the Summer Olympics of 1952. But numbers proved disappointing for tourism, with campsites such as that on nearby Lauttasaari, which had expected 6,000 visitors, receiving only 483. Nonetheless in that year the Palace Hotel opened, providing international amenities in the latest modernist style. Its interior, designed by Olli Borg, Olavi Hänninen and Antti Nurmesniemi made it a prototype for a display of Finnish design. It still functions today, despite the fact that its formerly glittering image of modernity has become tarnished by the rebirth of the Hotel Kämp.

Restaurants

Mika Waltari, known outside Finland for his much-translated novel *The Egyptian*, memorably celebrated the culinary tradition of 1960s

Finland. Gone now are the modest eateries "where the beefsteak was served with many onions, and the semolina pudding brought on in portions that might have stilled a giant's hunger," as Topelius had put it in the nineteenth century, but new ones have certainly sprung up in their place. Yet a century ago, Finnish fashions could raise eyebrows among more urbane travelers. As Mrs. Tweedie noted with a certain scornful disdain, the fashions of the city left something to be desired:

Flannel shirts and top hats are, to an English mind, incongruities; but in Suomi *fashion smiles approvingly on such an extraordinary combination... therefore, mashers strolled about attired in very bright-colored flannel shirts, turned down flannel collars, trimmed with little bows of silken cord with tassels to fasten them at the neck, and orthodox tall hats.*

British matrons were, of course, not the only visitors to Helsinki restaurants at the turn of the twentieth century. Shortly afterwards Lenin came to the capital more than once and stayed there in 1917, at which time he was a *stammgast* at the nearby Workers' Union at Säästöpankinranta near Kaisaniementori. This building, in the National Romantic style, was shortly to lose its tower during the Finnish civil war in 1918, when German troops assisting the Whites, fired upon it. It was later rebuilt and today the pub at the bottom, where Lenin's table can be seen, still provides locals with vast quantities of beer.

Restaurants enjoyed a revival during the early decades of the twentieth century. During the First World War the Kulosaari Casino opened at Hopeasalmenpolku, designed by Armas Lindgren. During the inter-war period, despite the introduction of Prohibition, a spate of other establishments followed suit, albeit officially dry. Even then, it seems, Helsinki's love affair with drink was flourishing. Presenting a medical prescription at any chemist gave access in 1932 to eight different champagnes along with 33 other types of wines, not to mention ten whisky varieties.

The restaurant-cum-café at the Kunsthalle, designed by Jarl Eklund and Hilding Ekelund in the 1920s, was the first artists' café in the Finnish capital and still carries on today. Another restaurant, established in 1932 and frequented by artists, musicians, dancers and literary figures as much today as then, is Elite, situated at Eteläinen Hesperiankatu 22 and decorated in a splendid *art deco* style worthy of a transatlantic steamer of the period. Another, even older, is Kosmos in the heart of Helsinki at Kalevankatu 3. It was founded in 1924 by Yrjö Teodor Lindfors and is still owned by his daughter today. Here among wooden booths in an often smoke-filled room, the Bohemians of the city gather for dinner or drinks in what is a veritable time warp from pre-war days. There is also a very interesting collection of pictures, including works by artists, such as Juhani Harri, Alvar Gullichsen and Martti Aiha. Unfortunately, the orchestral music that regaled guests in the 1930s is no longer performed and a minor remodeling of the restaurant occurred in 1993. Nonetheless, an authentic atmosphere of the inter-war years lives on in both these establishments, a corrective to mainstream European cafés where tourism or American coffee culture has swamped most in their wake.

One of the most fashionable restaurants of the late 1930s was the Savoy at Eteläesplanadi 14, designed by Alvar Aalto in his first public commission in Helsinki. Situated on the top of the Ahlström Building, it still accommodates up to 100 guests. When its roof terrace, popular with visitors to the adjacent Savoy Theater, is open during the summer months, a further 150 guests can be received.

Even during the wars of the 1940s, restaurants, hotels and other commercial establishments remained open, even if entertainment and dancing were now temporarily forbidden. Later, during the post-war years, new hotels began to grace the skyline of Helsinki. During the 1950s, for example, Hotel Vaakuna was built to the west of the railway station and its square was built in a functionalist style that won the praise of many modernists of the day, even if now it has fallen somewhat out of fashion.

The most innovative of Helsinki's modern restaurants, at least in architectural terms, is the two-story one built at the long-established Linnanmäki Amusement Park in 1999. Since the hamburger has become a primary ingredient in the modern Finnish diet, not least in the Linnanmäki Amusement Park, the foundation that runs the Park felt it only appropriate that the restaurant honor the dish in the very architecture of the building. To this end, the firm of the architect

Mauri Mäki-Marttunen provided designs for a circular building incorporating an open-plan restaurant area on its first floor, surmounted by a majestic convex wooden dome-type, the ribs of which supported the load while reducing the volume of materials required. The roof of the restaurant is of spherical shape, its laminated wooden dome forming a crisscrossing network of protruding arches and recessed rings, held in place by metal clips and incorporating a layer of mineral wool.

Another idiosyncratic watering hole worth mentioning is Kaurismäki's Café Moskva in Eerikinkatu. Designed as a copy of an old Soviet hard currency bar, its interior decoration harks back to the early post-war years, though few of its customers remember the hardships of those times, when food rationing was strictly regulated and coffee, Finland's favorite drink, was a luxury, the rationing of which was only abolished in 1954. It set the trend by which restaurants and cafés were given amusing names, often with a hint of irony

Yet one restaurant that continues in the old classical style is Sundman's, among Finland's finest. Established in the old Sundman House, built in 1817 on the waterfront at Eteläranta 16 for Captain G. W. Sundman by Carl Ludwig Engel, it offers some of the most beautiful dining rooms of the capital as well as its most splendid cuisine, a melange of French and Finnish dishes.

Car Ferries

One important aspect of the burgeoning modern tourist industry has been the improvement in transport to and from Finland, from the south and west. In 1959 the first car ferry started operation, utilizing a normal passenger ferry converted for that purpose, between Maarianhamina, the capital of the Finnish Åland Islands, and Stockholm. Thirteen years later, the *Aallotar* started to ply the route between Helsinki and Stockholm. By now at least some 170,000 people were arriving annually in Helsinki by sea alone. Within another decade this number had grown to 635,000; yet no end of the growth in sea travel was in sight. In 1998 over 4,300,000 arrived in the Finnish capital, many of these not only from Sweden and Germany, but Estonia as well, cut off from Finland before the break-up of the Soviet Union.

Popular Entertainment

The greatest popular entertainment has always been the quest for romance, and in this Helsinki was no exception. The most prominent outdoor venue for coquetry and romantic encounters was, and remains, the Esplanadi. As the Finnish playwright R. Frenckell put it in his comedy of manners, *Peter and Paul* (1846):

> *Both cat and the dog on promenade*
> *Swagger on down our Esplanade*
> *Whilst proud mothers sit in contentment and bliss*
> *Their daughters cast glances, which no man could miss.*

By the middle of the nineteenth century Helsinki was a city among the most social and cosmopolitan of northern Europe. In 1850, for example, twenty private balls were held in the capital. There were also numerous dramatic productions put on by traveling troupes, not to mention the public balls financed by lottery (though by invitation only) and four public concerts. Among these the higher officers of the Russian military stationed in or near Helsinki often took a prominent part. The mansion of the governor general at Eteläesplanadi 6 was the venue at which all of Helsinki high society made an appearance, whether Swedish, Finnish or Russian in tongue. The ball held there on August 9, 1885, in honor of the visit of Czar Alexander can perhaps be seen as the greatest social occasion at which all segments of the Finnish upper classes were brought together, before political issues came to trouble Finnish-Russian relations at this level.

That said, the capital's social life was characterized by a very subtle and graduated scale of social status and customs corresponding to that found elsewhere in continental Europe. As Topelius put it in 1885 in "Notes on a Vanished Helsinki" (Antäckningar om det Helsingfors gått): "the limited number of people who formed the pinnacle of society, the military, the lower civil servants, the university, burghers and craftsmen, each social segment had their own social gatherings, which distinguished them most markedly from the working classes who had none, only the pub as a place of recourse."

Red Light District and Night Life

While romance was an ideal almost all aspired to, some made do with less exalted experiences: visits to brothels. During the second half of the nineteenth century the red light district of Helsinki was situated around Iso Roobertinkatu, in whose vicinity gay venues were later to blossom. It has been calculated that 638 prostitutes arrived from Sweden alone during the years 1867-1900. One brothel, catering for students, was at the Green Villa adjacent to what is now the Villa Eläintarha at Eläintarhatie 14 in Töölönranta Park. This latter is today a house of artists, where visiting performers, writers and others can stay at subsidized rates while in Helsinki. Topelius, it is said, was a frequent visitor to this institution. Another was at Iso Robertinkatu 20-22, and had just under a dozen girls between 1860 and 1885. Here, as in other brothels, the red stained-glass windows were an advertisement for the trade plied within, a trade that grew over the following three-quarters of a century. Whereas in 1850 there were altogether fewer than 200 prostitutes in Helsinki, by the 1930s their number had quintupled to over 1,200, only to return in our own time to about 200, many of these from the ex-Soviet Bloc countries of Eastern Europe.

The seamier side of Helsinki notwithstanding, a fashionable nightlife also continued in the capital. For Kjell Westö, the interior world of the Café Adlon, tucked into the building housing the Helsinki Stock Exchange, assumed iconic dimensions as a terrestrial reflection in shocking dimensions of the wider world. He wrote in *Kites over Helsinki* "of the awesome shining globe, which each evening descended over the dance floor at Adlon like a symbol of the earth itself." Unfortunately, today it is a venue reserved for private functions, generally rented for the evening by prosperous companies for the entertainment of their employees and guests. But other nightspots still abound.

Alcohol

The Finnish government has for many decades wanted to restrict, rather than encourage, the consumption of alcohol. Many families in the nineteenth century suffered the ill effects of an addiction to it, and many reprobate acts were committed under its influence. Indeed, in all the Nordic countries, it was the *sine qua non* of most violent crime, both domestic and public, especially murder. Under the growing influence and political importance of evangelical movements with a strong temperance tradition, drinking habits were subjected to increased public scrutiny, and in 1906 an initiative was launched to prohibit its consumption. This movement gathered force in the post-independence period, as in many other parts of the western world, when a tidal wave of temperance swept through Finland. Strict prohibition was duly introduced in 1919.

Yet, as in the United States, prohibition from 1919 to 1932 proved worse than what it purported to remedy, encouraging a plethora of criminal activities relating to alcohol distribution and consumption. It was also profoundly unsuccessful. Loopholes were many; for one thing, prescriptions for alcoholic beverages could be filled at local chemists, later with bottles supplied by ALKO, the State Alcohol Company, founded in 1932 and which still controls the supply of wines and spirits today. Indeed, from 1924 a range of fine bottles was to be had, individually or by the case, with no fewer than 129 different labels on sale, including ten of sparkling wine and nine of whisky. By 1932 thirty different labels of brandy were on sale at these chemists, along with 41 varieties of fortified wines. For those with large enough purses, Château Haut-Brion (1924) and Château D'Yquem (1925) were available, and all on medical prescription.

As a result, the law was repealed in 1932. But it was still three and half decades later that some rural areas finally permitted the production and sale of alcoholic beverages. It was the 1970s, however, which witnessed a mushrooming of so-called 'drinking restaurants', once the sale of medium-strength beer was legalized in 1969. Even today the centralized national monopoly ALKO still provides the only outlet in Helsinki, indeed in all of Finland, for alcohol, even if beers of low alcoholic content can be bought in food shops. Spirits may today be outrageously expensive in western European terms, but wines are very reasonably priced so as to woo drinkers off beverages with stronger alcoholic content. In weekly consumption, Finns drink less than their American or British equivalents; yet they do their drinking in the course of two evenings—Friday and Saturday—rather than in smaller quantities throughout the week!

Contemporary Cafés

The Tamminiemi Café, for years now under the splendid management of a delightful Polish lady, is an establishment that reigns supreme in Helsinki as the queen of cafés. Here, in a charming old villa from the old Meilahti Estate, beautifully furnished with period pieces and with a flower-filled garden, tea is served constantly from a samovar with the most delicious of traditional cakes—all to the accompaniment of music by Chopin. Then there is Café Engel, opposite the Great Church of St. Nicholas, where all long-term visitors to Helsinki seem to end up, including Doris Lessing and other literary notables.

Café Socis, in a gray granite building designed by Armas Lindgren, in 1913, would formerly have figured proudly in this list. But long gone are the days when the great, the good and the terrible (Hitler, it is said, visited the café during the Second World War), filled its *art nouveau* salons as tangos played in the background. Even as late as the 1980s under the ownership of Elanto its philosophy of opening its establishments to as wide a public as possible gave it a richly varied clientele. During the day it was filled with elderly ladies and their grandchildren, in the evening with courting couples, and late at night with writers, musicians and others poring over books. Then, in the wee hours of the morning, tarts, insomniacs and other denizens of the dark hours made their appearance. Now all that is gone as it caters for sedate middle-aged tourists in the usual hours.

But all is not lost. Kappeli still functions, and new cafés spring up throughout the city. Most disappear not long afterwards but some continue, like chameleons undergoing a variety of outward changes as fashions dictate. For those interested in such aspects of life today, the Hotel and Restaurant Museum in the Kaapeli Factory at Tallberginkatu 1G provides an enduring explanation of a bygone period of Helsinki hospitality.

Saunas

The Russian chronicler Nestor (c. 1056-1113), a native of Kiev, wrote in 1112 of the sauna as a central feature of life in the forested regions of the north, and its usage in Finland was recorded not long after. Today, of course, it is viewed in the world at large as a primarily Finnish institution. The first known saunas in Helsinki were the two installed in the royal demesne at Vantaa during the course of the later sixteenth century. The nineteenth century witnessed the appearance of many more as the city grew in size, and by the mid-nineteenth century Marienbad in Kruununhaka had become the most famous sauna in Helsinki, one of several of its kind constructed in stone rather than wood. Yet even in Helsinki the sauna remained an essentially rural institution, as expressed by the great Finnish painter Akseli Gallen-Kallela in his painting *At the Sauna* (1889), displayed at the Ateneum. As the author I. M. Edelswärd put it:

> *The sauna is a ritual, in which a person may participate in various social transformations, cleansing being just one aspect of its total meaning... A critical symbolic quality of the sauna is liminality... Liminality refers to the threshold, the interstitial period between two states.*

Gallen-Kallela wrote in his autobiography of the sauna's sanctity, commingled with a certain sexual ambiguity:

> *It was still a common custom also in Satakunta in those days, for the male and female hands of even so-called gentlemen's farms to bathe together. When I was a brat I once took part in such a sauna and my eye chanced to fall on a fat, naked, red-headed servant girl who in all her splendor was descending the sauna platform. In my innocent indiscretion, I made an impertinent and indecent remark. Bailiff Tuomas who was in the bath rose from his bench and said sternly, "You... I'll show you!" I sneaked away ashamed from the sauna, and from that moment on I was awakened to respect the holiness of the sauna and nudity.*

For Aleksis Kivi, one of Finland's first great writers, the sauna was also a place of immense importance, a refuge from severe weather as well as the stresses of life. This is especially true in his groundbreaking novel, *Seven Brothers*, where some of the primary events take place in the sauna. It is a place of purification and regeneration, intimacy and meditation. When this fictional sauna burns to the ground through a series of misfortunes, it bodes disaster for all; its rebuilding, however, signals rebirth and when it is completed, it is as if a metaphysical phoenix has risen from the ashes.

During the Second World War, while Risto Ryti was president, a sauna installed at the Villa Kallio at Tamminiemi became a regular meeting venue for the president and his colleagues from the Bank of Finland. Later, at the beginning of President Kekkonen's term, a new sauna was erected in the gardens, to which in 1969 an indoor swimming pool was added. A veritable sports complex was thus installed at the Villa Kallio at a time when few presidential palaces in the world were equipped with such amenities. Politicians, scientists, artists and men of letters all participated in this Finnish national institution at a time when saunas were only just becoming popular in five-star hotels.

While Helsinki's twentieth-century saunas could not compete for authenticity with the earlier models, those from the 1920s like the Harjutorin Sauna (1928) in Helsinginkatu in Kallio come as close as one could hope in an urban area. This sauna functions much as it always did, fueled by wood-burning stoves, and even leech-like cupping for the curative sucking of blood of guests is still on offer for a modest price, along with massage and the more "new age" aromatherapy. All swimming pools also provide saunas, such as that at Helsinginkatu, but it is the great swimming complex at Yrjönkatu 21b that offers the greatest variety, including a large and small swimming pool where nude bathing for men and women is *de rigueur* on alternate days in autumn, winter and spring. Built in 1928, it was originally to be located at Kaivopuisto Park, near the old Ullanlinna Spa. But in the end, a more central situation was chosen, where it was constructed in the classical style of the period, with two-story colonnades along which private rest-cum-changing rooms are positioned around the large swimming basin. In the summer, it shuts down, its services replaced by the sauna and swimming pool connected to the Olympic stadium: not as attractive, to be sure, but open-air and a welcome experience on a warm and sunny day.

As for private domestic saunas in Helsinki, they number tens of thousands, tucked away in garden corners, cellars and lofts, and continue to confirm by their very presence that Finland is still the land of the sauna.

CHAPTER ELEVEN

Helsinki and the Visual Arts: Museums, Galleries and Artists

The history of Helsinki's museums is in many ways the history of artistic philanthropy, or the *largesse* of private patrons of the arts and the voluntary work they have contributed. Some of the first of such benefactors were the nineteenth-century grandees Baron Carl Johan Walleen, Otto Wilhelm Klinckowström, and Henrik Borgström, who assisted the Finnish Art Society, founded in 1846, when no public art collection existed in the country. The Society's own collection was first established for the benefit of the students who attended its Drawing School, but it was shown to members of the Society and other audiences. In 1868 it acquired official status and later formed the core of the collection in the Finnish National Gallery itself. By the 1880s Czar Alexander III, fully aware of the implications of such a gesture, himself contributed to the Society.

The Russian Czars, especially Alexander I, played an important role as benefactors of the arts and architecture throughout the nineteenth century. In the second half of that century locally funded public benefactions also played a significant part, with equally clear-sighted political overtones. It was not by chance that the first official public sculpture to be erected in Helsinki was that to the poet Johan Ludvig Runeberg, unveiled in May 1885 in the heart of the Esplanade park at a time when many felt that Finnish national identity needed to be reinforced.

It was also about this time and in the following decades that the most important Finnish national museums and other major public buildings devoted to the arts came to be built. Kluuvi, near the railway station, became the seat of some of Finland's most famous cultural institutions; of similar vintage are the Ateneum art gallery and the

National Theater, which opened in 1902. For the Russian educated classes in Helsinki, however, it was the Alexander Theater on the Boulevard, with its regular productions in Russian, that was the principal social, artistic and intellectual focal point.

Cygnaeus Gallery

A prominent artistic patron was Fredrik Cygnaeus (1807-81), who was also important in the Finnish Art Society, buying art and helping in the private support of artists, especially as the Society's president from 1863 to 1878. He had intended to donate his own collection to the Society, but disagreeing with plans to place both the fine arts and crafts together at the Ateneum, he withdrew his donation.

Cygnaeus' interests were not restricted to the visual arts, but included music, literature and theater. The Cygnaeus Gallery was formed around the collection he bequeathed to the Finnish nation, the gallery opening in 1882, one year after his death. It is situated at Kalliolinnantie 8 in a two-story yellow-painted wooden villa designed by the German architect J. W. Mieritz, and is the oldest art gallery in Helsinki. Today its principal collection is of Finnish artists of the nineteenth century, but temporary exhibitions are also held here along with the occasional concert. The painter Albert Edelfelt made the first donation with his famous work *The Burnt Village* (Poltettu kylä; Den brända byn) in 1879. This act helped fulfill Cygnaeus' ambition to form a complete collection of Finnish art that would continue to grow even after his death.

Ateneum

The literary historian Carl Gustaf Estlander (1834-1910) was also a key figure in the cultural life of Finland and first conceived of building the Ateneum, which he envisioned as "a house of the arts", in which painting, sculpture and crafts would flourish together under one roof. Herman Frithiof Antell (1847-93) was another great patron of the arts who was instrumental in forming the core of the Ateneum's future collection. His enormous and crucial donation included not only painting and sculptures, but old coins, archaeological objects, textiles and a wide range of other artifacts.

One half of the donation went to the Ateneum, the other formed the nucleus of the National Museum.

Helsinki's most important art gallery is the rightly famous Ateneum, which opened in 1888, named after Pallas Athene, the goddess of wisdom in ancient Greece. Designed by the architect Theodor Höijer, it originally accommodated two separate collections and two schools. With its façade adorned by the busts of Phidias, Bramante and Raphael, the glories of the classical European traditions of art were heralded within. Yet only in 1991 did it officially become Finland's National Gallery of Art, consisting of three museums: the Ateneum, the Sinebrychoff, and Kiasma. Among the Ateneum's most important works is Akseli Gallen-Kallela's *Aino Triptych* (1891), a supreme example of a work influenced by the imagery of the epic *Kalevala*. Also to be seen is Maria Wiik's evocative work *Out in the World* (1889), painted while the artist was at the artistic colony of St. Ives in Cornwall. Of no less importance is Hugo Simberg's *Wounded Angel* (1903), in which war, spirituality and good and evil can be seen to merge enigmatically into an allegory of Finland's troubled political position with regards to a centralizing Russia at that time. For an art historian like Marjatta Levanto, however, the wounded angel is no political symbol, but firmly rooted in the physical milieu in which it has been painted.

The National Museum and Sinebrychoff Museum

If the Ateneum was eclectically inspired and continentally European in style, Eliel Saarinen, Herman Gesellius and Armas Lindgren chose to build the National Museum (1906) in National Romantic vein, symbolically matching its contents, much of which had been donated by Antell. Like the Pohjola Insurance Company (designed by the same triumvirate), the entrance to this solid gray edifice is adorned by a richly carved sculpture of a bear guarding its portals. Situated at Mannerheimintie 34, a vast array of objects, archeological and folkloric, from Finland's ancient past to the present is on show. These focus upon a plethora of aspects relating to the country's culture, society and moral values.

Yet another important museum foundation, in Helsinki, was that bequeathed by Paul and Fanny Sinebrychoff of the brewing family, who in 1921 left their large collection of mainly foreign masters to the Finnish nation under the auspices of the Finnish Art Society. The paintings of the great eighteenth-century Swedish portrait artist Alexander Roslin are among the most evocative in the collection. It was ultimately established in 1980 in a mansion at Bulevardi 40. The building, which now accommodates permanent and temporary collections, was built in 1842 to the designs of Jean Wik for Nikolai Sinebrychoff. The smaller house behind was an earlier family home, actually moved to this site from the fortress of Suomenlinna in 1823; today it houses offices.

Sinebrychoff's significance was as the main collector in the Nordic countries of Swedish portraits in general and miniatures in particular. After his wife Fanny's death, the house was opened to the public in 1921. It closed during the Second World War, but reopened in 1960. It has been thoroughly renovated recently and reopened in 2003, with the interiors once again decorated and hung as they were in Sinebrychoff's time. The collection features portraits by Roslin and David Krafft, both father and son, as well as Dutch and Flemish portraits. The acquisition of many of these works was facilitated by two other important art world figures of the time, the Polish-born art dealer Henryk Bukowski, whose name still features in the company names of auction houses in Helsinki and Stockholm, and the art historian Osvald Sirén, both of whom lived in the Swedish capital.

Sinebrychoff's wife, who had been an actress before their marriage in 1883, also took an avid interest in collecting porcelain, silver and bronze *objets d'art*. As she recounted to the Finnish newspaper *Suomen Kuvalehti*, in 1921, the year of her death, after which the collection was bequeathed to the state: "I do not generally become vexed or out of sorts. In fact, the only thing that may do this is the long list we have kept over the years of all the works we desired but which fell into the hands of others."

The Kunsthalle

One new venue for art exhibitions that opened shortly before the Great Depression erupted in Finland was the Kunsthalle Helsinki, designed by Jarl Eklund and Hilding Ekelund in the classicizing style of the 1920s and completed in 1928. Situated at Nervanderinkatu 3, it contains three large galleries full of contemporary art in its numerous temporary exhibitions. It was established with the help of the artists' unions to provide an alternative venue to the Ateneum for a wide range of cultural exhibits. Although it has no permanent collection, these exhibitions include a wide range of works focusing upon design, the visual arts and architecture from both Finland and abroad. It also contains one of the oldest artists' restaurants in Helsinki.

Finnish-Russian Cultural Links

Fin-de-siècle Helsinki had close cultural links not only with Scandinavia, in particular Sweden, but also central Europe, especially Berlin and, of course, Paris. Yet the political problems confronting Finland because of its difficult relationship with Russia should not mask the close relations it also enjoyed with the imperial capital. The rise of a keen interest by Finnish patrons and local government officials in aspects of Finnish cultural history in the late nineteenth and early twentieth century did not express a complete polarization of relations between native Finns and representatives of Russian cultural expression. For despite growing antagonism between Russia and Finland in the 1890s because of the "Russification" of the Grand Duchy, many friendly cultural contacts between the two nations continued unabated. In 1898, for instance, the great Russian impresario Sergei Diaghilev traveled to Finland, seeking to foster contacts between Finnish avant-garde artists and his own World of Art Movement (Mir Iskusstva). There he visited the Finnish Artists' Exhibition, accompanied by the Russian writer Dimitry Filosofov and one of Russia's greatest stage designers, the painter Leo Bakst. It was perhaps Bakst who had originally introduced Diaghilev to the Finnish National Romantic artist Albert Edelfelt in Paris in 1895, for Bakst had been a student there at Edelfelt's studio in the years 1893-6.

Such a relationship expressed Diaghilev's long-latent desire to achieve an artistic *rapprochement* with the west of Europe. Indeed, in the early years of the decade he had already exclaimed amid his many travels to European cultural centers: "I want to nurture Russian painting, clean it up and, most importantly, present it to the West, elevate it in the West." And the exchange of artistic ideas and values in the opposite direction was also of interest to him; not only did he write favorably about Finnish art in the first issue of a journal published by the World of Art Movement, but he also put on an exhibition of Nordic art in St. Petersburg in the autumn of 1897. For Diaghilev Finnish art was distinctive, showing limited connections with both Russian and Scandinavian art; it possessed its own identity, based upon its unique cultural past, infused with a rich oral, epic tradition.

Diaghilev was especially keen on the works of Albert Edelfelt because of their successful application of French stylistic methods to northern themes. He was also aware that Edelfelt had made quite a splash in the Parisian art world of 1880 and in 1881 had became a member of the Imperial Academy of Arts and Architecture in St. Petersburg. He also took an interest in the works of Gallen-Kallela, in which the aesthetic values of Symbolism merged with the National Romantic after an initially naturalistic period. When Diaghilev organized a specifically Russian-Finnish exhibition of painting in St. Petersburg in January 1898, Gallen-Kallela's *The Defence of the Sampo* (1896) and *Lemminkäinen's Mother* (1897) provided the focus, causing a sensation because of their morbid Karelian themes taken from the Finnish epic *Kalevala*. The International Exhibition organized by Diaghilev in St. Petersburg in January the following year exhibited further works by Edelfelt and Gallen-Kallela and also Magnus Enckell, a leading figure of the so-called "Group of Seven", and Eero Järnefelt, a landscapist who had himself studied in St. Petersburg and Paris, where he was deeply influenced by the Barbizon School of Art. After the publication of the October Manifesto that same year and the assassination of Governor General Nikolai Bobrikov, however, these contacts entered a dormant period.

World's Fair, 1900

Still, many Finns and especially the art world of Helsinki now looked to Paris, not St. Petersburg, as their European showcase for bringing their conception of Finnish national identity into the European public eye. This showcase was, in the literal sense, the Finnish pavilion of the World's Fair in 1900. Designed by the firm Gesellius, Lindgren & Saarinen, all architects in their early twenties, *au fait* with the latest European architectural trends yet keen to foster Finnish identity, they employed the sculptor Emil Wickström to execute exterior surface decoration utilizing the motifs of Finland's flora and fauna. Gallen-Kallela himself provided the frescoes that adorned the interiors of the domes of the ceilings, focusing upon themes derived from the *Kalevala*. These were later repainted in the National Museum with the help of Jorma Gallen-Kallela, the artist's son. The pavilion also beautifully integrated the textile fabrics and other features used for the interior decoration, which won great accolades from the Czech painter Wassily Kandinsky. Yet the main claim to fame of the Finnish Pavilion was the works of art, both painting and sculpture, produced by more than thirty native artists. These included not only fourteen members of the Young Finland society, but six women artists as well.

The Kaivopuisto Spa "Colony"

Not all Finnish artists worked independently. Some preferred to join forces, at least in the sense that they chose to live and work together within a single artistic colony during the summer months. The Kaivopuisto Spa had had its heyday in the days before the Crimean War, when aristocratic Russians from St. Petersburg flocked to Helsinki to enjoy its health-giving waters and summer social life. After a lengthy period of decline, the city had reclaimed both the spa and its park from private lease-holders, hiring it cheaply for other uses. One such use was the establishment in the early 1890s of an artists' colony during the winter. Here some of Helsinki's leading young painters and sculptors could live and work in a quasi-communal atmosphere that helped to forge a special identity, one in which a pride in being Finnish played a key role.

Among those who formed the community were Venny Soldan-Brofeldt, one of the leading women painters of her time, and her husband Juhani Aho, author of the novel *To Helsinki* (1889). They lived on the second floor of the building. As she remembered: "in the quiet room divided by a huge old wardrobe into sleeping and working quarters we enjoyed undisturbed working peace at a partner's desk, longing at the same time for the wider world, where Paris and Italy were enticing."

An understanding of Aho, as well as his wife, can best be obtained by a visit to Ahola, a museum dedicated to their memory on the shores of Lake Tuusula, outside Helsinki. Ahola is not far from Järvenpää, where the Järvenpää Art Museum exhibits many of her works. Also in the vicinity is Halosenniemi, the former home of the Finnish artist Pekka Halonen, built in 1902 in a National Romantic "Old Karelian" style.

Many of the members of the Kaivopuisto colony were also involved in the informal cultural group "Young Finland", which took a militant approach to the maintenance of Finnish cultural and political identity. Apart from the spa, customary meeting places included the offices of the daily liberal newspaper *Päivälehti* (the predecessor of today's *Helsingin Sanomat*) as well as the Kappeli and Kämp restaurants.

Havis Amanda: Public Sculpture

Sculpture, too, was growing as a medium of expression for Finnish identity and by the dawn of the twentieth century it witnessed a major revival, as infused with national and romantic symbolism as its sister art, painting. One major work of this ilk and a symbol of still-considerable significance especially during sporting events in the capital, when it is draped with the national colors, is *Havis Amanda*, a bronze nymph rising from the sea, surrounded by sea lions, dolphins and other denizens of the sea who lap at her feet. May Day is the highlight of the nymph's year, when university students gather around the statue, wearing their traditional white caps, one of which they attempt to place on the nymph's head. The great National Romantic painter Edelfelt was instrumental in commissioning the work, but the actual sculptor was Ville Vallgren, long active in Paris and Finland's most important sculptor at this period. He had already been identified as the artist most appropriate to carry out the work as far back as 1880.

Adorning the large fountain erected in 1908 at the Market Square, *Havis Amanda* had a mixed reception at first, even from those devoted to the propagation of Finnish national identity. Moreover, its name became a matter of great bewilderment for many people, a confusion only clarified in the 1930s by the sculptor himself. As he confessed, he had derived his inspiration not from any Finnish source, but from the old Germanic fable "Amanda and Herman". Yet he felt the association appropriate since, like Amanda, rising up from the sea like a Nordic Venus, so Helsinki had risen from the Gulf of Finland, a veritable daughter of the sea and jewel of Finland's south coast.

Similarly, the siting of a statue of Aleksis Kivi by Wäinö Aaltonen in front of the National Theater was appropriate for this leading figure of Finnish literature, whose great work *Seven Brothers* (1870) is an almost epic tale of Finnish country life and cultural values in the middle of the nineteenth century. Later, twentieth-century sculptures of important figures in Finland's cultural history were to follow and these include that of J. W. Snellman, from 1923, the first of a Finnish senator and statesman. Politicians, by contrast, took second place to cultural personalities, as the fact that the new country's presidents only came to be sculpted after the Second World War demonstrates.

Many modern sculptures take as their subject matter the fauna of Finland, and more sculptures of animals than of men have been produced in post-war Finland. A significant number depict the bear, an animal of great significance and religious awe in old Finnish-Karelian mythology. Elk are also a subject in many Finnish works of art of the period, and one of the most striking of these was made by Jussi Mäntynen in 1923, now in front of the Museum of Natural History.

Amos Anderson: Private Patrons

Amos Valentin Anderson (1878-1961) was one of Finland's most important patrons of the arts during the first decades of its independence. He had had no formal artistic or architectural training, was educated at business school in Helsinki, and later furthered his economic studies in both Göttingen and London, where he worked in insurance. After his return to Finland and a successful business career in Helsinki, Anderson acquired the ownership of Finland's most important Swedish-language newspaper *Hufvudstadsbladet* in 1920. Eight years later he became its editor-in-chief, a position he held until 1936. Anderson also was actively involved in politics. From 1922 to 1927 he was a Member of Parliament, representing the Swedish People's Party.

A self-made magnate of Finnish-Swedish background, he first made his presence known as a patron of the arts through the renovation and reconstruction of the numerous residences he acquired in and near Helsinki. One was the Villa Nissen at Tammisaari, which had been the home of Ernst Sundgren between 1914 and 1924. Anderson mostly lived at Yrjönkatu, in the heart of the city, but was keen to have a nearby country retreat as well, suitable for occasional visits. But in the event he rarely visited the Villa Nissen and so let it to Consul Johan Wilhelm Cadenius, who lived there until his death in 1939. But the villa was ultimately to become famous for a different reason, the result of Anderson's close connections with Finland's president since 1937, Kyösti Kallio (1873-1940). It was Kallio who suggested to Anderson that he should donate the Villa Nissen to the government of Finland. The president, a man of relatively limited means, had lived in rented accommodation in the capital before his election and was keen to have a less formal venue than the presidential palace elsewhere in the vicinity. Anderson acquiesced and the villa was duly handed over to the state for at least 25 years, along with 190,000 marks for important renovations. He also stipulated that the city of Helsinki should make its own contribution, if only 10,000 marks, for having installed a bunker in the villa during the Winter War in January 1940. The architect Toivo Pelli carried out the work and the villa, in its new presidential role, was re-christened the Villa Kallio in honor of the late president who, prevented by war from living there, stayed instead with Sigrid Krogius at the Villa Larsro at Granö. As a result, the villa only received the new president, Risto Ryti, in January 1941.

Anderson had, in any case, long been a munificent supporter of charitable causes throughout Finland. Towards the end of the 1920s he had supported the construction of the Kunsthalle. In the following decade he greatly assisted the Swedish National Theater, undergoing a major restoration and renovation. He later established his benevolent Art Foundation, through which many of his vast assets were channeled in a range of property and other financial investments to benefit the arts, then and now. These include a significant stake in Stockmann's Department Store as well as in Forum, a vast commercial block on Mannerheim Street. Here *Hufvudstadsbladet* has its office, as does the Mercator printing house, both of which are owned by the Art Foundation.

Forum also contains Anderson's own private house, built in 1913 and designed by the architects W. G. Palmqvist and Einar Sjöström. Established as an independent museum in 1965 and situated at Yrjönkatu 27, it is one of the largest private art collections in Finland. The exhibition hall on the ground floor was later enlarged in 1985, when the shopping complex was built. More recently a renovation occurred in 1998-9 when an auditorium and other exhibition spaces were incorporated into the attic. Among the museum's most important works is the collection of the architect Sigurd Frosterus, which has been on permanent display since 1994, as well as paintings by Magnus Enckell and A. W. Finch. There are also works by Signac, Bonnard and Vlaminck. Latterly Felix Nylund's sculpture collection has been acquired, as have the collections of Birger Carlstedt and Santeri Salokivi. Part of the Amos Anderson collection is also held at the Söderlångvik Museum in Dragsfjärd on the island of Kemiö, Anderson's beloved summer residence.

Though not an academic in any formal sense, Anderson nonetheless devoted much time to publishing his insights into the ecclesiastical art of Finland's medieval period and even wrote a theatrical production, *Vallis Gratiae*, in 1923, based on Finland's ancient past. His scholarly interests also extended to Italy, where, keenly interested in antiquities, he helped to establish the Finnish Institute in Rome in 1954, located in the magnificent Villa Lante atop the Gianicolo Hill in the heart of the city.

The Amos Anderson Gallery, like other private institutions that sprang up in the post-war years, was indicative of the fact that the attitude of private patrons was changing. Before the wars almost all private collectors had donated their collections to the Finnish Art Society, but now they began establishing their own museums.

Villa Gyllenberg

Another prominent patron of the post-war years was the banker Arne Gyllenberg (1891-1977), a keen collector of Tyko Sallinen, many of whose works adorned his study. With his wife Signe, he endowed the Villa Gyllenberg, formerly his family home at Kuusisaarenpolku 11, with an excellent collection of Finnish art as well as some early foreign works. Funded by a foundation established by the banker and his wife, the villa, originally built to the designs of Matti Finell in 1938 with a later extension added in 1955, opened in 1980. Situated on the shore of Laajalahti Bay, on Kuusisaari, it also enjoys splendid views towards the Gallen-Kallela Museum on the opposite shore. Among its principal treasures, which include works by Titian and Tintoretto, is one of the largest collections of work by the Finnish artist Helene Schjerfbeck, who was deeply influenced by Japanese silk-screen printing.

Didrichsen Art Museum

Put together by the Danish couple Marie-Louise and Gunnar Didrichsen, who settled in Finland, this collection is housed in an annex at their home, the Villa Didrichsen, which was designed in 1958 by the architect Viljo Revell. Located at Kuusilahdenkuja 1 also on the island of Kuusisaari, it contains works by twentieth-century artists from Finland and abroad. Among the former are paintings by Albert Edelfelt, Alvar Cawen and Helene Schjerfbeck, as well as works by more modern artists like Juhani Linnovaara, Eila Hiltunen and Laila Pullinen. From a wider international world, works by Picasso, Kandinsky and Miro as well as Léger, Moore, Giacometti and Arp all figure prominently. Finland's only pre-Columbian collection of art works is also to be found in its basement, along with a number of important examples of Chinese art from the Shang to the Ming dynasties.

Venues Old and New

Leaving aside the major art galleries, Helsinki is well endowed with exhibition venues. An interesting collection of Finnish painting, put together by the German-born Lauri Reitz and his brother Lasse, is situated in a flat in Töölö on the second floor of a block at Apollonkatu 23, above the famous Elite Restaurant, which artists have long made their haunt. In 1992 another new art gallery, specializing in Finnish art of the late nineteenth and early twentieth centuries, opened in a flat at Pohjoinen Hesperiankatu 7. This is the former home of Dr. Juhani Kirpilä, a medical doctor specializing in rheumatic illnesses, who bequeathed the collection to the Finnish Cultural Foundation. Most of the works are figurative and are by some of Finland's most famous artists: Albert Edelfelt, Akseli Gallen-Kallela, Hugo Simberg and Tyko Sallinen. To this list must also be added the names of more modern artists, whose works appealed even more to Kirpilä, including Yrjö Saarinen, Åke Mattas, Ahti Lavonen and Kain Tapper.

One venue of particular interest in the past was Artek. This interior design company not only produced a wide range of furniture and other items of interior design but also organized groundbreaking exhibitions of foreign art. Among those who had their works exhibited in Helsinki through Artek in the 1930s were the Frenchmen Henri Matisse and Fernand Léger as well as Pablo Picasso and the American Alexander Calder.

The Museum of Finnish Architecture, located at Kasarminkatu 24, was one of the first museums of the post-war period to signal an artistic renaissance, opening in 1956. It was established in a building that had previously served as the headquarters of various scientific societies, built in 1899 and designed by Magnus Schjerfbeck. In 1979 the newly established Museum of Applied Arts added to the capital's artistic repertoire. Located in a three-story former school designed in 1895 by Gustaf Nyström, it was renovated by Olli Borg and has since been enlarged by a special center for temporary exhibitions.

The Helsinki City Art Museum is formed by two venues: one in Tennispalatsi at Fredrikinkatu 65, originally built as the Automobile Palace in 1937 by the architect Helge Lundström, and one at Tamminiementie. The former is a barrel-vaulted building, the top floor fitted with indoor tennis courts, the lower floors containing a cinema, restaurant, café and exhibition spaces. These hold important exhibitions of ethnography and anthropology. The latter is based at Meilahti, where the core of its collection was donated by Leonard

Bäcksbacka, a collector of Tyko Sallinen. Bäcksbacka was the owner of the Konstsalongen at Bulevardi, still run by his family today, and was not only an important art dealer but a major collector.

Kiasma

The most important new gallery in decades is the Kiasma Museum of Contemporary Art, part of the National Gallery of Finland, which opened in 1998. Designed by the American architect, Steven Holl, its name Kiasma is derived from the Greek letter "X" (chi). The word itself signifies a crossing ("decussation") of the optic nerve and has stimulated almost as much debate as the new gallery itself. The art displayed is international in scope, even if Finnish art forms the heart of the permanent collection. Some artists whose works are displayed focus on the indigenous fauna of the far north. Jussi Heikkilä's sculpture *Puffin* (Fractercula Arctica) is one such example. Others like Mario Merz's *Untitled (Igloo)* takes its theme from Inuit (Eskimo) culture though, of course, there are no Inuit in Finland. Other works are more general in subject, such as Jon Arne Mogstad's *Voice of Spring* and Lea Whittington's *Chicken Bone Chandelier*. Other displays have been produced in more high-tech media, such as the digital art contributions of Mathias Fuchs and Sylvia Eckermann, who have merged electronic elements into their works of art. There is also a multimedia aspect to their art as well, for music plays an important role, and they have also spent considerable time at the Sibelius Academy. Nor has the role of architecture been neglected as a means of binding the whole together:

> *The connecting architecture between the rooms resembles staircases, passages, elevators, hidden doors or portals, each of them referring to the nature of the connotation. Quite contrary to web-based databases and hypertext structures, the links therefore possess a quality of their own, carrying much more information...*

As Fuchs-Eckermann (as they like to style themselves) have put it: "Our main goal is to develop artistic edutainment environments for the representation of complex scientific fields of content. We try to cross-breed art, science and fun and want to come to terms with former

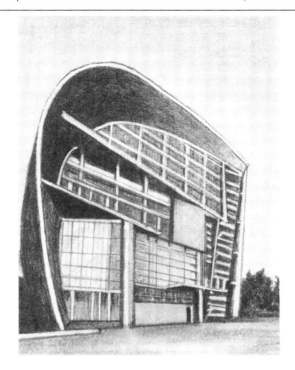

experiences we made in the dry field of media art, research and popular science."

This is the only public building in Helsinki designed by a foreign architect since Engel and it has not been without its detractors. For some, it looks more like a Zeppelin shed than an art gallery. Be that as it may, the architect has very much taken a hands-on approach, designing not only the fabric of the building itself, but its interior decoration, including wall hooks, door handles and many pieces of furniture such as the striking green chairs in the café. Others such as Stefan Lindfors have also made their own contributions, in this case to three so-called *Star Trek* highchairs.

Although the main exhibition space is on the first floor, Kiasma is a multi-story building that includes a seminar room, reading corner, café and shop. Temporary exhibitions are primarily devoted to modern art since 1960. There is also a picture archive and library of considerable scope on contemporary art. The Kiasma Theater puts on a vast array of dramatic, dance and musical performances, as well as multimedia happenings and video art. Perhaps the performances of *Kaspar*, written in 1968 by the Austrian playwright Peter Handke, have been the most significant of those recently held in the theater. As its title suggests, the play alludes to both the nineteenth-century German "wild boy" and the character of a clown, but in such a way that language and communication become the principal themes. There is also an outdoor stage, designed by the Finnish architect Roi Mänttäri, where a variety of summer events are staged.

With a gallery such as this newly opened, Helsinki was in an excellent position in the year 2000 to become the official European City of Culture, with a whole range of cultural events to celebrate that occasion. In any case, Helsinki is a city where the quantity of museums—if not always the quality—is unparalleled, since it has more museums *per capita* than any other city in the world—one for every five thousand inhabitants.

Art and Crafts

Helsinki can also boast of a wide range of schools for higher training in the arts and theater. These include the Academy of Fine Arts, the Helsinki University of Art and Design, and the Theater Academy. The Academy of Fine Arts has a School of Sculpture, originally founded in 1871 and now situated in what was up until 1981 a girls' school at Yrjönkatu 18. After suffering financial difficulties soon after its founding, the institution's plight was resolved when the newly founded Finnish Society of Crafts and Design assumed the support of both the school and related museum. This was, in any case, a period of revival for the Finnish handicraft tradition, which had undergone a decline in the face of growing industrialization. Fanny Churberg, for example, unable to make a living for herself as a professional artist because of public hostility to professionally independent women at this time, turned instead to the craft tradition. She founded the famous Friends of Finnish Handicraft in 1879, which encouraged the revival by focusing on Finland's special cultural heritage.

The country has traditionally enjoyed a high level of skilled craftsmen with respect to wood, but it should also not be forgotten that Helsinki had extremely gifted jewelers as well. From the early days when, in 1850, the city acquired its first master jeweler's workshop to the turn of the twentieth century when it achieved the highest standards, there was a rapid acquirement of luxury tastes in Helsinki. Some jewelers later made their mark in St. Petersburg, where among the Finnish craftsmen the master goldsmith August Holmström actually taught Peter Carl Fabergé, becoming chief jeweler at Fabergé from 1857 to 1903. His mantle was then taken up by his niece, Alma Pihl, who in 1913-14 designed two magnificent Easter eggs for Czar Nicholas II. Other items she designed included a variety of jewelry which the Swedish Nobel Company commissioned as gifts for the families of important clients.

In the 1970s another revival occurred in Helsinki, as workshops dedicated to different handicrafts once again blossomed. The most famous, Pot Viapori, was founded at Suomenlinna in 1973, and craftsmen such as Åsa Hellman and Hilkka Jarva carried out their old ceramic traditions there. Other artists' studios were added in 1981, designed by Severi Blomstedt. Four years later, the Nordic Art Center, renamed the Nordic Institute for Contemporary Art since 1995, was established in the old Russian barracks, the restoration of which was designed by Pekka Helin and Tuomo Siitonen.

A new audio-visual department has recently been created at the University of Art and Design, situated in the so-called Helsinki Virtual Village at Arabianranta, where, surrounded by such neighbors as IBM and Sonera, a virtual community has taken shape. It is also an area, adjacent to Arabia itself, where art, design and industry enjoy a unique and mutual symbiosis.

CHAPTER TWELVE

Helsinki and the Performing Arts: Music, Opera and Ballet

Helsinki's innovative musical life can be said to begin at the tail end of the sixteenth century when Michael Bartholdi Gumerus, a schoolmaster during the years 1598-1606, became a pioneer of Finnish church music. He wrote some 95 hymns along with a large Finnish-language collection of antiphons, supplanting the more or less ubiquitous Gregorian chant that had previously been the mainstay of ecclesiastical music in Finland. Nonetheless, much of his music had traditional, even Catholic roots, with sources in Latin chant, albeit with texts derived from the Bible translation of reforming bishop Michael Agricola. Gumerus later became vicar of Vanaja, where he continued to perform his ecclesiastical music.

The composition and performance of secular Finnish classical music really began during the course of the eighteenth century as a significant number of amateurs—priests, merchants, and country gentlemen—took a keen interest. One of the earliest professional musicians was Bernhard Henrik Crusell (1775-1838), the son of an impecunious bookbinder. Originally trained as a musician in a military band based at Suomenlinna fortress, he went on to become an internationally acclaimed clarinetist after moving to Stockholm, producing at least three significant concertos for that instrument. Another important figure in the world of music was Thomas Byström (1772-1839), the son of a local merchant who later became Mayor of Helsinki. Most of his youth and early manhood were spent abroad, first in Tallinn and later in St. Petersburg, where he was a cadet at the Imperial Military Academy. Commissioned as an officer in the

Swedish military in 1793, he eventually became a Senior Adjutant to the King in Stockholm while continuing to compose music, including three violin sonatas (1797). He also composed some pieces for the piano, among which the *Aire russe variée* is perhaps most famous. Even while abroad he continued to maintain a close connection with Helsinki. Then, when he was seconded to Suomenlinna, he continued his musical activities, becoming involved in a number of private musical societies, despite their political overtones. After the transfer of Finland from Sweden, however, he lived permanently in Stockholm, where from 1818 he took up teaching piano and organ at the Royal Academy of Music (he had been a member since 1794). Among his pupils was Crown Prince Oscar, son of the French-born King Carl Johan.

Early Musical Venues

During these early years the hotel known as the Society House, adjacent to the Market Square, provided the venue in its ballroom for many musical performances. Here it was that Helsinki's first Orchestra Society (later to be re-christened The City of Helsinki Orchestra, the first permanent symphony orchestra in the Nordic countries) commenced its performances under the leadership of the great conductor Robert Kajanus, who began giving regular concerts in 1882. The City of Helsinki Orchestra was eventually to become the Helsinki Philharmonic, but it was still the Society House that provided the venue where all Sibelius' symphonies, except for the Seventh Symphony, were given their premieres. Kajanus had studied music in Leipzig, Dresden and Paris and was no mean musician. But his greatest fame is due to the multitude of orchestral events that he organized for the capital. These attracted not only the nobility and privileged middle classes, but a wide public drawn from different segments of society.

The newly built Hotel Kämp also provided another, even more all-encompassing venue in terms of productions, though not with respect to the audience. Here, everything from the Swedish poet-cum-musician Carl Michael Bellman (1740-95), once a student at the Åbo Akademi, to operettas, vaudeville and magic acts, were staged for socially prominent gatherings.

Fredrik Pacius

Of greatest importance to the Helsinki's nineteenth-century musical scene was the German Fredrik Pacius (1809-91), who had migrated to Finland from his native Hamburg. A bust of him (1885) by the sculptor Emil Wickström can be seen in the Kluuvi Gardens, behind the railway station. Appointed music teacher at Helsinki's recently established Alexander University in 1834, he arrived in the capital the following year and promptly proceeded to revolutionize the world of music. He founded a new musical society while establishing both a new university choir and orchestra and assisted in the organization of a vast range of musical events in the city, including costly oratorios and symphonies. He also did not hesitate to take advantage of the popularity of the German band, which entertained guests at the fashionable Ullanlinna Spa. In the meantime, Henrik Borgström, the entrepreneur who had helped establish the spa, also made major contributions to the new musical society.

Pacius' most significant musical contributions were yet to come. In 1848 he composed the music, while Runeberg wrote the words, of what is today the much-loved Finnish national anthem, *Our Land*. He also devoted himself to opera, and in 1852 his historical opera, *The Hunting of King Charles*, with a libretto written by Zacharius Topelius, was first performed. Based on the life of Sweden-Finland's great king, it was the first opera ever composed in the Grand Duchy, albeit in a German idiom. Here, the influences of the early Romantic German composers Ludwig Spohr and Carl Maria von Weber, famed for his opera *Der Freischütz*, are clearly felt. Yet certain other works such as *The Princess of Cyprus* reveal certain Finnish elements, as does his third opera *Loreley*, along with numerous other pieces both symphonic and vocal.

By now, foreign operas were also making their appearance in Helsinki. In fact, those of Offenbach were presented in Helsinki only a year or so after they first made their debut in Paris. More intimate private musical soirees were also very popular. Many of the residents of Helsinki could play musical instruments or sing, while the local production of sheets and books of musical scores was considerable. Some of these were produced by Eduard Fazer, one of the Swiss family who owned the confectionary company.

By the early twentieth century, operettas from Germany and Austria-Hungary had become extremely popular. Many of these were performed during the summer months in open-air venues, enabling the public to enjoy the splendors of the bright midnight sky.

Kantele

The late nineteenth century was, of course, the period of the *Kalevala*, the great Finnish epic composed by Elias Lönnrot, so it is not surprising that the ancient Finnish musical instrument, the *kantele*, a lyre-like object, should also have received renewed interest from among the intelligentsia. The Russian Karelians Iivana Bogdanoff-Vihantola and Iivana Shemeikka become the musical icons of this Karelian tradition, their interpretation of the songs of Väinämöinen (the elderly bardic hero of the *Kalevala* epic) at the 1900 Helsinki Song Festival winning them cultural immortality. By then, when big was beautiful, twenty- or thirty-string instruments had come into fashion, replacing the earlier ten- to fourteen-string instruments that had, in turn, supplanted the more historically authentic five-string *kantele* of previous centuries. Today, more than a hundred years later, the Värttinä group has pioneered a revival, along with others such as Sikiät who are still carrying on this ancient tradition. *Kantele* music is taught both as theory and for performance by Professor Heikki Laitinen at the Sibelius Academy, and graduates play not only in Helsinki but throughout the country and abroad. CDs of Finnish *kantele* music can now be found in London, Paris, New York and Tokyo, where visiting groups occasionally play.

Merikanto and Wegelius: National Tradition

While *kantele* music was the genuine article from an ancient Finnish tradition, Oskar Merikanto chose to write modern pieces of music, both vocal and for the piano, but drawing more indirectly from a folkloric reservoir. As a child he studied with Lauri Hämäläinen, the organist of the Old Church, but moved in 1888 to Germany, where he studied in Leipzig and Berlin. Then in 1892 he returned to Helsinki, where he assumed the post of organist at St. John's Church, a post he occupied until his death some thirty years later.

Altogether, Merikanto wrote about 150 solo songs and fifteen duets. Most have Finnish texts, but some are written in Swedish and

German as well. A significant number, such as "Where the Sun Shines", have become known as "Evergreens" because of the naturalistic beauty of their words. As for his piano pieces, "Summer Evening Idyll" proved to be one of his most popular but he also contributed compositions for other musical instruments; his "Passacaglia" for the organ was one of the first major pieces produced in Finland for that instrument.

A keen opera enthusiast, one of his great contributions to Helsinki's music was his foundation of the Domestic Opera (later to become the Finnish National Opera) in 1911. He himself produced a number of operas, some of the first ever written to be sung in Finnish including *The Maiden of the North* (1898), first premiered in 1908, and *The Death of Elina* (1910), but these were far less successful than his songs and piano compositions.

A contemporary figure in Helsinki's nineteenth-century musical world was Martin Wegelius. He opened the Helsinki Institute of Music in 1882, the forerunner of what was to become the Sibelius Academy, where Merikanto also became a teacher. That same year, two other important educational establishments for ecclesiastical music were established: the Helsinki Organists' School and the Church Musical College. Interestingly, Wegelius had studied philosophy and literature at Helsinki University but, having acquired some musical training, he later studied in Vienna with the organist Rudolf Bibl before moving on to the conservatory at Leipzig. It was during this period that he became a devotee of Wagner's music, later establishing a short-lived society in Helsinki devoted to the propagation of Wagner's musical values. It is as a musical mentor that he is most remembered, not least for his analytical work, *The History of Music*, published in 1893.

Sibelius

By contrast, Jean Sibelius (1865-1957) has become a household name in the international world of music, not as a teacher but as Finland's greatest genius of musical composition. A Swedish-speaking native of Hämeenlinna, where his father was a doctor, he had first arrived in Helsinki in 1885 in order to study law, but that same year he entered the Helsinki Conservatory, where he remained for four years. Having then won a scholarship, he traveled abroad to pursue musical studies first in Berlin and then in Vienna.

It was no continental European theme that took his fancy, but those of Karelia and the *Kalevala* which were to be the primary subject matter of his musical repertoire, especially in his early period. In fact, much of his early music has a folkloric emphasis. First came his *Kullervo* symphony of 1892, then the suites *Saga*, *Karelia* and *Lemminkäinen* continued these themes. Two further symphonies also followed. Most famous is now *Finlandia*, a tone poem of 1899, the title of which was suggested by Sibelius' close friend Axel Carpelan, himself later the subject of an eponymous novel by his relation Bo Carpelan. Its haunting tones seem to embody the very spirit and fortitude of the Finnish nation at a time when its very identity and existence were threatened by the centralizing measures of the Russian imperial government in St. Petersburg. Yet it should not be forgotten that it was also at this time—around 1910—that Russian balalaika music was introduced to the Finnish public, and performers continue to play to enthusiastic audiences to this very day.

Sibelius, together with his wife Aino and daughter Ruth, made his home at Ainola, to the north of Helsinki, in 1915. Sadly, no idyllic happiness awaited him there, as alcoholism, especially an uncontrollable thirst for whisky, devastated both his life and his marriage, which was in crisis by 1924. Still, it was then that he composed his *Seventh Symphony* (1924-5), followed by *Tapiola* (1926), which won him great acclaim and financial security, and facilitated his travels in the following years. After 1931, however, he remained at home in Finland, the embodiment of Finnish nationalism in its best sense, producing little in the way of formal compositions except for his mysterious and unfinished last *Eighth Symphony*, burnt by the composer himself under mysterious circumstances. Perhaps his alcoholism played a role in this, or perhaps his dissatisfaction with the political circumstances of his beloved Finland. On the other hand, the reasons may have been more musical; some had criticized his ability for scoring, declaring that he was not as gifted as his fellow composer Gustav Mahler. Sibelius might have felt the symphony unsuitable for publication; in any case, he no longer had to publish in order to earn his daily bread. Others dispute this, so the matter remains an enigma and one still hotly debated. Its loss may be a musical tragedy, but there are still a further 116 musical works left to us today.

Fittingly, Sibelius was buried at Ainola, and today the house is a museum, nestling in the woods of the surrounding countryside. The composer is also commemorated by Eila Hiltunen's Sibelius Monument (1967), an abstract tubular work in the Sibelius Park on

the western side of the city. Visitors can walk both inside as well as around the monument, which took five years to complete, and as such they become part of the musical imagery of the composition. A more immediate legacy is the Sibelius Festival, first held in June 1951 and repeated annually since then.

Sibelius' reputation as one of the world's greatest composers is now secure, a far cry from the days in 1906 when Rosa Newmarch had introduced Sibelius to an English public by means of a lecture. His popularity there and in the United States was much greater than in the rest of Europe for years to come, but now his genius is recognized across the world.

Later Composers

Other Finnish musicians were to be deeply influenced by Sibelius, including Erkki Melartin and Leevi Madetoja, the latter best known for his opera *The Ostrobothnians* (1924). Selim Palmgren turned aside from the symphonic interests of these colleagues, preferring to devote himself to chamber music, while others like Yrjö Kilpinen drew their inspiration from different sources (in Kilpinen's case from the *Lieder* tradition of Austria and Germany). Aarre Merikanto, son of Oskar Merikanto and Väinö Raitio, meanwhile, turned to the world of opera, employing a continental atonality in works such as the opera *Juha* (1922), in which the great Finnish diva Aino Ackté performed.

Disdained for its too heightened "modernity" by the public of the time, it had to await the 1960s for its first performance.

By this time other musical trends were coming to the fore, once again frequently harking back to themes of the *Kalevala*. This is true of the works of Uuno Klami, whose *Kalevala Suite* has been called an orchestral fresco, with a texture not unlike that of the Russian Stravinsky's orchestral works. This was also true of the next generation of Finnish composers, Einojuhani Rautavaara and Usko Meriläinen. The latter, together with Erik Bergman and Paavo Heininen, came to prefer a so-called "post-serial" medium.

Bergman became one of the leading figures in the post-war modernist school of music; in the 1950s he introduced the so-called "twelve tone technique" and in the 1970s turned towards a self-conscious primitivism in music. This led him to take inspiration from exotic international sources, instrumental in the development of his aleatoric and coloristic musical modes. His opera *The Singing Tree* (1986-8) is arguably the crowning achievement of this development. When Anna-Lisa Jakobsson, Peter Lindroos and Marianne Harju sang it in 1995, it achieved significant international acclaim.

These were not the only Finnish composers of the time to experience Russian influence. Einar Englund rejected the National Romanticism of Sibelius, drawing inspiration from the music of Dmitri Shostakovitch. Joonas Kokkonen, on the other hand, looked to Hungary for his inspiration, notably the music of Béla Bartók. Made a member of the Academy of Finland in 1963, his dodecaphonic (twelve-tone) Third Symphony was a great success. He is also noted for his opera *The Last Temptations* (1975), which also has some roots in continental Europe, even if its musical relationship to key religious questions in nineteenth-century Finland cannot be denied. Englund's former villa, the Villa Kokkonen near Järvenpää, designed by Alvar Aalto, contains a museum dedicated to his life.

By the 1970s the modernist tradition had once again come into disfavor, as a renewed interest in harmonious tonalities came to the fore. Previously modernist figures like Rautavaara and the more recent generation of musical composers like Kalevi Aho have since changed their focus, adopting what has come to be called a post-modernist medium.

Rautavaara's compositions are hard to characterize since they are an eclectic mix of stylistic sources. Like so many other highly gifted Finns, he had been a student at the Sibelius Academy, but he, too, had training in continental Europe and the US, which further broadened his musical horizons. Then he became immersed in the so-called constructivistic style, which had encouraged the introduction of twelve tones in musical composition during the 1950s and 1960s. During the 1970s Rautavaara became professor at the Sibelius Academy and went on to produce some seven operas. In his mature years a richly syncretic form of music has emerged, most in evidence in his operatic productions of the mid-1980s. These include the operas *Thomas* (1985), *Vincent* (1987), and *The House of the Sun* (1990), all of which reveal rich spiritual depths. Most recently, an opera based on one of the Finland's leading literary figures, *Aleksis Kivi* (1997), has achieved wide popularity in the Finnish capital.

Aulis Sallinen achieved the greatest fame among contemporary Finnish composers in the 1990s. His most celebrated operas are *The King Goes Forth to France* (1984) and *Kullervo* (1992), both commissioned not by any musical foundation or house in Helsinki, but by the Royal Opera House, Covent Garden, and the Los Angeles Opera House, respectively. Other contemporary composers of note include Magnus Lindberg and Kaija Saariaho. Both were members of the musical group *Ears Open*, along with the conductor Esa-Pekka Salonen and Jouni Kaipainen. All have turned, to some degree or another, to computer-generated musical tones for their inspiration while still incorporating a sense of harmony and the romantic into their works. Kaipainen also worked on opera compositions, joining forces with the great Finnish modernist poet Paavo Haavikko, who wrote at least eleven of his libretti.

Performers and Conductors

Helsinki has long been a city rich in composers, but it has also been a place blessed with splendid musical performers. Ackté, as we have seen, was one of the first opera singers to achieve international fame after her debut in Helsinki. A soprano of considerable skill and great expression, she first performed at the Paris Opera House in 1897 to great acclaim. Invitations from other important European opera houses followed, and in 1904-6 Ackté performed at the Metropolitan Opera House in New York, later singing the role of Salome in the eponymous opera by the German composer Richard Strauss in 1910. Once returned to Finland, she helped establish the Finnish National Opera in Helsinki, as well as the Savonlinna Opera Festival in the southeast of the country. Both institutions still flourish today.

Other opera singers of international importance in Helsinki include Monica Groop. Trained at the Sibelius Academy, her debut at the Royal Opera House, Covent Garden, where she sang as a mezzo-soprano in Wagner's Ring Cycle, gave her almost instant fame. Perhaps such a success has its roots not only in the talent of the performer but in the fact that music is nurtured within Finnish education with splendid children's choirs, such as the world-renowned Tapiola Choir. In this sense, the Finnish musical tradition can be compared with that of Hungary and the dominant role Kodály has played there with respect to education, much as Sibelius did and continues to do in Finland.

Among conductors of the late twentieth century it is Paavo Berglund who has achieved the greatest acclaim. He was one of the first to complete the recording of all Sibelius' symphonies in Europe, the first of which was performed while Berglund was conductor of the Bournemouth Symphony Orchestra, whose director he became in 1972. Three years later he also became chief conductor of the Helsinki Philharmonic Orchestra. A litany of other Finns who are among the world's leading conductors includes not only Esa-Pekka Salonen, but also Jukka-Pekka Saraste, Leif Segerstam, Osmo Vänska, and Hannu Lintu. Many of them owe their success to the training provided by Jorma Panula.

The Finnish Ballet

Although the National Ballet was founded in 1922, Helsinki's ballet had long benefited from its proximity to St. Petersburg and that city's extraordinarily rich dance culture. The arrival in 1908 of Anna Pavlova, star of the Mariinsky Theater, at Helsinki's National Theater was the sensation of the year. The organizer was, of course, none other than Eduard Fazer who opened his own company with a production of Tchaikovsky's *Swan Lake*.

The Russian Theater Company had originally been founded in 1868, taking premises in the old Arkadia Finnish theater and opening its doors for the first Finnish opera company, founded by Ackté and Fazer. The latter was instrumental in bringing the Russian impresario Serge Diaghilev's Ballet Russe Company to Helsinki in 1909. (Fittingly, Fazer later became first director of the newly founded Finnish Opera.) This Russian company later moved to the Alexander Theater on the Boulevard, which became its permanent home. Built in 1879 in a neo-Renaissance style with a monumental portico by the architectural team of Benard and Koshperov, both engineers in the Russian Engineering Corps, it is a rectangular building containing a large amphitheater that seats five hundred. With the establishment of the Finnish Opera there in 1911 and then the National Ballet in 1922, it provided the country's most prominent venue for such productions until well into the mid-1990s. Leading opera singers, including not only Ackté but also Alma Fohström and Hortense Synnerberg, charmed their audiences for decades. It served Helsinki as its principal opera house until the 1990s, when the new Helsinki Opera House superseded it. Yet even today it still hosts a variety of operatic and other productions, many from abroad.

Other performers like Maggie Gripenberg preferred to look across the Atlantic for inspiration. The unconventional American dancer Isadora Duncan had already performed at the National Theater in 1905, and so it was that Gripenberg took her primary inspiration from Duncan's "natural and free" athletic movements. Lengthy studies in Germany and Switzerland widened her perspective still further, making her keenly aware of the idiosyncratic influences Finland's musical scene exerted upon her. Not surprisingly, she turned to Sibelius for inspiration, choreographing some of his music in 1939, surprisingly the first to do so.

But it was primarily the classical repertoire of St. Petersburg's Mariinsky Theater that remained for many Finns the model for Finland's National Ballet. Indeed, its two most important *maîtres de ballet* had themselves been trained at the Mariinsky: the St. Petersburg-born George Gé and Alexander Saxelin. Whereas the former composed ballets in the idiom of Diaghilev, Saxelin took a more traditional approach, which continued into the next generation, when Elsa

Sylverstersson assumed the reins of the National Ballet, influenced by such diverse but international figures as George Balanchine and the Swede Mats Ek. Much less classical were the performances organized by Riitta Vainio. For now modernism began to make modest inroads into the Helsinki's world of dance, culminating in the 1970s in the works of the choreographer Marjo Kuusela. In particular, her ballets like *People Without Power* or *Salka Valka*, based on the eponymous novel of the Icelandic Nobel Prize winner Haldur Laxness and performed by her recently established Raatikko Dance Theater, sought a more social realist subject than previous Finnish ballet productions. In fact, even such Finnish-inspired productions as *Seven Brothers* (1980), based on Kivi's novel, had starkly realist elements.

Later, during the 1980s, a new dawn for modern dance in Helsinki broke when Jorma Uotinen developed a far more experimental aesthetic, drawing upon his experiences as a dancer in Paris with Carolyn Carlson. He assumed control of the Helsinki City Theater in 1980, turning it into a showcase for modern dance. This theater, a noted piece of architecture, is situated at Eläintarhantie 5 and was built in 1967 by the architect Timo Penttilä. Accommodating up to 920 people in its principal auditorium and 300 in its studio auditorium, this building, which seems all granite and glass, lies on a stepped slope as if embedded in the rocky terrain like an ancient amphitheater.

The long-term importance of the choreographer Jorma Uotinen must be underscored, for his influence on the modern dance scene in Helsinki has been enormous, producing the choreography for the principal works of both the Helsinki City Theater and the Finnish National Ballet. His choreography for Milan's La Scala won plaudits, but it is perhaps his work at the Paris Opera for the opera *Frozen Dream* (1987), based upon Magnus Lindberg's instrumental composition *Kraft*, which has won him the greatest international fame, along with *a La Nuit Gelée* (1995), produced for the Vienna Dance Festival.

Others have taken dance to the limits of the western tradition in a quest for novelty and new impulses. This was certainly true of the Swedish dancer and choreographer Kenneth Kvarnström, who came to Helsinki from Stockholm, taking up the artistic directorship of the Helsinki Theater Dance Company in 1996. Kvarnström had trained at the Stockholm Academy of Ballet from 1984 to 1987, but found influences as far afield as in American rock and Asia, where martial arts had a strong impact on his perceptions of movement. His most noted productions include the bizarrely titled ...*that was all I wanted so I stuck my finger in his eye*...(1991) and its sequel ...*and the angels began to scream*...(1996). Since then other works created for the Helsinki City Theater include *Liquid* (1994) and *Nono* (1996). This work deals with themes of social alienation and isolation as well as violence as a product of consumer materialism and its growing presence in modern human relationships.

Oriental influences, and especially the Japanese dance form of *butto* were also taken up by Ari Tenhula, who knew both India and the Pacific from considerable first-hand experience. Others have looked further north, even to Siberia, where Arja Raatikainen found inspiration in shamanism. On the other hand, her fellow women choreographers, Sanna Kekäläinen and Kirsi Monni, chose to take as their themes elements from the domestic world of women in Finland.

The Sibelius Academy

Of vital significance for the continued musical excellence of Helsinki has been the foundation of the Sibelius Academy, the most important musical academy of higher learning in Finland. Founded in 1882 as the Helsinki Institute of Music under the directorship of Martin Wegelius, Sibelius himself studied composition and the violin here. In 1911 it became a conservatory, under the leadership of Erkki Melartin and in 1924 was re-christened the Helsinki Conservatoire. Two years later a department of military music was incorporated within it. Then, on the eve of the Second World War, it was renamed the Sibelius Academy. It remained in private hands until 1980, when the state assumed control. In 1998, it achieved university status and started awarding degrees in the technological aspects of music.

As the third largest classical musical academy of university standard in Europe and with a list of graduates who have reached the highest levels of the musical world internationally, its fame is justly great. Under the directorship of Professor Jorma Panula, its 1,700 students, both undergraduate and graduate, focus upon a truly vast range of musical studies including early religious music, classical, ethnic, jazz and musical theater.

In the world of classical music Magnus Lindberg has achieved considerable renown. His early compositions in a so-called "post-serial style" include the piano quintet ...*de Tartuffe, je crois* (1981). Later works such as *Kraft* (1983-5), as its name implies, exude an aggressive power. More recently, complex harmonies dominate in other works like *Marea* (1989-90) and *Arena* (1995). Another important figure is Olli Mustonen, both a pianist and composer. Having begun his composing at the age of five, he studied first with Ralf Gothóni, and then with Eero Heinonen and Einojuhani Rautavaara. Aside from performing with the great orchestras of the world, he has also been involved in the establishment of a new one for the capital, the Helsinki City Orchestra.

As for folk music and dance, the Folklore Center at Tomtebo, a charming nineteenth-century villa set in a garden at Tamminiementie 1, has become one of the main venues, with performances taken not only from Finnish folk tradition but the wider world as well.

Theater Life in Helsinki

Drama also has a long tradition in the Finnish capital, in the two official languages of the country, Finnish and Swedish. The first theater that Helsinki could claim was built in 1826-7, a yellow wooden edifice at the western end of the Esplanade, the designs provided by Engel, the German-born architect of Alexander I's imperial city. It could hold 400 spectators in its horseshoe-shaped auditorium, in which the loges were traditionally arranged along the sides. One adjacent wing contained a buffet, another a cloakroom, but the fact that neither was heated, even in winter, limited their popularity. Superseded by new concepts of comfort a mid-century clientele was beginning to demand, it was dismantled in 1866 and removed to Arkadiankatu, where it began to cater for a Finnish- rather than Swedish-speaking public. In its stead, the current Swedish Theater was built, at Pohjoisesplanaadi 2, designed by Nikolai Benois, professor at the Imperial Academy of Art and Architecture in St. Petersburg. Eliel Saarinen also added an extension in the 1910s. Its current appearance, however, dates from 1936 when Eliel's son Eero Saarinen and Jarl Eklund undertook a major renovation, rebuilding both end wings while replacing the auditorium's central aisle with two side ones. In 1978 a winter garden annex was incorporated into the restaurant by the architect Olof Hansson. With its adjacent terrace, it is one of the city's most popular venues in both winter and summer.

Yet the most important venue in Helsinki was perhaps the Finnish Theater, later known as National Theater (Kansallisteatteri), constructed opposite the Ateneum in 1902. Built in the National Romantic style, with two flanking Romanesque-inspired towers, it used rough-hewn granite blocks, like so many similar buildings in Helsinki at that time, but much of its skeletal structure is also made of reinforced concrete. One of the largest theaters in Finland, it can seat 1,100 spectators. Frescoes for the foyer were provided by Juho Rissanen and Yrjö Ollila. More recently in the 1960s two smaller auditoriums were appended to it, thereby allowing three productions to be held at the same time.

For those interested in Finnish theatrical history, the Theater Museum at Tallberginkatu, set up in the old Cable Factory, provides a very worthwhile insight into its permutations.

Finlandia Hall

Famous as the National Theater is, the buildings designed as musical venues by Alvar Aalto have come to supplant it in the public eye. His House of Culture in Sturenkatu (Sturegatan), built between 1955 and 1958, was the first great musical venue to appear in the Finnish capital since before the Second World War. Basically composed of two separate units, one side contains the concert hall, with its voluptuous curves and richly textured red brick walls. The other is a five-story office block, adorned by a copper-plated façade, somewhat withdrawn from the street and joined to the other unit by a canopied bridge-like section at the rear.

More important in architectural terms is Aalto's Finlandia Hall at Mannerheimintie 13, by the Hesperia Gardens in Töölö. It provided the city with the most important concert hall since the White Hall was constructed for that purpose on Senate House Square in 1925. With a façade decorated by a mélange of Carrara marble and black granite, the main auditorium was built in 1971 and the Congress wing, with a number of conference halls, completed some four years later. As such, it is the only building in Aalto's great plan for Helsinki of the years 1967-71 to be constructed. The principal auditorium of the concert hall accommodates 1,750 people—a sharp contrast with that of the White Hall, which only holds 400; a smaller hall for chamber music, seating 350, was also provided at Finlandia Hall.

Another venue, Kanneltalo, the Cultural Center of Western Helsinki, was erected in 1992, designed by Pekka Salminen and his partners. It includes not only a 250-seat auditorium where concerts and theatrical productions are held, but a library, café, workers' institute and youth club. Two years later the similar and so-called Malmitalo, the Cultural Centre of Northern Helsinki, was finished, its larger auditorium seating 212 people for concerts and films. The newest cultural venue of this type is the Vuosaari House, while smaller but also of note is the Villa Aino Ackté, the former home of the famous soprano. Situated on Tullisaari Island, a wide range of concerts is held here during the summer months. A new opera house on Mannerheimintie at Töölönlahti finally opened in 1993. Designed by the architects Eero Hyvämäki, Jukka Karhunen and Risto Parkkinen in an idiom more reminiscent of a factory than an opera house, it has two auditoriums, seating 1,350 and 450 respectively. Beautiful it certainly is not, with its unrelenting white surfaces and sharp angularity, but its functionality is indisputable, comprising numerous rehearsal rooms, workshops and a ballet school, all built into the complex.

Circuses

With Helsinki's proximity to Russia, it is not surprising that circuses made an important mark on the Finnish capital, especially as Russia was and remains the home of some of the world's great circus troupes. This was especially true in the late nineteenth century, when the circus of Gaetano Ciniselli visited Helsinki on repeated occasions from its headquarters in St. Petersburg. With regular and convenient rail and shipping links, people, animals and other equipment could be transported relatively easily and cheaply.

In actual fact, the circus had first arrived in Finland from Sweden as far back as 1787, but the most famous of the earlier circuses was that of the brothers Jean Baptiste and Pierre Louis Fouraux, which arrived in 1828. Then there was also Magnus Hinné's spectacular show which visited Helsinki three times between 1858 and 1871, on the final occasion with no fewer than 100 circus artists, a 26-piece orchestra and 60 horses. Even in the twentieth century circus troupes, mainly from abroad, continued to provide much sought-after entertainment in a rapidly growing Helsinki. These included the Swedish circus of Trolle Rhodin and the Danish one of the Schmidt brothers in the first half of the century. Later, the homegrown circus known as Finlandia, under the leadership of Carl-Gustav Jernström, also achieved a modicum of success. But not all were so fortunate; the circus of Sariola, founded to synchronize with the 1952 Olympics, proved unable to cope with the harsh economic realities of post-war Helsinki.

Jazz and Tango

Jazz has a long and venerable tradition in the Finnish capital. The Rhythm Boys, under the bandleader Eugen Malmsten, and the Ramblers, led by Klaus Salmi, were very popular during the heady days of the 1930s, even if the ascetic wartime decade that followed led to a severe setback for such musical expression. Only in the 1950s did jazz recover, but then in quite a different medium with a significant input from swing.

Even so, other popular musical ensembles were taking their place in the sun, including the Harmony Sisters, Raija Avellan, Maire Ojanen and Vera Enroth, who were at the height of their popularity in the late 1930s. Many of the most popular songs at this time were written by Toivo Kärki, who achieved his zenith of fame in 1939 when he won the competition set up by the British *Melody Maker* magazine with the wistful song "Things Happen That Way". Of equal importance were the singer Olavi Virta, in vogue at this time, Ossi Aalto and his crowd-pulling swing orchestra, and Olli Häme, a byword for be-bop.

During the Winter War and Continuation War a variety of musical events were held, and special concerts for the troops were an especially prominent feature during the dark year of 1944. It was from this background that the rock and roll tradition was also to emerge, and it was the jazz musician Onni Gideon who released Finland's first instrumental rock and roll record, *Hawaiian Rock*, in 1957. Two years later Kai Järnström was crowned the King of Finnish Rock under the stage name of Rock-Jerry.

But jazz was by no means dead and in 1975 the UMO Jazz Orchestra was established in Helsinki, giving the capital an important organization dedicated to the performance of jazz. An expensive undertaking, it required the financial support of not only the city's administration but that of the Ministry of Education. The Finnish State Broadcasting Company has also provided much assistance. This latter, located at Pasila in a building of architectural note, is not far from the new Exhibition Center, as well as the site of a commercial television station, MTV.

More recently in the 1990s the Töykeät Trio, featuring the pianist Iiro Rantala, as well as the Krakatau Ensemble with the guitarist Raoul Björkenheim, have won critical plaudits.

Tango, which arrived in Finland during the early years of the twentieth century, became the veritable national dance of the country during the inter-war years, with a melancholic aspect even exceeding that of the Argentine tango. Though more a rural than urban phenomenon, such Kings of the Tango as Olavi Virta, Henry Theel and Eino Grön have won Finnish fans with tragic songs like "The Golden Tango" and "Love, Suffer and Forget".

The Live Music Society
With respect to the younger generation, tango has largely gone the way of the dodo in Finland in general and especially in Helsinki, which prefers to follow the fashions of the various tides of rock and pop that emanate from New York and London. Rock goes back to the 1950s, but it was the establishment of the Live Music Society or ELMU in May 1978 that has most helped to stimulate the modern pop scene in the capital. This is especially true of Suomi-rock, that is rock music sung with original Finnish lyrics. These lyrics, articulated as they are in the modern idiom of international popular music, also have roots that can be traced directly to the more traditional genre of Finnish folk music. In fact, it is the unique blend of the traditional and modern that gives it its texture and richness.

A still more "alternative" dimension was added to the Helsinki rock world when the organization acquired the so-called Cave of Bats, a derelict building in which the capital's first techno raves were held. Both it and another venue, the Cable Factory, drew vast crowds of young would-be political activists. The latter, really a disused hostel for the homeless not far from Nokia's cable-producing factory, had been secured through a tenancy agreement with the Helsinki City Council. By taking the radical musical movement, with all its social overtones, under its wing, the city's administration was also able to tame it by close supervision and by keeping its more radical and dysfunctional elements at arm's length.

Today the Nokia Cable Factory is, in turn, an "establishment" monument to contemporary culture, which extends far beyond its original musical remit. It contains a theater for musical and dance performances, a hotel and a restaurant. There are also two museums and at least a hundred artists now maintain studios and other workshops there. A last resort for down-and-outs has thus been transformed into a showpiece of the city government.

Contemporary Music

Helsinki is now a city noted for its modern popular music. Long gone are the days of the 1980s when Helsinki's selection for the Eurovision Song Competition came in last, even if Finns remain for many the laughing stock of that jamboree. In June 1993, for example, the renowned Finnish rock group Leningrad Cowboys joined forces in unlikely fashion with the Red Army Choir on Senate Square to create the so-called Total Balalaika Show. More than 80,000 fans occupied the square and its adjacent streets to participate in this extraordinary event, inconceivable in the political climate only two years before. Groups such as Värttinä have also traveled abroad, where they have enjoyed considerable success, playing distinctive music and not aping the worst of Eurovision popular music.

More recently, high-tech artists such as the Austrians Mathias Fuchs and Sylvia Eckermann have married their digital art to the visual, as at Kiasma, Helsinki's new museum of modern art. Based at the Sibelius Academy, their electronic displays now form digital bridges between the visual arts and music.

Today Helsinki is a city enormously rich in musical venues. There are now at least four large symphony orchestras in or within a ten-mile radius of the town center. There are also a further three orchestras, albeit of more modest proportions, not to mention numerous chamber ensembles and string quartets. As for the musical world beyond the classical, the city abounds with jazz, tango and ethnic music, not to mention legions of pop bands, playing everything from 1960s disco music to acid house and other more high-tech varieties.

Techno music has also made inroads, with groups like Movetron and Aikakone both selling hundreds of thousands of CDs in the 1990s. The new role of computer technology in music is also putting Helsinki on the map, especially in the work of the composer Kaija Saariaho, whose composition ...à la Fumée has utilized the latest electronic techniques of tonal reproduction for its richly dramatic qualities.

Films

The film industry in Helsinki was a slow developer, even if such a wonderful venue as the Savoy Theater, with room for 700 people, had been built in the 1930s, as had the 800-seat functionalist Bio Rex Cinema at the Glass Palace. Only towards the end of the twentieth century could it be said that this lengthy period of relative obscurity was coming to an end. This was helped by the fact that Helsinki, with neoclassical architecture similar to that of parts of St Petersburg, often stood in as a substitute stage set for that Russian city during the Cold War years, gaining special prominence in MGM's production of *Dr. Zhivago* (1965), based on the novel by the Russian poet Boris Leonidovich Pasternak.

The change in Helsinki's cinematic fortunes is largely due to the films of Aki and Mika Kaurismäki. The rock documentary, *The Saimaa Phenomenon* (1981), for example, was a particular trendsetter and was to take the brothers, especially Aki, on the road to international fame. Many of his other works, however, focus upon those living a marginalized and impoverished life in modern society. *Shadows in Paradise* (1986) considers the plight of working people, while *Hamlet Goes Business* (1987) and *Ariel* (1988) look to Shakespeare for inspiration. While each of these is still an essentially Finnish film, more recent ones such as *Leningrad Cowboys Go America* (1989), set in the US, *I Hired a Contract Killer* (1990) located in London, and *Drifting Clouds* (1996) are in a more cosmopolitan style. Most recently, his film *Man Without a Past* did extremely well at the 2002 Cannes Film Festival and was widely praised by reviewers throughout Europe and America.

Aki's brother, Mika Kaurismäki, studied film in Munich where his diploma work, *The Liar* (1981) was an instant success. This was followed the next year by *Worthless* (1982), another small-scale work in which the illusions of film and reality itself are juxtaposed. Interestingly, such later works as *The Clan* (1984), *Rosso* (1985) and *ChaChaCha* (1989) seem more traditional by contrast and almost in a Hollywood tradition, while in *The Last Border* (1993) Mika Kaurismäki enters the world of science fiction.

City of the Future

Today, Helsinki is one of Europe's richest and most beautiful cities, with a plethora of amenities, cultural and sporting, to match its status. It is a city rich in history; yet it also looks towards the future with great optimism. Unusually, while many of the world's great conurbations extend outwards and upwards, Helsinki, on the cutting edge of high technology and urban planning, is now extending downwards, under the earth, for a vast complex of underground shops and other facilities just behind the old Lasipalatsi, on Mannerheimintie, is being built at this very moment, deep into the earth. From the gangways and footpaths which circumnavigate it, visitors can watch with fascination as this new subterranean world, known already as the New Kamppi Centre, is born. This is a blessing in a city where for almost six months of the year the snow and cold can be oppressive, despite the recent introduction of underground heating of streets in the center. At the same time, Helsinki is making the most of its natural milieu, to the benefit of both residents and visitors, while doing its utmost to safeguard the environmental resources that make it unique among European capitals as a city truly embedded in its countryside.

Helsinki has also largely succeeded in recent years in escaping much of the civil upheaval that often accompanies the migration of foreigners into a society whose citizens feel themselves threatened, economically and socially. In fact, it has begun to treat their arrival as an asset, a logical response on the part of Finns in general and Helsinki dwellers in particular, as the city is truly a bridge between east and west. Whereas in the past it often served as the last defensive bulwark of western Europe against the east, today it offers a gateway through which much of the best of art, culture, science and even spirituality pass, in a distinctive creative symbiosis. Nature, technology, cultural diversity: these have now become bywords for Helsinki on the cusp of the new millennium.

Further Reading

Aho, Juhani, *Helsinkiin.* Helsinki, 1889.

Alho, Olli (editor-in-chief); Hawkins, Hildi and Vallisaari, Päivi (eds.), *Finland: A Cultural Encyclopedia.* Helsinki, 1997.

Beijar, Kristina, Henrik Ekberg, Susanne Eriksson, and Marika Tandefelt, *Life in Two Languages—The Finnish Experience.* Jyväskylä, 1997.

Bell, Marjatta and Marjatta Hietala, *Helsinki, the Innovative City: Historical Perspectives.* Helsinki, 2002.

Carpelan, Bo, *Axel.* Helsinki, 1986. (English translation also available).

Hawkins, Hildi and Siola Lehtonen, (eds.), *Helsinki: A Literary Companion.* Helsinki, 2000.

Herring, Peter (ed.), *High Technology Finland 2001.* Helsinki, 2001.

Honko, Lauri, Timonen, Senni and Branch, Michael, *The Great Bear: A Thematic Anthology of Oral Poetry in the Finno-Ugrian Languages.* Trans. Keith Bosley, Helsinki, 1993.

Illonen, Arvi, *Helsinki, Espoo, Kauniainen, Vantaa: An Architectural Guide.* Helsinki, 1990.

Jussila, Osmo, Seppo Hentilä, and Jukka Nevakivi, *From Grand Duchy to a Modern State: A Political History of Finland Since 1809.* London, 1999.

Jutikkala, Eino and Kauko Pirinen, *A History of Finland.* Trans. Paul Sjöblom, Juva, 1996.

Kent, Neil, *The Soul of the North: A Social, Architectural and Cultural History of the Nordic Countries, 1700-1940.* London, 2000.

Kent, Neil, *The Triumph of Light and Nature: Nordic Art, 1740-1940.* London, 1987.

Kirby, David, Merja-Liisa Hinkkanen, and D. G. Kirby, *The Baltic and North Seas.* London, 2000.

Kirby, David and D. G. Kirby, *The Baltic World, 1772-1993: Europe's Northern Periphery in an Age of Change.* London, 1995.

Kirby, David (ed.), *Witness to History: The Memoirs of Mauno Kovisto, President of Finland, 1982-1994.* Trans. Paul Sjöblom, London, 1997.

Klinge, Matti, *The Finnish Tradition: Essays on Structures and Identities in the North of Europe.* Helsinki, 1993.

Klinge, Matti and Laura Kolbe, *Helsingfors. Östersjöns dotter. En kort biografi.* Helsinki, 1999.

Kuusi, Matti, Keith Bosley, and Michael Branch (eds.), *Finnish Folk Poetry: Epic: An Anthology in Finnish and English.* Helsinki, 1977.

Layton, Robert, *Sibelius.* London, 1992.

Lönnrot, Elias, *The Kalevala: Or the Land of Heroes.* Trans. Keith Bosley. Oxford, 1999.

Nevakivi, Jukka, *The Appeal That Was Never Made: The Allies, Scandinavia and the Finnish Winter War, 1939-40.* London, 1976.

Piri, Markku, *En trilogi om Helsingfors.* Helsinki, 1996.

Screen, J. E. O, *Mannerheim: The Finnish Years.* London, 2000.

Taagepera, Rein, *The Finno-Ugric Republics and the Russian State.* London, 1999.

Tingdal, Birgit, "Torparsonen som fick Helsingfors att blomstra". *Finlands Svensk,* Årgang, January 2002.

Westö, Kjell, *Drakarna över Helsingfors.* Stockholm, 1996.

Index of People

Index of Places & Landmarks

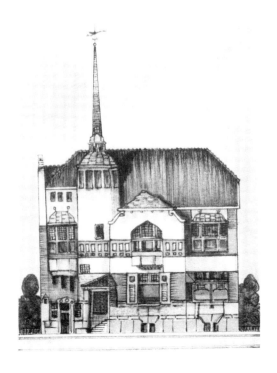

914.8971   Kent, Neil.
K
        Helsinki.

/5.00

DATE			

BAKER & TAYLOR